Illegibility

Illegibility
Blanchot and Hegel

William S. Allen

BLOOMSBURY ACADEMIC
NEW YORK • LONDON • OXFORD • NEW DELHI • SYDNEY

BLOOMSBURY ACADEMIC
Bloomsbury Publishing Inc
1385 Broadway, New York, NY 10018, USA
50 Bedford Square, London, WC1B 3DP, UK
29 Earlsfort Terrace, Dublin 2, Ireland

BLOOMSBURY, BLOOMSBURY ACADEMIC and the Diana logo are trademarks of Bloomsbury Publishing Plc

First published in the United States of America 2021
This paperback edition published 2023

Copyright © William S. Allen, 2021

For legal purposes the Acknowledgments on p. ix constitute an extension of this copyright page.

Cover design by Eleanor Rose
Illustration © Fabienne Verdier, Vide Vibration n°5, 2017, Acrylic and mixed media on canvas, 183 × 350 cm, Courtesy Waddington Custot

All rights reserved. No part of this publication may be reproduced or transmitted in any form or by any means, electronic or mechanical, including photocopying, recording, or any information storage or retrieval system, without prior permission in writing from the publishers.

Bloomsbury Publishing Inc does not have any control over, or responsibility for, any third-party websites referred to or in this book. All internet addresses given in this book were correct at the time of going to press. The author and publisher regret any inconvenience caused if addresses have changed or sites have ceased to exist, but can accept no responsibility for any such changes.

Whilst every effort has been made to locate copyright holders the publishers would be grateful to hear from any person(s) not here acknowledged.

Library of Congress Control Number: 2021935683

ISBN: HB: 978-1-5013-7675-7
PB: 978-1-5013-7678-8
ePDF: 978-1-5013-7677-1
eBook: 978-1-5013-7676-4

Typeset by RefineCatch Limited, Bungay, Suffolk

To find out more about our authors and books visit www.bloomsbury.com and sign up for our newsletters.

En los desiertos del Oeste perduran despedazadas Ruinas del Mapa, habitadas por Animales y por Mendigos

In the Western deserts tattered Fragments of the Map remain, providing shelter for Animals and Beggars

Borges, 1946

Contents

Acknowledgements	ix
Abbreviations	xi
Introduction: marks of experience	1
1 Roussel and Lautréamont	21
2 Derrida: infinite outline	55
3 Hegel: uneasy infinite	91
4 Blanchot: nothing doubled	127
5 Blanchot: wholly impossible	167
Notes	207
Index	241

Acknowledgements

Chapter One draws upon works published before: 'A Semblance of Life: Raymond Roussel's Speculative Prose', *MLN* 129.4 (2014): 955–2; and, 'Blanchot and Lautréamont', *Qui Parle* 29.1 (2020): 95–143. My thanks to the Johns Hopkins University Press, and Duke University Press, for permission to reuse this material here. I must also thank the two anonymous readers of this work, whose recommendations helped tighten up the argument substantially, as well as my hard-working colleagues in the inter-library loans department at the University of Southampton who managed to secure access to essential materials despite the straitened times. But, above all, my thanks go to the team at Bloomsbury, and especially Haaris Naqvi, whose support and enthusiasm for my work has been indispensable.

Abbreviations

Where double page references have been used, they refer to the French or German text and then the English versions, as translations have generally been modified.

AO   Maurice Blanchot, *L'Attente l'oubli* (Paris: Gallimard, 1962); tr. John Gregg as *Awaiting Oblivion* (Lincoln: University of Nebraska Press, 1997).

AT   Theodor W. Adorno, *Ästhetische Theorie*, ed. Gretel Adorno and Rolf Tiedemann (Frankfurt am Main: Suhrkamp, 1971); tr. Robert Hullot-Kentor as *Aesthetic Theory* (Minneapolis: University of Minnesota Press, 1997).

CJE   Raymond Roussel, 'Comment j'ai écrit certains de mes Livres', in *Comment j'ai écrit certains de mes Livres* (Paris: Pauvert, 1963); tr. Trevor Winkfield as 'How I Wrote Certain of My Books', in *How I Wrote Certain of My Books and Other Writings*, ed. Trevor Winkfield (Cambridge, MA: Exact Change, 1995).

CM   Isidore Ducasse, le Comte de Lautréamont, *Les Chants de Maldoror, Poésies I et II, Correspondance*, ed. Jean-Luc Steinmetz (Paris: Flammarion, 1990); tr. Alexis Lykiard as *"Maldoror" and the Complete Works of the Comte de Lautréamont* (Cambridge, MA: Exact Change, 1994).

D   Jacques Derrida, *La Dissémination* (Paris: Éditions de Seuil, 1972); tr. Barbara Johnson as *Dissemination* (Chicago: University of Chicago Press, 1981).

DG   Derrida, *De la grammatologie* (Paris: Éditions de Minuit, 1967); tr. Gayatri Chakravorty Spivak as *Of Grammatology* (Baltimore: Johns Hopkins University Press, 1976).

DS   Adorno, *Drei Studien zu Hegel*, in *Gesammelte Schriften 5*, ed. Rolf Tiedemann (Frankfurt am Main: Suhrkamp, 1971); tr. Shierry Weber Nicholsen as *Hegel: Three Studies* (Cambridge: MIT Press, 1993).

ED   Derrida, *L'Écriture et la différence* (Paris: Éditions de Seuil, 1967); tr. Alan Bass as *Writing and Difference* (London: Routledge, 1978).

EDB	Blanchot, *L'Écriture du désastre* (Paris: Gallimard, 1980); tr. Ann Smock as *The Writing of the Disaster* (Lincoln: University of Nebraska Press, 1986).
EI	Blanchot, *L'Entretien infini* (Paris: Gallimard, 1969); tr. Susan Hanson as *The Infinite Conversation* (Minneapolis: University of Minnesota Press, 1993).
EL	Blanchot, *L'Espace littéraire* (Paris: Gallimard, 1955); tr. Ann Smock as *The Space of Literature* (Lincoln: University of Nebraska Press, 1982).
ENZ	G. W. F. Hegel, *Enzyklopädie der philosophischen Wissenschaften im Grundrisse (1830)*, ed. Wolfgang Bonsiepen and Hans-Christian Lucas (Hamburg: Felix Meiner, 1992); §§1–192: *Encyclopedia Logic*, tr. T. F. Geraets et al. (Indianapolis: Hackett, 1991); §§193–299: *Philosophy of Nature*, tr. A. V. Miller (Oxford: Oxford University Press, 1970); §§300–477: *Philosophy of Mind*, tr. W. Wallace and A. V. Miller (Oxford: Clarendon Press, 2007).
FP	Blanchot, *Faux pas* (Paris: Gallimard, 1943); tr. Charlotte Mandell as *Faux Pas* (Stanford: Stanford University Press, 2001).
G	Derrida, *Glas* (Paris: Galilée, 1974); tr. John P. Leavey and Richard Rand as *Glas* (Lincoln: University of Nebraska Press, 1986).
GS	Jean Hyppolite, *Genèse et structure de la "Phénoménologie de l'Esprit" de Hegel* (Paris: Aubier, 1946); tr. Samuel Cherniak and John Heckman as *Genesis and Structure of Hegel's "Phenomenology of Spirit"* (Evanston: Northwestern University Press, 1974).
IA	Roussel, *Impressions d'Afrique*, ed. Tiphaine Samoyault (Paris: Flammarion, 2005); tr. Mark Polizzotti as *Impressions of Africa* (Champaign, IL: Dalkey Archive Press, 2011).
LE	Hyppolite, *Logique et existence* (Paris: Presses Universitaires de France, 1953); tr. Leonard Lawlor and Amit Sen as *Logic and Existence* (Albany: SUNY Press, 1997).
LS	Blanchot, *Lautréamont et Sade* (Paris: Minuit, 1963); tr. Stuart and Michelle Kendall as *Lautréamont and Sade* (Stanford: Stanford University Press, 2004).
MP	Derrida, *Marges de la philosophie* (Paris: Éditions de Minuit, 1972); tr. Alan Bass as *Margins of Philosophy* (Chicago: University of Chicago Press, 1982).
ND	Adorno, *Negative Dialektik*, ed. Rolf Tiedemann (Frankfurt am Main: Suhrkamp, 1972); tr. E. B. Ashton as *Negative Dialectics* (New York: Seabury Press, 1973).

P	Derrida, *Positions* (Paris: Éditions de Minuit, 1972); tr. Alan Bass as *Positions* (Chicago: University of Chicago Press, 1981).
PA	Derrida, *Parages* (Paris: Galilée, 1986); tr. as *Parages*, ed. John P. Leavey (Stanford: Stanford University Press, 2011).
PAD	Blanchot, *Le Pas au-delà* (Paris: Gallimard, 1973); tr. Lycette Nelson as *The Step Not Beyond* (Albany: SUNY Press, 1992).
PF	Blanchot, *La Part du feu* (Paris: Gallimard, 1949); tr. Charlotte Mandell as *The Work of Fire* (Stanford: Stanford University Press, 1995).
PG	Hegel, *Phänomenologie des Geistes*, ed. Wolfgang Bonsiepen and Reinhard Heede (Hamburg: Felix Meiner, 1980); tr. A. V. Miller as *Phenomenology of Spirit* (Oxford: Oxford University Press, 1977).
VP	Derrida, *La Voix et le phénomène* (Paris: Presses Universitaires de France, 1967); tr. Leonard Lawlor as *Voice and Phenomenon* (Evanston: Northwestern University Press, 2011).
WL1/2	Hegel, 1: *Wissenschaft der Logik. Die Objektive Logik (1812/1813)*, ed. Friedrich Hogemann and Walter Jaeschke (Hamburg: Felix Meiner, 1978); 2: *Wissenschaft der Logik. Die Lehre vom Sein (1832)*, ed. Friedrich Hogemann and Walter Jaeschke (Hamburg: Felix Meiner, 1985); *Science of Logic*, tr. A. V. Miller (London: Allen & Unwin, 1969).

Introduction: marks of experience

A text can be illegible because its language is too complex, too foreign, or too obscure to be read, but these obstacles can to some degree be overcome with time and patience. But a text can also be illegible because it cannot be read in any summative way, and in a text like this what is in play is structurally unreachable, that is, it cannot be read because doing so would require more (in whatever way this 'more' might be measured: time, effort, thought, etc.) than is possible. How is it possible to write a text like this, and what would be the effects of reading it? A text that is somehow beyond comprehension offers itself to thought in other ways, which not only indicates a different sense of writing and reading but also a different way of relating language and thought, and thus a different way of language existing within the world. A text like this could perhaps be termed infinite, in that it exceeds the capacities of the finite, but the very notion of an infinite text is problematic. In some ways, all texts can substantiate a potentially endless reading, but the infinite text is one that is structured as such, which is to say that even beginning to approach it requires a negotiation with its lack of finitude. But a text and a language, as well as its apparent author, are not ordinarily considered to lack finitude but rather to be socially, materially, and historically grounded and limited. An infinite text thus appears in a very different form, and with very different consequences, for insofar as it is not limited then there is no border to approach, no limit that separates it from the world or the reader. It is this lack of boundary that needs to be considered, and that informs the problematic of its reading, since if reading cannot begin, on the basis that there is no place that would form a natural starting point, then how can it proceed? Therefore, what has to be addressed is not just the difficulty of beginning but the nature of the challenge that its language poses to thought.

Conversely, this puts into question the nature of what we call philosophical language, especially when it becomes apparent that the language of thought bears no intrinsic relation to the language in which we approach thinking, for in what way is thought able to bring to expression the path by which it proceeds?

What happens to thinking when it seeks to come to terms with itself (as it is said)? When thinking is brought up against the dissipation of its own language, when it is forced to put it and itself into question, what happens to it? The manner in which these questions surface around a set of issues concerning language and thought, finitude and infinitude, and the nature of experience leads to the realization that the problematic of illegibility lies at the heart of a certain response to Hegel, in particular to the response by Blanchot who understood that philosophy, in concerning itself with its own language, was concerning itself with the limits of finitude, with death and the infinite, which is the experience that occurs when thought attempts to think its relation to language and is necessarily brought out not by philosophy alone, but through literature. It is to this discussion that the following work will attend.

I The life and death struggle

Let us consider a scenario: A subject is called to a challenge, at which they fail and are killed, nevertheless they have risked their life in facing this challenge. At the moment of death everything is at stake in an instant of suspense and freedom. Both life and death are held in abeyance at this point of extreme possibility, the possibility of possibility. A place opens up between life and death that is also the point at which they come to meet, one comes to touch against the other and in that moment both are suspended or neutralized. There is no assimilation or conversion of one to the other, no mixture or overcoming, but a double negation by that which lies outside both life and death and is neither one nor the other.

In more detail, a young man is asked to complete a linguistic test over which he has struggled. After much hard work he tries again, fails, and is killed. But the moment (of death) becomes immortalized, frozen at the point where there is neither life nor death, at which we too hold our breath. The dice have not yet landed, the cards have not been turned over, the trigger has not been pulled, the acrobat soars from one trapeze to the other, there is a moment of absolute tension, which is itself paradoxical. We say that the moment of death has become immortalized, but does that mean that death has become endless or that it has been defused, denatured, neutered? And, if the tension is absolute, then it is not only at the most extreme point but also without relation, but how can there be tension without relation? It is no surprise that time seems to stop and we hold our breath, for as witnesses we are also drawn into this impossible moment. But the man has been killed, defeated by the challenge, he has faced death and been found wanting. The scenario is of course oppressive; he has been forced into this situation, but is such a challenge ever just, or avoidable? In its dimensions it thereby becomes a primal scene of endeavour.

For Hegel, the primal scene is also a life and death struggle, but in this case it is a struggle for recognition in which the stakes are raised to such a degree that it becomes a question of who is willing to risk everything, to give up all reservation or restraint in order to gain this recognition, whether it is your life or mine. One side blinks, retreats, folds, the challenge was not one for which they were willing to put everything at risk, and in doing so they show their comparative weakness, which leads to subservience. This is a rather one-dimensional encounter, as all means of recognition are subordinated to that of force and coercion, which has the result of leaving the relation of master and slave empty of all but their mutual dependence through the reiteration of this force.[1] The master controls the slave through the threat of force and the willingness to raise the stakes to their ultimate degree, and thereby wins freedom since he is now able to get the other to work for him, but this leads to a contradictory tension of complacency and responsibility, which can undermine his freedom. The slave has discovered their own limits in being forced into obedience, but this also grants them the strange freedom of irresponsibility, and the illusory escape of internal emigration that leads to stoicism or *ressentiment*. Thus, the mutual dependence is unstable and shallow because it derives only from the threat of force, but is this risk ever absent? At some point, all challenges that are worth anything become escalated to the point of becoming critical, where it is necessary to risk everything, and so it is the presence of the shadow of death that is to be considered. For Hegel, one side of the agon claims this shadow while the other shrinks from it, but can death become the *mode d'emploi* as well as the *raison d'être* of life? Is the life and death struggle only to be solved by seizing it?

Blanchot seems to explore a number of primal scenes, which should be distinguished from his occasional autobiographical notes: aside from the passage in *L'Écriture du désastre*, there is the account in the introduction to *Faux pas*, the descriptions of solitude and night in *L'Espace littéraire* (which is in part an extended meditation on this encounter), and some of the episodes in *Thomas l'Obscur*. There is also the narrative related in *L'Instant de ma mort*, which provides a third version of the challenge that is in question here. During a wartime skirmish a young man is brought before a firing squad by enemy soldiers, and at the last moment he escapes:

> There remained however, at the moment when the shooting was no longer but to come, the feeling of lightness that I would not know how to translate: freed from life? the infinite opening up? Neither happiness, nor unhappiness. Nor the absence of fear and perhaps already the step beyond. I know; I imagine that this unanalysable feeling changed what remained of existence for him. As if henceforth the death outside him could only collide with the death in him. 'I am alive. No, you are dead'.[2]

The moment cannot be crossed, it is not crossable, there is no beyond, no other side that can be reached. There is only the rift without borders that it exposes, which is thus without moment or place. At the point of death there is neither awareness nor experience, only suspense, without any further determination.

As is made clear, this is as much a struggle about language as anything else, about the possibility of narration and recollection, of *histoire*, given the absence from experience. And so the only words that can be found that may approximate what happened are all evasive of the terms of experience: beatitude, ecstasy, lightness, elation, as is its strange relation, which is described in the loosest of ways as a friendship, 'he was bound to death by a surreptitious friendship', a relation of death with death, in which any subject-relation (with time, language, self) is unravelled. Thus the primal scene is in no way a pre-existing origin or primordial source, it is no *Urszene* in any psychoanalytical sense but absolute negativity, in which 'everything solid and stable has been shaken to its foundations' by 'the vertiginous knowledge that nothing is what there is, and first of all nothing beyond' [PG: 114/117; EDB: 117/72]. In being put to the test in facing this challenge it is not only existence that is at stake but the ability to master it, to make its possibilities one's own, to have the ability to be as well as to be as such. This is the extent to which existence becomes one's own existence in being the existence of a self with an identifiable position. Without language this ability is compromised in advance, but with language there is the risk of its complete collapse, of its touching upon what is not, as this challenge is inherent in every sentence.

To make a connection or relation within syntax is to essay its possibility, to be caught up in that which it is attempting to circumscribe. A sentence is always potentially a death sentence, since it is in its articulation that we can be called to defend ourselves, to give an account of ourselves, which in its failure can lead to disaster. But equally, the sentence can skirt this collapse by holding itself to the moment of its dissolution, the moment where there is neither this nor that. Prose is the language of the slave, Hegel is said to have written, the language of mere external relations, which is perpetually forced to confront a challenge to its own existence, as it does not enjoy the freedom of rhythmic limits but has to endure the lack of any intrinsic structure, to be pervaded by non-existence as intimately as by existence.[3] The example of the young man faced by a linguistic test comes from Raymond Roussel's novel, *Impressions d'Afrique*, where the man is a Spartan helot called Saridakis, and not only is he killed for failing in this challenge but the moment of death is also recorded in a bizarre statue [IA: 34–36/7–8, 292–95/259–61]. While Hegel's version of the struggle occurs between two individuals as they seek recognition, Roussel finds a more complicated interaction, since the challenge is set to the slave by his master, and then repeated in the construction of the statue itself, which is also issued as a challenge to a prisoner on pain of death. Furthermore, as will be shown in the next chapter, this collision between the construction of the statue and the story that it memorializes is itself an attempt to solve another linguistic challenge [CJE: 14–15/7]. The implication that seems to arise is that the triangulation of the struggle through language and art leads to its reflexive proliferation, which removes it from the one-dimensionality of Hegel's model.

The death of Saridakis is an explicitly colonial rupture, a manifestation of the gap that arises when it is found that the subaltern cannot be made to speak, but it would be too much to assert a political dimension to Roussel's writings, instead, the challenge for him is unavoidably existential, which means that it is only to be grasped under conditions of extreme risk; as Hegel's discussion made clear, the challenge is always escalated to the point of death. It is not the case that the refiguring of this struggle by Roussel and Blanchot sublimates its terms but rather that it finds its ineradicable linguistic supplement, the very articulation through which the struggle persists. And in its failure, it does not simply give on to its impossibly contingent grounds but exposes the point of its illegibility, whose experience gives rise to an entirely different form of relation. Hence this is a kind of syncope of language, a form in which the sentence marks the experience of its own illegibility, its opening on to that which cannot simply be read. An experience in language of that which is perhaps 'beyond' language, leading to 'a writing, the riskiest there is, subtracting something from the order of language that it, in turn, yields to with a very gentle and inflexible rigour' [PA: 26/15].

Language becomes the arena in which this escalation to mortal extremes takes place, as if the slogan 'Liberty or Death!' were not only to become its own death sentence but would be emblematic of the status of language as such. Death runs through language not just in the sense of the tragic or traumatic inexpressible that impossibly grounds its possibility but as that which permeates through every word as the ubiquitous border of its utterance. This border is not before or after or, in some spatialized sense, outside language, but is the very ridge across which language exists in its occurrence, its appearance as language. In the sentences at the end of Blanchot's account, the appearance of death is intrinsic: 'I know; I imagine that this unanalysable feeling changed what remained of existence for him. As if henceforth the death outside him could only collide [*se heurter*] with the death in him. "I am alive. No, you are dead".' However, the status of this account is unclear, especially in its conclusion, for although the last two sentences appear to be a paraphrase of the preceding thought, they offer a different formulation, and primarily because they are recorded as a quotation. They thereby appear as narrative, a narrated and recalled phrase, which is to that extent literary, a quotation that removes it from the context while appearing to offer itself as an exemplary condensation of it. Its status is thus one of self-contestation, making it impossible to know exactly what it refers to or what its truth status might be.

If we place these doubts aside for the moment and consider that the statement about the collision between the death outside and that within is in some way restated in the quotation that follows, then we are immediately placed in further uncertainty, as the collision between the two deaths is now rendered as that between life and death. Moreover, the quotation asserts this repositioning by way of two different voices, so that there appears to be a coincidence between the perspective of the first person and that of being alive, and, conversely, that of the second person and that of being dead: *Je suis vivant. Non, tu es mort*. 'I am living. No, you are dead.' From where does this second voice arise? As part of the same quotation it cannot arise from a different place or subject position, so it is perhaps a form of reflective reconsideration, or epanorthosis, a retrospective correction. Thus, there would be two moments at issue, that of the living, and that of its realization as becoming dead, as if the transition were literally taking place within this quotation, with language becoming the means of realizing this fact. And, in becoming dead, the first person has disappeared, even as language still maintains the possibility of its being said. Hence the collision of two deaths is that of language and within language; that which occurs in language as such and that which takes place through its occurrence: the first arising in the voice that claims to say, 'I am living', and the second that phrases this as its discovery of being dead. These sentences are not speculative in Hegel's sense, in that they would actualize a higher truth about identity by demonstrating its unstable and contradictory nature; rather, the ontological predicates of these sentences are rendered singularly concrete. This is not a formula about being as such, about the abstract status of the subject in general, but about the relation between language and death, about the language of life death as Derrida might say, that evacuates its ontological universality in favour of its actual experience, which can neither be translated nor analysed.[4]

Blanchot's lines here do not make exactly the same point as that which Derrida made in his reading of Husserl, where he had spoken about the structural necessity of my death for pronouncing the I: 'The statement "I am living" is accompanied by my being-dead [*être-mort*] and its possibility requires the possibility that I be dead – and conversely' [VP: 108/82–3]. Blanchot has doubled the statement and thereby complicated its temporality, which is why it is not simply epanothortic, for not only has the subject position changed from one sentence to the next but there is also no reason to assume that the second statement eradicates the first, despite the negative around which it pivots. Indeed, the negative indicates precisely that the relation between life and death is not established once and for all but remains subject to its negativity. Hence in saying, 'I am living. No, you are dead', Blanchot is moving beyond the quasi-transcendental grounding that Derrida is discussing into the narrative distortions that are granted to this linguistic thanatology by way of literature, which gives us a world of which it is its immanent border. Literary language provides the short circuit that Blanchot referred to in saying that, from now on, the death outside could only collide with the death within. The death inherent in the subject position is brought up against the death made sensible in the experience of language as that which constitutes its reality and unreality, its separation from things and the signification of things in the 'luminous opacity' of its appearance, as Blanchot describes the reality of words: 'To the extent that their meaning is less guaranteed, less determined, that the unreality of fiction holds them apart from things, and places them at the edge of a world forever separated, words can no longer be content with their pure value as signs [...] and at the same time take on importance like verbal paraphernalia [*attirail*] and make sensible, materialising what they signify' [PF: 81/76]. Such a language, in its relation to the world, is both alive and dead and yet, in itself, is neither; it is the image of that which neither lives nor dies but bears its own living death.

Coming to enounce this language in a statement about oneself is thus to meet the point of this short circuit as that which remains, as Blanchot had emphasized. It does not extinguish or dissolve itself but persists as the experience without experience of this 'without' (*sans*), the neutrality of that which is neither this nor that. And the strange status of this experience can then only be formulated tentatively as that which is (a) step/not beyond, a form of (infinite) liberation from life that is neither really beyond nor liberated. It is thus that the nature of the finite and infinite becomes rethought, just as the borders of life and death are complicated. For 'every writer who grapples with the experience of death as transcendence can only fall into the ordeal of the symbol, an ordeal he can neither overcome nor remove'. The symbol becomes significant for Blanchot as it is the key to the strange status of literary language as both contingent and general. While being made of many ordinary details, symbolic language (in which all literary language, and so all language of narration, participates) renounces these particularities in favour of the emptiness that it puts in their place, for, as a symbol, it is that which presents what is in its absence, and also undercuts this appearance by presenting itself as the immensity of the possibility of negation as such. The symbolic nature of literary language is thus an experience of nothingness as the search for a negative absolute that does not and cannot succeed: 'A writer who accepts to express himself in the symbol, whatever the theme of his meditations, can finally only express the demand of the symbol and measure himself by the misfortune of a contradictory negation, seeking to surpass all particular negation and to assert itself as universal negation, and not as an abstract universal but as a concrete emptiness, a realised universal emptiness' [PF: 86/81]. Such a close reformulation of Hegelian thought (especially in regards to the symbolic emptiness of prose as that which bears only inadequately developed relations, and the symbolic nature of the thought of finitude itself) requires considerable investigation, which is what this book will seek to deliver, but it can be seen how complex this will become when the experience of literature and of death are so intimately imbricated.[5]

And not only for the writer: if we are to read Blanchot's narrative then it is to the degree that the neutrality of its step, which is neither beyond nor not beyond (whether it be of experience, life, thought, or language), can be read, which is also inherent in the ordeal of the symbol. To read this narrative is to realize its singular logic in all the contradictory demands that it puts into play. Part of this challenge is implied in the final part of the extract from *L'Instant de ma mort* in its step beyond the text, which perhaps becomes the sentence in which it realizes its response to the challenge of the text as a whole: not to narrate or to recall so as to memorialize but to expose the point at which the death within and that without are brought together (without relation) in language.

The life and death struggle develops out of the failure of mutual recognition, and it is worth rehearsing the details of Hegel's thought here in order to understand how Blanchot takes it up, since it will prove to be a critical focus for his examination of the experience of literature as one in which its dialectics is ruptured by death. Optimally, the encounter with the other leads to mutual recognition, for each party not only recognizes the other but also sees themselves recognized by the other. Rather than finding that the subjectivity of self-consciousness is simply reflected in the gaze of the other, which in its one-dimensionality diminishes both the other and the self, the position of subjectivity is developed as a mutual interplay of recognition. Much as the speculative sentence undermines the simple predication of subject and object (as will be discussed in the next chapter), recognition operates across both self-consciousnesses as a movement of shared and reciprocally structured subjectivity:

> The middle is self-consciousness, which disintegrates into the extremes; and each extreme is this exchange of its own determinacy and an absolute transition into the opposite. However, as consciousness, it does indeed come *outside of itself*, but in its being-outside-of-itself it is at the same time kept back within itself, *for itself*, and its self-externality is *for it*. It is for it that it immediately *is* and *is not* another consciousness; and likewise this other is only for itself as it sublates itself as being-for-itself, and it is for itself only in the being-for-itself of the other. Each is the middle for the other, through which each mediates and integrates itself with itself, and each is for itself and for the other an essence immediately existing for itself, which at the same time is for itself in this way only through this mediation. They *recognise* themselves as *mutually recognising each other*.
>
> PG: 110/112

Part of this recognition comes from the awareness and demonstration of freedom, since a self must show that it is a self by demonstrating its freedom from dependence on others. While this is a starting point for the development of mutual recognition it does not become so peacefully, for in the demonstration of freedom the self shows its independence by also proving that the other is not independent. It is as such that there arises a fight to the death, as each self seeks to show that it alone has the freedom and independence of being its own self. Recognition thus depends on the willingness to risk everything in order to show that one is not tied to anything, not even to life, whether this is one's own or another's. And, by showing that its freedom is not dependent, the self compels the other not only to recognize itself but also its own concomitant lack of freedom.

Thus the life and death struggle leads to the master and bondsman relation, in which the master continues to exist as the freedom of pure negation while the bondsman mediates this existence because, in his failure to demonstrate the freedom of complete independence he is forced to negotiate his dependence on things through his labour or work. However, the bondsman retains a latent awareness of the negativity that the master enjoys, for he has experienced the fear of death, of becoming nothingness, of being dead, that has shaken him to the core. Although he has not been able to realize this negativity, it remains within him by way of this fear and is explicated in his working through of the negative. To this extent the bondsman is granted a greater awareness of the role of negativity in self-consciousness than the master, who remains dependent on the bondsman for his enjoyment.[6] The encounter with the (literary or philosophical) work condenses this challenge for the writer or reader, who is presented with that which, finally, has no concerns or relations other than with its own negativity, and towards which the labour of mediation becomes a way of negotiating the fear of death that it comprises. This struggle is thus less for mutual recognition than it is an encounter with a form of language that brings negativity as such to a critical point.

II The ground of Cratylism

This understanding of literature by way of the life and death struggle is a key part of Blanchot's thought and it is useful to offset it with the reading developed by Foucault – in this case, in regards to Roussel – in order to see the important differences that are brought about by the Hegelian model. Foucault's approach to Roussel begins from the point of view of the enigma, so everything that follows has to do with the relation between a secret and its key, between what is inside and what is outside, what is hidden and what is revealed, and also with the nature of the threshold or transition that divides and unites the two aspects. Furthermore, the notion of the enigma gives rise to a suspicion about the revelation itself, about what is not revealed, or, indeed, whether the enigma of the enigma is that it bears no secret. So, insofar as the enigma is perhaps only an enigma, that is, one that bears no hidden meaning but is merely structurally enigmatic, then language only conveys 'itself' in the proliferation of its (non-)secret. Such an approach resembles Heidegger's thought of unconcealment, but without Dasein, as if the essence of language could be uncovered in itself as the simple structure of revelation without sense. Literature then becomes a formal exercise that has neither goal nor limits, much like an infinite puzzle, and whose experience is radically desubjectifying. The death of the subject is thus revealed as its displacement in and by language, which is, however, only to re-essentialize it in linguistic terms. As will be seen, Roussel's works may lend themselves to such an approach but this should not suggest that Foucault's formalism is the only way to approach them, as it is based on two unconsidered assumptions: that Roussel's writings are structured as enigmas and that these enigmas have no secret; that all they contain or reveal is their own enigma. Hence there is a further assumption that, in conveying nothing but its own structure as an enigma, language thereby reveals 'itself' as the mere structural possibility of sense, without purpose or reason, as if there could be such a 'self', which would have some formal identity, some ideal or transcendental form or structure. As Foucault makes clear, there is a kind of Cratylist image at the root of his reading:

> The labyrinth of words, constructed according to an inaccessible architecture and referring only to its own play is at the same time a positive language [...] it is the neutral discourse of objects themselves, stripped of complicity and of every sentimental kinship, as if entirely absorbed by the exterior. Spread over a world of possible forms that hollow out a void in it, this language is more than any other proximate to the being of things. And it is just there that one approaches what is really "secret" in Roussel's language: that it is so open when its construction is so closed, that it has so much ontological weight when its morphology is so aleatory, that it looks out over a detailed and discursive space when, with decided purpose, it is enclosed within a narrow fortress.[7]

Such an illusion of reality, of 'objects themselves', needs to be examined carefully. The contingencies of Roussel's writing procedure do not allow us to say that his language opens itself to objects, and even less to their being. Indeed, the very formation of such an opening is to be reconsidered, deriving as it does from the nature of the enigma. The associations in Roussel's writings are formed from word to word, and sentence to sentence, but there is no necessity or essentiality to these associations, which can just as easily disappear or never arise.

The Cratylist thought, that of the natural, original, or given relation between names and things, is as hard to refute as it is to demonstrate. Certainly, there is no way of showing that names derive in some onomatopoeic or mimetic manner from things, in that they somehow resemble them, but this illusion is equally hard to dismiss. There is a strong investment in this belief, which persists despite its untenability, as it counters the all-too obviously arbitrary nature of names, which seems too difficult to accept. It is as if there is a fear that names themselves would become untenable if their lack of grounding were to be acknowledged and that the whole structure of language would then unravel as a result. But the notion that names need to have a material grounding belies their inherent abstraction, so Cratylism works against the general movement of language as such, while also suggesting that the abstract nature of language development is insufficient. So, although the Cratylist belief is wrong in substance it reflects a more profound uncertainty about the nature of names, about what we might mean by the arbitrary and abstract form of language, and how such a thought is sustained. The division that Socrates attempts to arbitrate in the *Cratylus*, between the idea that the meanings of names are conventional or that they are natural, is clearly too crude and only leads to an aporia, which has not only remained but also distorted the approach to language by obscuring the more important point about abstraction. As Foucault shows, the interest in exploring the apparent material topography of language arises from the notion that language, in its grounding, needs to be immanent to the world of things, with all the Borgesian paradoxes that then emerge about the nature of such correspondence. However, the problem of abstraction, which is taken up in Blanchot's understanding of the negativity of language, indicates a concern with the non-relation with the world; not the range and necessity of connection but its distance and deviation, its removal from things, which becomes a question of its experience. For if there is no given or necessary relation between names and things then to what are names referring, not just in their meanings but also in their likeness?

Foucault's reading does not quite follow this Cratylist thought for, as he has emphasized, there is a double deviation from sense and things, which takes place through the rupture of immanence by death. In Roussel's language there is only an artificial isomorphism between language and the world: between words that have become emptied of meaning, which can thereby approach things that have become dead or merely potential, as if in a parallelogram of images, extraneous from both language and the world:

> As if language thus ritualised could only accede to things already dead and disburdened of their time; as if it could not at all reach the being of things, but only their vain repetition and that double in which they might faithfully be recovered without ever recovering the freshness of their being. The narrative hollowed out from the interior by the communicative process with things hollowed out from the exterior by their own death, and so separated from

themselves: on the one hand, with the apparatus of their repetition pitilessly described, and on the other hand, with their existence definitively inaccessible. There is thus at the level of the 'signified' a symmetrical splitting of what separates the description of things and the secret architecture of words in the 'signifier'.[8]

Despite its distance from any asymptotic immanence there remains a symmetrical architecture of estrangement here that is still bound to its unequivocal meaninglessness, as if the specular nature of language and thought were now reflecting (on) itself to infinity, which would be no more than empty repetition, a multifarious figuration without sense or purpose or bearing. This would be a charade of Cratylism, merely gesturing towards but not connecting to the world, except in an illusory relation as a fantastic simulacrum of things.

The problem with Foucault's reading of Roussel, although it is largely accurate on this point, is that there is no place for finitude in it. Language operates like a Möbius strip, in that it is infinite and one-dimensional, and yet able to draw out the displacement of its aspects by way of its infinite distortion. But this is not language in any human sense, let alone that of any form of literary narrative, and it is as such that it is so elusive; it looks readable and yet in its infinite form it cannot fully be read. Foucault is thus correct to draw our attention to the morphological changes that occur as a result of the tropological transformations in the text, for Roussel works with the structure of linguistic tropes to expose a form of textuality that is not simply literary.[9] In doing so, however, his writings are removed from any sphere of human resonance, which is not fully taken up by Foucault. It no longer makes sense to speak of language here as that which draws out the being of things, or that of language itself (if such a thought has meaning), for whatever language has become in this textual form it is not certain that it bears any essence or ontological weight. Instead, Roussel's writing is like the virtual language of mathematics, which is only potentially legible, as it is based on the meaningless epiphenomena of rhyme, which in turn leads to nothing more than the empty rhapsody of the bad infinite (*das Schlecht-Unendliche*). And this becomes the importance of Roussel's works, for they demonstrate what the form of an infinite literature would entail, and what it leaves out. The play of death that Foucault focuses on is not, in the last instance, that of finitude and mortality but that of a phase transition: a displacement or translation of the subject by the text. Insofar as it is understood in terms of the enigma, death does not take place in any more substantial sense than as a change of state, which is why there is no real difference between the performances of the artistes in *Impressions d'Afrique* and those of the living-dead machines in *Locus Solus*; death is no more of a challenge to art than it is an end to life. Death is merely an aspect of the enigma, in the same way that the Möbius strip bears its own alternating aspects.

The death that Foucault discusses is to be understood as an aspect of the relation between language and the world: it is an effect of what he calls the poverty of language, the fact that there are fewer words than things, and that there is thus a form of anxiety inherent to language as it cannot achieve immanence with the world. This finitude comes to override what occurs in the limitation of existence, so although death appears to be central to his reading of Roussel it is not death as such, as it were, but only an aspect of the finitude of sense. It is perhaps as a result of this structural deficiency that Roussel moves to make his own world in the form of a fantastic Cratylism in which language is constantly expanding rather than being limited, but this means that death has again become displaced and defused, and so removed from the absolute negativity that shakes consciousness to its roots, which is Hegel's understanding of death. For Foucault, Roussel's procedure is designed to obscure finitude and mask death and to convert this fact into a resource for the replication of images, and this is made clear by the way that he begins his study with the coincidence of Roussel's own death and the appearance of his last text, and by considering this coincidence as a rebus, a puzzle that both yields and conceals.

However, the reaching beyond the world that is the conceptual or abstract movement of language is not simply for the discovery and invention of fantastic resemblances, for through this movement consciousness is driven beyond the limits of natural life and, in Hegel's words, 'this uprooting entails its death'. The experience of consciousness is one in which it goes beyond itself by doing violence to itself, since what consciousness learns occurs by way of the negation that arises through the concept, a negation of what is that is not simply nothing but is the nothingness of that from which it results, a determinate nothingness [PG: 57/51].[10] This ongoing negation shows that language is not only engaged in the abstraction of new relations but also the negation of previous ones, a negation that is more than their erasure or occlusion as it involves the anxiety of real suffering. And so, because the life and death struggle of recognition is ongoing within the structure of consciousness, in the movement of the understanding, the fear of death that troubles the slave is one that can never be shaken off but remains part of their experience. Hence the understanding, as the determinate and determining form of experience, becomes that which endures death and maintains itself in it, as the labour of its negativity cannot ever be relinquished or completed. Language, in conveying consciousness beyond its natural state, thereby bears this experience of death, which compromises its movement beyond and prevents the possibility of its full or successful transition to abstraction. It should then be recalled that the fear of death is that of absolute negativity, which is to say that it is not in relation to anything, and perhaps cannot be so at all, and as a result it cannot be assimilated or reduced to any thought or form of consciousness.

If Roussel's writings give the appearance of mimetic affinity as a fantastic simulacrum of immanence, then they are still of considerable significance in that they indicate how language proceeds by way of this affinity, whether real or assumed. In doing so they expose the obverse case, the distance that is opened by negativity, and in particular the removal and estrangement of abstraction, which is in no way merely conceptual or innocuous but bears, as Hegel made clear, a demanding and disturbing upheaval. Roussel's work is thus useful as an example of how language might be perceived to relate to the world in its Cratylist illusions, which is then ruptured by the eccentricity of abstraction, and leads to its own experience that recapitulates the false appearance of immanence as absolute negativity. In the following chapters I will explore the consequences of these modes of language, first through Roussel (where the sense of affinity will be found to be materially speculative rather than simply mimetic) and then Lautréamont, who will show the extremes to which the estrangement of metaphorical language can be taken and its effects on experience, which are not only metaphorical, before going on to examine the implications of these issues as they are exposed in Derrida's and Blanchot's readings of Hegel. Although this book is primarily a study of the ways in which Blanchot has taken up Hegel's thinking, particularly in reference to the relation of the finite and the infinite, I have started with these examples of the experience of literary language in order to situate the subsequent analysis. As such, this book picks up from my earlier readings of Blanchot's relation to Hegel in *Aesthetics of Negativity* and *Without End*, which are here extended to his later work in *Le Pas au-delà* especially, but in doing so I also take account of the parallel reading of Hegel that occurs in Derrida's early writings, which would prove critical for Blanchot's later thinking.[11] Integral to this reading will be an analysis of the development of the terms *différance* and *aufheben*, for by way of these terms both Derrida and Hegel are seeking to think through the transformation of thought in language.

In short, this investigation is seeking to approach that which Blanchot spoke about when he wrote that Roussel's work – through its series of intervals in which descriptions, explanations, and narratives perpetually open onto each other – represents 'the infinite navigation from one kind of language to another'. In this crossing there is a transformation in which the language of philosophy is exposed to change, which is drawn out in the fact that it cannot address its movements except by way of another language, thereby revealing a constitutive lack or void that keeps it in excess of itself, since its attempts to circumscribe this lack only call forth a further excess. As he concludes, in a tacit criticism of Foucault's reading, this does not lead to an endless reversal or mirroring effect, but rather to the play of displacement without place, reiteration without repetition, infinite passage [EI: 496–7/338]. What is being addressed here is a problematic that Blanchot also touches on in his 1968 article on Althusser's reading of Marx, which is that the challenge of language as such is brought out by the conflict of discourses that characterizes philosophy (which is partly historical, partly scientific, and partly speculative), a conflict that is not sublated or defused in thinking but rather estranges thought. Blanchot's most considered discussion of this topic comes in an essay on Merleau-Ponty from 1971, where it becomes a question of what takes place when philosophy finds that its own language is that which prevents it from achieving its aims, when it finds that in speaking of being, for example, it does so without right since it only changes that which it speaks of in speaking of it. Thus, what is encountered in this problem is the movement of language contesting itself as it seeks to evade its own categories and formations while yet pursuing its aims. In the ongoing (self-)interrogation to which philosophy then commits itself, its language changes, but to such a degree that it now risks becoming estranged from thought or, indeed, estranges thought itself. This risk is made tangible in the fact that the form of this language has itself become anomalous, for, as philosophical language, it is still attempting to develop an account of being, as well as trying to avoid this position in being part of being.

It is thus that Blanchot approaches the language of Merleau-Ponty's late works, in which this problematic becomes central and that led to his search for an 'indirect language', which would be able to respond to and express what he called wild being (*être sauvage*) – that is, being as it is outside or before the forms of reflection and signification – a language in which being would be able to speak in all its vibrant indeterminacy. But such a language, if it were possible, thereby raises the question of the very status of philosophical discourse:

> It seems to me that we should ask the question even more simply: there is perhaps no philosophy, just as we can doubt the validity of the word literature,

but, speaking, not speaking, writing, not writing, there is, in our modern societies, even under the modest appearance of the most modest professor of philosophy, someone who speaks in the name of philosophy that perhaps does not exist, and keeps empty, in order to disappear there, the empty place of a speech always other than that which he pronounces. It is thus, whatever he says, that the philosopher teaches, in obscurity or in renown, this philosopher, who has no right to his title, is always the man of a double speech: there is that which he says and is important, interesting, new and proper for extending interminable discourse, but, behind what he says, there is something that withdraws his speech from him, this *dis-course* precisely without right, without signs, illegitimate, unseemly, ominous and, for this reason, obscene, always deceptive or rupturing and, at the same time, passing beyond all prohibitions, the most transgressive, the closest to the untransgressible Outside – in this sense linked to that brute or wild (or lost) something to which Merleau-Ponty referred. The philosopher must in a certain way respond to this other speech, speech of the Other, which he cannot however understand directly: responding to it, he knows, not knowing it, that it is not only itself unjustified, without guarantees and without attachments and in some way struck by inexistence, but always in relation with what is *prohibited* in society where it has its "function", since he himself only speaks in speaking again over this insolent, inert, dissident non-discourse that, as Hegel suggested for another use, is, in broad daylight, the decision of "evening" and, in broad daylight, nightfall, like the collapse of language in appropriate, suitable, and cultivated language.[12]

I have cited this passage at length to show how Blanchot negotiates this point, and because this important essay remains untranslated. It is apparent that the language that Blanchot is referring to is related to the crepuscular, to the twilight moment, when philosophy begins to take flight in Hegel's words, but in which it is irretrievably after the fact and coloured by its inextricable ambiguity. In becoming a thought *of* change the genitive provides an ambivalence that cannot be resolved, as the thought of change cannot coincide with the thought that change itself brings about, and yet they are linked, almost as the *Abschattungen* of the moment, its protential and retentional tendencies, which reverberate around its null point.

Therefore we should understand that, in stating that philosophy only takes flight with the falling of dusk (*beginnt erst mit der einbrechenden Dämmerung ihren Flug*), both the negative and positive aspects of flight are being marked, alongside the conditional necessity of ambiguity.[13] As Blanchot points out, this moment can occur in broad daylight, at any moment in which language endures its own collapse, and it is thus that he concludes his article: 'Philosophical discourse always loses itself in a certain moment: it is even perhaps no more than an inexorable manner of losing and losing itself'. The double tension of the moment makes itself apparent in the movement of philosophical language that necessarily leads to one losing oneself and itself, just as it loses its way and itself, which only partially resembles a dialectic insofar as a dis-course is revealed in any discourse. This emergence is marked idiomatically in Blanchot's article by the phrase 'ça suit son cours', which indicates that which is ongoing or running its course, a work in progress, and shows that discourse, especially philosophical discourse (in that it seeks to interrogate the right of its own language), is always undermined by the permanently inconclusive and evasive (dis)coursing that marks its language. For, as he has emphasized, and despite the verb in this phrase, the course of language is only ever a dis-course, 'always broken and not followed', and so there is no mediation to its putative dialectical transformations, only rupture and deviation without the possibility of summation. This inconclusiveness is not merely provisional or accidental but arises from the fact that language, as language, can never be abstract enough to rid itself of ambiguities and uncertainties, or of the fact that its speech is without justification or reason, and so it always appears unseemly and illegitimate, fundamentally out of place, as if it were somehow barbaric to the very concepts of form and order, forbidding and untranslatable, and seemingly foreign to any system of thought. The 'disgusting murmur', as Blanchot terms it, that the ancient Greeks heard in the language of foreigners, which led to them being called barbarians, is the mark of the alterity and exteriority of this form of language, which barely even qualifies to be called language.[14] It is thus that it can only be registered as a dis-course and be treated as an affront in principle, as insolent and obscene to the very notions of philosophical discourse, just as death irrupts as a raw and offensive violation to the order of things. This is not to refer to the way that the language of philosophy is diverted by poetry or literature, or occasionally punctured by the contingent and everyday, but to a much stranger and more elusive violation that occurs when language, of its own accord, as it runs its course, exposes and is exposed to a mode that is foreign to its very order, as if it were to become suddenly unintelligible.

Philosophy, for Blanchot, is then the interrogation and experience of this transformation, its task being no more than that of losing itself and enduring how and where it goes. This is a significant change in tone, for rather than suggesting that there is the language of philosophy and also that which exceeds it, whether by way of madness or poetry (as he may have sometimes intimated),

Blanchot is saying that there is only one discourse and that it is perhaps philosophy that is most sensitive to its deviations. It seems likely that this change in emphasis is a result of Derrida's criticisms of Blanchot's language, although the notion of there being only one language was already evident in Blanchot's early writings, for example, in 'La littérature et le droit à la mort'. Furthermore, it is apparent that in saying as much Blanchot is also responding to Foucault's comments in his inaugural lecture, which had urged a change in direction away from the study of writing and signification and towards that of discourses as regular and distinct series of events. Blanchot's reservations in relation to the notion of the event are marked by his preference for the notion of disaster but, as with his earlier criticisms of *Les Mots et les choses*, he is also drawing attention to the strangeness of a language that does not entirely depart from the sphere of the human in being referred to its structures and displacements [EI: 373–4/250].[15] Instead, there is the arrival of something more peculiar and disruptive, which cannot be extricated from its experience and thought, and it is philosophy, as Blanchot rather surprisingly suggests in a formulation that is at once very close and yet also very far from Hegel, that is most thoroughly engaged in these transformations, even to the extent of losing itself.

1

Roussel and Lautréamont

I Torn lining

The transformation of language that occurs in Roussel's writings requires more explanation and doing so reveals that it presents a rigorous if unexpectedly materialist version of Hegel's notion of the speculative sentence. This literary parallel indicates a profound point about the relation of language to experience, which will be explored further through the work of Lautréamont, and particularly through Blanchot's reading of the literal nature of metaphor, in which each of these terms are found to be catachrestic. What then becomes apparent is that in the works of both Roussel and Lautréamont a form of language emerges that is not fully legible but instead takes place as a transformation of experience, a transformation that bears its own form of thought, which occurs by way of language but is not limited to it.

Roussel is not a writer of the order of Kafka or Proust, but what he has done is of importance because it is so unusual, for in attempting to write according to what seems like an algorithmic procedure he has not only produced some extraordinary literary works but has also brought out the relation between literature and language by treating literary language as something that can be produced by a serial technique. This is to treat literature in a way that divorces it from inspiration and in doing so exposes its own poetics, as it were, a poetics apparently drawn from language, rather than being imposed on it. In order to investigate the implications of this discovery I will first outline Roussel's literary procedure before turning to Hegel's speculative logic of sentences, and there is perhaps no better place to start than the summary given by Foucault of a short story entitled *Chiquenaude* (Flick of the finger) that Roussel published in 1900:

> One evening, a farcical play is put on; but it is already no longer the premiere (reproduction of a reproduction). The spectator who is going to narrate it has composed a poem that one of the characters must recite several times on stage.

But the celebrated actor who has taken the role has fallen ill: an understudy replaces him. Thus, the play starts with the "verses of the understudy in the play of Red-Heel the Pirate" [*les "vers de la doublure dans la pièce du Forban talon rouge"*]. This twice-copied Mephisto comes on stage and recites the poem in question: a proud ballad in which he boasts of being protected from all blows by his marvellous scarlet clothing that no sword in the world can pierce. Taken with a beautiful girl, one evening he substitutes himself – a new doubling – for her lover, a highwayman and an incorrigible swashbuckler. The bandit's fairy godmother (his clever double) uncovers the devil's plan in the reflection of a magic mirror (that unmasks the double by repeating him); she gets hold of the enchanted clothing and sews into its lining some moth-eaten material of the same colour (a torn lining). When the bandit returns to challenge the devil to a duel (confronting his double played by an understudy), his rapier has no trouble passing through the cloth, once invulnerable but now split and separated from its power by the lining – more exactly by "the worms in the lining of the material of the strong red trousers" [*"les vers de la doublure dans la pièce du fort pantalon rouge"*].[1]

The play begins and ends with the same phrase subtly transformed, and the story is seemingly merely the texture that joins the two together, and so despite the baffling series of reversals and duplications that take place there is a sense in which nothing happens. Instead, there is only the concatenation of a set of images that appear to return to themselves without remainder, as if the genie of the story after being released from its lamp finally returns and is once more sealed immaculately inside it. This is far from being Roussel's most developed work, but its significance lies in the fact that it is the first to employ his *procédé* (device or technique), which will in his later writings become thoroughly transformed.

In these later works Roussel takes the *procédé* a step further by making the explanations for each of the narrative twists into narratives themselves, which are then woven into the main story. This has a disorientating effect on our reading, as the explications are equally perplexing and only seem to call for further explications, which leads to confusion over what is meant to be explanatory in the narrative and what is to be explained. Highlighting this uncertainty, the first edition of *Impressions d'Afrique* included a note from Roussel to advise those readers 'not initiated into the art' of the author to start with chapter ten, proceed to the end and then return to the beginning. In doing so, the reader is presented with the narrative chronologically and thereby given the explanations that will supposedly unravel the descriptions in the first half of the book.[2] This novel was Roussel's first large-scale work to use the *procédé* and it emerged out of an unpublished short story called 'Parmi les Noirs', which was structured around the transition from its opening sentence, '*Les lettres du blanc sur les bandes du vieux billard*' (the white letters on the cushions of the old billiard table), to its transformed echo, '*Les lettres du blanc sur les bandes du vieux pillard*' (the white man's letters on the bands of the old plunderer). Although the latter sentence describes some of the features of *Impressions d'Afrique*, its terms have largely been abandoned, and the first sentence has disappeared entirely, such that in the transition from short story to novel the clues to the *procédé* have been lost. So, while the earlier text follows the same logic as *Chiquenaude*, where a particular sentence opens and closes the narrative by means of the slight displacement that it carries, this mechanism has become concealed within the novel in the form of the stories that it relates. But this additional layer of explanatory concealment would not be revealed for another twenty-five years, when Roussel finally explained it in his posthumous work, *Comment j'ai écrit certains de mes Livres*. Up until then the novel simply presented its narrative alongside a rationale that only duplicated it with a further series of stories.

But there is more to these stories than their mechanics for, despite the conventional forms in which they appear, Roussel's texts follow a logic of persistent absence. *Chiquenaude* emphasizes this logic by way of the series of deferrals and displacements that mediate the narrative of an actor who is only an understudy, playing a part in which he only repeats lines about success while impersonating someone else within the play, only to be discovered and to lose himself when the truth of his appearance is replaced with a fake lining. Thus, although there is a methodological conversion that takes place in the transformation from short story to novel, in which the *procédé* becomes concealed, this not only arises out of the experience of the richness of linguistic associations and resonances but also out of their withdrawal, which is to indicate that the experience of writing is double: that there was an *experience* of (literary) fulfilment is only evidenced by the fact that there *was* an experience. Its evidence lies in the mark that it leaves behind and it is this infinitesimal trace (Marcel Duchamp would call it *inframince*) that arises in the transition from *billard* to *pillard*, or *Forban talon* to *fort pantalon*, which means that despite initial appearances the *procédé* does not immaculately return to itself like the genie to the bottle but leaves a remainder, a subtle displacement. It is this shift that is the trace of the experience, as it indicates that there is no absolute return but rather a transition, an experience, if only of the most minimal kind, and this is the experience of writing, as it is only out of this experience that there is writing.

The *procédé* used in *Chiquenaude* was only the first stage for Roussel, since by starting with a word bearing two distinct meanings he could then go on to construct sentences where each subsequent word would extend the duplicity of reference by bearing further double meanings. In this way, he could move away from the transparent schema that structured his early works to a more buried network of associations, as the expanding series of references within each sentence would provide the space for a narrative to develop without the *procédé* having to be indicated. So, while the genesis of *Impressions d'Afrique* 'consists in a rapprochement between the word *billard* and the word *pillard*', this relation only takes place by way of the ever-expanding series of ambiguous resonances that each word reveals. For example, *billard* led to *queue* (cue/train), which might bear a *chiffre* (monogram/numeral); equally *reprises* could refer to the darning in the *bandes* (cushions) of the old billiard table or the melodic repetitions of a song; and the *colle* (glue) sticking the paper to the base of the chalk (*blanc*) was also a slang word for detention. These terms could then be combined into phrases by the use of the preposition *à*, which meant that the *queue à chiffre* was both the monogrammed billiard cue, and the numeral sewn onto the train of the bandit's gown; the *bandes à reprises* could either be the repaired cushions of the billiard table, or the repetitions in the song sung by the old plunderer's bands [CJE: 13–14/5–6]. It is as if beneath the ordinary scenario of an old billiard table a new and strange world has been revealed as each word now appears like a door that opens onto ambiguity. Occasionally, these phrases can be found within the text, thereby partly illuminating its mechanics, but often the chains of associations are too hidden or too long so that we are only presented with the cipher and very little hope of fathoming it and so, although Roussel does provide some clues by giving numerous examples of these lexical matrices in *Comment j'ai écrit*, much of what goes on remains unexplained.

Consequently, it is possible to think of the text as operating like a loom weaving together the fabric of the narrative out of the threads of the words' ambiguities. Viewed from one side, the fabric reveals one story, viewed from the other a different story is uncovered, but the fabric is necessarily the same: one single stream of words, yielding under a slight deviation of perspective to two utterly different narratives. In fact, such an image is used in *Impressions d'Afrique*, as the engineer Bedu has constructed a loom that is operated by paddles like a watermill, such that the passage of water through the paddles controls the movements of its spindles, which weave a large multi-coloured cloth embroidered with an image of Noah's Ark [IA: 109–15/76–82]. Thus, an autonomous machine (loom/*procédé*) reveals by way of the currents (river/language) an image of harmony (Ark/loom) also resting on the movement of the waters. Such self-referentiality is difficult to fathom but what this indicates is the impossibility of determining a hierarchy between the different narrative levels. We might see one image and feel that we can perceive another buried beneath it, but the relation of depth is not given, for even if the images seem to refer to the *procédé*, this in turn simply refers back to the images it generates. Once the existence of this linguistic machinery has become apparent, it becomes difficult to say at what level its train of associations is operating, for there is a sense, driven by language's referential function, that this concatenating logic is actually picking out the internal rhymes of objects and that language is simply a more mobile and ambiguous reflection of this objective logic. After all, why would *billard* and *pillard* be near homonyms unless there was some ontological necessity to their affinity, unless there was actually some relation between their referents? This is the logic that appears to drive the machinery of Roussel's works, but it is necessary to be wary about such Cratylist illusions, as the way that Roussel's writings reflect on their own origin in the *procédé* is simply the way that their relation to the world of things is *indirectly* demonstrated, for it indicates that language is not just a system of reference but bears the marks of its sonorous material generation, and thereby shows itself to be a thing. Hence there is no secret, encrypted meaning, for the designations of these words simply convey their material contingency.

The lack of a distinction between the designed and chance elements of the text helps illuminate the nature of the *procédé*, for although I have been describing its operations as mechanical, this is not accurate, as it is not comprised of separable parts that are causally and extraneously linked, but nor is it fully organic, since it does not generate any kind of coherent body. Rather, it fits the designation of being an artwork, insofar as it appears to have arisen naturally even though it is artificial, that is, it seems to bear a purposiveness without actually having any purpose. For the basis of the *procédé* lies in the affinities it uncovers between certain words and phrases, such that its operation comes simply from examining how the necessity of this contingent affinity might manifest itself. Affinity is thus construed as a problem or idea that can only be understood by putting it to work and it is in this way that it becomes the engine or heart (or genius) of the process, so that the *procédé* can be seen as a machine (in the abstract, non-mechanical sense) only insofar it is the means by which what is at issue in affinity can be realized. For as long as language is viewed as consisting of discrete parts that are only extraneously connected through the imposition of a syntactic order, then affinity can only be viewed as accidental and insignificant, but if language is seen as bearing its own immanent material order as a thing in the world like any other, then affinity becomes an issue whose necessity has to be examined. This is not to slip into linguistic animism since affinity is no less contingent than it is necessary, instead, its significance lies in what it conveys about the nature of the relation it expresses, rather than in any meaning stated.

This is not the end of Roussel's *procédé*, which he felt it was his 'duty' to reveal, 'since I have the feeling that writers of the future may perhaps be able to exploit it fruitfully' [CJE: 11/3]. The third stage – following on from the use of near-identical sentences to frame a narrative and the subsequent doubling of phrases through a sequence of variations – was to move on to a process in which a phrase could be transformed if it was parsed differently. As was seen in the move from *Forban talon rouge* to *fort pantalon rouge*, the meaning of a phrase can be manipulated by slight changes to its vocalization, which then enabled Roussel to draw the material for his writings from all manner of found sources. For example, an advertisement for a machine called a Phonotypia yields 'fausse note tibia' (wrong note tibia, whence Lelgoualch's flute in *Impressions d'Afrique*); the first line of a folksong, 'J'ai du bon tabac dans ma tabatière', becomes 'jade tube onde aubade en mat a basse tierce' (jade tube water aubade in matte third bass, whence the first scene shown on Fogar's cinematic reed in *Impressions d'Afrique*); and a phrase from the Book of Daniel, 'Mane Thecal Phares', becomes 'manette aisselle phare' (handle armpit spotlight, whence the mechanism by which Fogar initiates his cinema) [CJE: 20–1/12–13, 23/15]. Each phrase exposes a matrix, from which the narrative then arises with the task of drawing together each of the elements mentioned. It is easy to see how the Surrealists might take this 'evolved' version of the *procédé* (as Roussel termed it) for some form of alchemy that turns base linguistic materials into the gold of poetry, thus revealing that poetic truths apparently lie buried within the objects around us. But Roussel is much less concerned with the manner of this revelation, as his offhand remarks about these transformations indicate: any of these phrases could be read in any number of alternate ways, leading to very differently parsed meanings.

And, from Duchamp to the Oulipo, it is this part of Roussel's *procédé* that has undergone the most extensive elaborations – since for writers like Georges Perec, Michel Leiris, or Jacques Roubaud, this malleability is the key to a mnemotechnics, to a personal language-memory – but the arbitrary nature of these transformations means that we should not approach Roussel's works as bearing some kind of philosophy of language. However, this should not also lead us to forget that there is something mysterious at work in his writings: although the *procédé* involves a rigorous and methodical experimentation, within a work like *Impressions d'Afrique* we are simply presented with the end-products of this manipulation of language; the chains of re-imagining that led to it and the sources from which it may have been derived are mostly lost, and indeed might not have been suspected without the revelations of his final work. The process of dismantling phrases and reconstructing them at a remove under a different order of sounds uncovers something like a curious form of vitality within language, a non-human, non-organic life that seems to mimic the movements of the life we are familiar with, but from a far remove, such that it has become transformed into something quite distant and unrecognizable, but that is nevertheless a reflection of the life that we know. This bizarrely reconstituted existence would seem to be no more than a fantastic mockery of life, were it not for the rigorously executed lines of extrapolation that link it at every point with the world, and the inescapable facticity that attaches itself to this recapitulation by virtue of the chance that innervates it. Although the distance referred to here is internal to language, as it is the space between one reading and another, the one lying latent within the other as its invisible lining, this is a language reconceived as every bit as materially ambiguous as the things that surround us.

II Speculative sentences

As we have seen, Roussel's *procédé* operates by taking everyday phrases and transforming them and this *procédé*, once learned, can be used by anyone to create works in which 'imagination is everything' [CJE: 27/20]. So, rather than seeing his works as straightforward if bizarre adventures, they can also be read as experimental manuals of literary creativity, which is how they have been responded to by the Oulipo. In fact, reading his novels straightforwardly is unsatisfactory because of their 'literary' limits, their lack of conventional narrative artistry, thus it is only by taking account of their construction that their significance becomes apparent. But the presence of the *procédé* is not immediately evident, so reading Roussel is not like reading an instruction manual, as the *procédé* only appears figuratively by the way that it contorts actions as well as the narrative strategy, such that its appearance has to be uncovered and decoded even by those who are aware of its mechanisms. (It is notable that the problem of the hidden relation between the *procédé* and the narrative is resolved in the work of the Oulipo by delineating the different types of constraint and emphasizing the fact that a text should in some way discuss the constraint it is using, as can be seen in Perec's *La Disparition,* for example.) In that case, what does the presence of the *procédé* mean for reading? By changing linguistic phrases such that they reveal alternative meanings and, by applying this approach to a series of phrases, it is possible to develop a narrative that links these original phrases to their variant meanings. In this way, the narrative figuratively carries out an analogous *procédé* of its own in drawing out these linkages, and this is how the *procédé* is carried out to its fullest extent. In a sense this is the entirety of what the *procédé* means, for both readers and writers.

The difficulty comes with the attempt to understand the nature of these linkages, for if they are connections, then what is it in the narrative that is being connected and what is the relation between the connections and the connected; and if they are transitions, then does this signify an innovation or degradation, what has been left behind and what has been achieved? It is easy to see how the *procédé* leads to reflections about the ontological status of the text's language, and then to essentialize or psychoanalyse the nature of the relation between the different sides of the connections or transitions, but this should not distract us from the relation that the *procédé* opens up within the text itself and that is tacitly recapitulated in its reading. The *procédé* does not stand outside the text as an abstract set of instructions, for it is only insofar as it is executed, which means that it operates within the text as its means of development to the extent that there is nothing more to it than its execution. Moreover, this execution does not take place of its own accord, as it depends on the reader for it to be carried out, since it is only in being so carried out that the *procédé* comes to its fuller meaning as that which actualizes variant meanings in the text without defining their relation.

In *Impressions d'Afrique*, we are introduced to a one-legged musician by the name of Lelgoualch, who has learnt to play the tibia from his amputated leg like a flute and entertains the audience at the Gala with a range of folk tunes from his native Brittany. Many years later Roussel explained this appearance by referring to an advertisement for a record player called a Phonotypia, whose name he transformed into *fausse note tibia* (false note tibia) [CJE: 21/13]. If we are to understand this relation, then we need to look at how Roussel has transformed the word Phonotypia into the phrase *fausse note tibia*, that is, aside from the relation between the name and the actual record player, Roussel has reconceived the word through its transformation, so in what way can we say that Phonotypia *is fausse note tibia*? Without Roussel's later explanation, no hint of the Phonotypia would have been apparent, and even with it the appearance of Lelgoualch seems just as arbitrary, especially when it is discovered that despite its provenance the tibia produces sounds that are far from false. On its own, the description from *Impressions d'Afrique* amounts to very little, but coupled with Roussel's later explanation (which explains nothing) it becomes fascinating because of the transformation by which the two phrases are linked. This transformation suggests that, beneath the basic fact of homonymy, another relation lies concealed from which the narrative is drawn, for from this perspective it is possible to see how a randomly selected word from everyday language can be changed into a fantastic scenario and, conversely, how such a fantastic scenario can find its basis (however contingently) in a word drawn from the material of everyday life. Thus there is a possibility of reading 'Phonotypia is *fausse note tibia*' as a speculative sentence, albeit of the most secular, non-idealist kind, in that what we might understand as the 'essence' of the sentence's subject is expressed *by* its transformation into the predicate, which itself becomes a subject, unsettling the basis from which we might determine a relation of predication, since each expresses the 'essence' of the other. Although this perspective is not apparent from a reading of *Impressions d'Afrique*, the relation that the *procédé* activates between the two levels of Roussel's writing amounts to a profound inquiry into the nature of linguistic identity, in which it becomes possible to say that Phonotypia *is fausse note tibia*. While this shows how mimetic affinity needs to be understood speculatively, as a thought of materiality, and vice versa, grounding the speculative in the quotidian, it also indicates the mimetic basis for linguistic autonomy.

But surely this is to confuse two very different sentences? Roussel's example is simply a pun, two words or phrases that sound similar but have very different meanings, whereas for Hegel the speculative sentence has a specific metaphysical sense. For example, when he writes 'God is being', Hegel is claiming that the copula in this sentence has a radically different sense from that which is found in sentences like 'Canada is large'. The latter sentence has a copula that bears a relation of predication in which the object determines the subject, while in the former sentence the copula bears a relation of identity as both its terms are concepts, such that each is to be understood *as* the other. The subject in the sentence 'Canada is large' is characterized by its predicate, but it nevertheless pre-exists this determination and can be alternatively characterized, hence the subject is separate from its predicates and supports them passively, even though without them it remains undetermined. Within the former (speculative) sentence there is no equivalent separation between its terms, so that one could be said to be the subject of the other, for instead of the subject being determined by its predicate the second term in a speculative sentence indicates the essence of the first. While the sentence 'Canada is large' involves a particular and a universal, in sentences like 'God is being' there are two universals that the copula relates through a movement of identity as each is an expression of the essence of the other. As such, the term that lies in the position of the predicate itself becomes the subject, so that the ordinary movement of predication from passive, pre-existing subject to characterization is halted and suffers a counterthrust (*Gegenstoß*), as Hegel writes. For when the predicate itself is a subject it casts the relation between the two into a mutually-determining dialectic in which thought is forced into reconsidering the place of the subject, finding it first here and then there, and thus reconceiving the status of the object and its relation to it:

> Thinking, instead of making progress in the transition from subject to predicate, feels itself even more inhibited, as the subject is lost, and is thrown back on to the thought of the subject because it misses it; or, as the predicate itself has been expressed as a subject, as *the* being, the *essence*, which exhausts the nature of the subject, it finds the subject also immediately in the predicate; and now, instead of preserving the free position of reasoning as it goes into itself in the predicate, it is still absorbed in the content, or at least the demand to be absorbed in it is present.
>
> PG: 44/38–9

Thus, in the speculative sentence the subject does not safely stand apart from the predicate but finds its essence expressed through it so that it can only be understood by way of it: there is no unilinear movement of specification in which a pre-existing particular is characterized by a universal, but an oscillation in which a universal finds its essence expressed by another, which in turn refers back to the first term in a new expression. This reversal of the movement of predication leads to a reconception of the subject in which it is now understood by way of what the copula conveys as its identity, so that it is itself *only insofar* as it is expressed in its essence as other. Thus, the subject is *and* is not expressed through the predicate, for it is itself only through what it is not, so the essence of the subject is neither term in isolation nor is it their synthesis. Therefore, the significance of the speculative sentence lies in the way that it expresses a different relation of logical thought, in which the identity and difference of subjects can only be articulated through a mutual determination, which means that it has no inherent terminus, no point at which stability and unity could be finally declared, which then affects the position and nature of thought in relation to language and its object.³ Indeed, the speculative movement cannot rest in its reversal onto the subject-term but must move on by way of further sentences to make this movement itself become explicit (as was also the case for the *procédé*), such that it is only through reading the text as a whole that there can be a dialectical explication of this movement:

> That the form of the proposition is sublated must not only happen in an *immediate* manner, through the mere content of the proposition. Rather, this oppositional movement must become expressed; it must not only be this inner inhibition, but the concept's return to itself must be *set forth* [dargestellt]. This movement, which constitutes what otherwise the proof should accomplish, is the dialectical movement of the proposition itself. It alone is *actual* speculation, and only the explication of it is a speculative presentation.
>
> PG: 45/39–40

On the face of it, Roussel's puns would seem very remote from Hegel's analysis, but the nature of the movement that is disclosed in Roussel's *procédé*, between Phonotypia and *fausse note tibia*, for example, suggests that his writing bears an equivalent sense of the alternative logical forms that arise when language is treated differently. The sentence 'Phonotypia is *fausse note tibia*' does not of course appear in Roussel's writings, but the relation between its terms governs his understanding of how the *procédé* operates, and this is not a relation of predication. The Phonotypia may be a particular, but *fausse note tibia* is not a characterization of it, instead both terms operate *like* concepts in that Roussel has abstracted them from their context in order take advantage of what they may bring to his literary experiments. In effect, these words and phrases are the conceptual and linguistic materials of his writing – conceptual because they provide a certain way of thinking about his work, and linguistic because this is the manner in which their effects operate as part of an objective network of determinate relations – from which he then develops his narrative, and to which they are in turn oriented. Clearly, however, these terms are not logical categories in the way that Hegel requires, since they are not universals, but this indicates their resolutely contingent particularity: Roussel finds these words in banal everyday contexts but treats them as if they were imbued with the same conceptual force and metaphysical vitality as if they were terms in a transcendental lexicon. This would undermine the idealism of the concept as that in which the network of concrete relations and conceptual articulations is realized as a whole, and in which the system is realized in the concept as its structure of self-comprehending reflection.

Admittedly, for Roussel this force and vitality are aspects of a *procédé* that is merely a way of generating poetic texts, which means that it finds itself endlessly returning to its own mode of generation. But such a return is never simple, for if it is correct to associate the relation between Phonotypia and *fausse note tibia* to that which is brought out in speculative thought, then the two terms are identified through a relation that does not posit their identity. Instead, this is a doubled relation in which each is the inverse of the other, insofar as each expresses what the other is not but could be, opening the exclusive nature of the predicative relation to what Deleuze saw as the endless disjunction of identity. It is this form of expression that is suppressed by the instrumental use of language, which would insist on a fixed form of identity in which the term Phonotypia can only be Phonotypia and never *fausse note tibia*. But in doing so, the way that language differentiates itself through its material affinities is excluded in favour of a conceptual domination, which imposes its own notions of identity. Thus, by showing that Phonotypia is also not-Phonotypia insofar as it is *fausse note tibia*, Roussel shows that the instrumental understanding of identity omits the alternative modes of relation that language potentially conveys.

Consequently the sense in which 'Phonotypia is *fausse note tibia*' can be understood as speculative is not only one in which everyday elements are expressed in other forms but also that these literary expressions refer back to their material and historical contexts, and thereby reveal that thinking operates out of a linguistic dialectic in which the non-conceptual material affinities of language yield their own 'metaphysical' vitality. This is the language-like quality, or linguisticality (*Sprachähnlichkeit*), which Adorno finds in artworks, but that is here found in language itself: its way of expressing non-conceptual relations through its language-like affinities, which is activated by the speculative reading of the copula [AT: 171–2/112, 211/140, 274/184, 305/205].[4] The importance of the phrase 'Phonotypia is *fausse note tibia*' lies not in what it connects, as much as in what it conveys about the nature of their connection as a transition – as the very possibility of thinking through the material aspects of language in their language-like capacity – which finds that language bears meanings that are only indirectly comprehensible. So, by foregrounding the *procédé*, Roussel shows how its connective and transitional facility is the means by which thought comes into relation with things and is thus the basis for a speculative thinking of the material. For through the copula in this phrase, thought comes up against the material affinities of language as that which both subtends thinking and obtrudes through it, and it is as such that the *procédé* demonstrates how the linguistic medium of thought is neither fully transparent nor fully opaque.

This approach enables us to understand the literary 'flatness' of Roussel's writing, for in focusing on the *procédé* to the expense of the narrative he has developed a mode of writing that is only intent on making apparent its aesthetic material; what it is and how it is constructed. But doing so has changed the quality of his writing by putting in question the perceived relation between literal and figurative language. On the one hand, his writings are entirely lacking in rhetorical figures, although they can also be seen as operating out of an almost entirely figurative perspective through the use of the *procédé*. On the other hand, there is nothing in his writings that could be understood literally, although they also offer nothing but the most direct and non-metaphorical language. It is this quality of literary flatness that would be so influential for the writers of the nouveau roman, but Roussel goes further in finding a mode of language that fails to be literal or figurative, insofar as it finds the figurative quality inherent to language; its own intensive composition of material forms. Ordinarily, we take figurative language to be that which is embellished with rhetoric, beneath which subsists a direct, literal meaning. But such a notion of non-figurative language is a myth, as is the case with the notion that rhetoric merely overlays a pre-existing language. In their place, Roussel finds a language in which thought comes up against a 'natural' rhetoric. This would be a rhetoric that subsisted within language as its mode of material affinity and would thus take on the role of what is understood as the literal, in that it offers access to what *is* through the way that it expresses the ongoing history of material engagements and inclinations of language. It is through this sense of rhetoric that we can come to a non-mythical sense of the literal, which does not lead to an immediate access to objectivity, but to the rhetorical communication of objectivity in language, granting a form of relation grounded in the material ambiguity of the language-like.

For Hegel, thinking comes to a halt in encountering the object, which prevents it from dissipating into formlessness by persistently turning it back on itself so that it becomes materially and reflexively complicated. Equally, although the *procédé* unveils this speculative relation inherent to language, it also acts as a *frein*, as Annie Le Brun points out, a check or brake on the movements of thought by bringing it up against the refractory nature of its material form.[5] So, while the *procédé* reveals the formal possibilities inherent to the materiality of language, this facility arises out of the very method of rational thought, that of using a technical *procédé*, which is what leaves Roussel's writings with the appearance of mechanical artefacts. But, out of this constructed formality, there comes an element of the unconstructed, that which is not made but found, not artistic but natural, that which cannot be formulated and yet which animates his works [AT: 198–9/131]. Roussel has thus found a way of treating literature as a linguistic artwork, in that it has no meaning other than what it conveys about its (linguistic) conditions. It is partly because of the difficulty of apprehending this material formation of meaning that the *procédé* is repeated again and again, but the simple and almost mechanical mode of its operation also makes it seem no more than a technique, and it is this suspicion that makes it so difficult to respond to his writings as works of art.

However, it is precisely because they contest their own status and present themselves as merely material arrangements that his works appear ambiguous (as this material ambiguity is what we are most unused to encountering when we approach a work of language) and thereby demonstrate their status as artworks, which are pre-eminently ambiguous. While this demonstrates the persistent objectivity of the work – as it appears to be both wholly material and yet also wholly worked over, thus leaving it unclear whether it is a work of nature or of art, which is the ambiguity that renders it an artwork in all its intransigence – it would be a mistake to treat this autonomy as immaculate. Roussel makes it clear that the *procédé* is closely linked to the everyday in its most banal and mundane forms, for he uses items drawn from the quotidia of his existence: the address of his cobbler, a caption from a cartoon, lines from folksongs and advertisements, etc., as well as references to the Bible and to scatological slang. This is not a language wholly abstracted from the world but one that touches upon it at every point, drawing out the peculiar resonances to be found in the prosaic, while at the same time grounding its most fantastic inventions in the most ordinary fragments of life. The *procédé* then becomes a way in which the mimetic lining of language can be reflected and reflected upon in order to expose the swarming undercurrents of its affinities in all their objective dimensions.

This peculiarity is also the mark of the seemingly desperate utopianism of his writings, the bizarre and incredible machines that are intent on pursuing some impossibly faint suggestion of vivacity, and it is necessary to emphasize the faintness of this suggestion as it is the source of both the joy and the latent horror of their stoical and eccentric efforts (Roussel's machines are not that remote from the apparatus featured in Kafka's *In der Strafkolonie*). There is a possibility of glory here, as Roussel was so committed to achieving, but at the cost of almost everything human, since it is only by way of inordinate efforts that it can be glimpsed. Furthermore, while the mechanisms that Roussel makes use of are part of the methods of conceptual thought, they are put to the service of that very aspect of thought that conceptuality has sought to expunge in order to be conceptual: its mimetic affinity. It is as if, out of the ongoing suppression of this mimetic aspect of language, by which conceptual thought asserts its authority, Roussel has found a way to draw out the still breathing possibilities of its half-dead form.[6] This semblance of life is what makes the performances in *Impressions d'Afrique* so compelling, for it indicates how each artiste struggles to recapture a moment of vivacity from out of their airless existence, as well as the nature of the space that is thereby opened up, which leads to its own form of experience.

III Viscous reading

To understand how the experience of literature forces a rethinking of the nature of experience as such, and thus of the apparently metaphorical relation between objects and their meanings, it is necessary to turn to one of the most formidable experiments in metaphor, Lautréamont's *Les Chants de Maldoror*. The strangeness of this work issues a challenge to the very nature and form of the literary work, and so it is unsurprising to find Blanchot discussing it, but what is of particular importance is the way that it became a touchstone for his thinking of literature as permanent contestation. In his reading, Blanchot pursues the problem of literary reality and the experience that pertains to it, and it becomes evident not just that the issues of metaphor and experience are the figures around which his later thinking of the image and the outside will develop, but that Hegel's thought will be critical to this development.

From the start *Les Chants de Maldoror* presents itself as an anomaly, since it is a novel made up of songs that are further divided into strophes or stanzas. To begin from such a point is already to show the distance taken from generic distinctions and the concomitant distance from the style and form of any particular genre. Moreover, this distance is not absent from the course of the writing itself, where it is persistently thematized and contested and thereby finds its way into the structure of each sentence and the range of each phrase. As a text that is divided into songs it would appear to operate in the framework of the epic poem, and the constant presence of the narrative voice seems to support this positioning. But, as the beginning of the first song makes clear with its warnings to the reader, it is also a text. Equally, these warnings bear the hope but also the doubt that the subsequent pages will not prove illegible, which issues in a peculiar challenge or contract: this text is not for everyone, we are told; only those who can become as fierce as what they read, and who can bring to their reading a rigorous logic and concentration, will be able to cross its pages without losing themselves entirely. More timid souls should now avert their eyes and turn back, or, rather, in the face of the impending storm, learn to tack back and forth in order to find a safer and more philosophical course. This last admonition is developed by way of an extended analogy about a flock of migrating cranes, which suggests that reading will proceed with the greatest sureness if it can also tack back and forth, moving into and out of the images of the text, which in turn bears out the movement between the voice of the song and its deviations across the page [CM: 99–100/27–8]. Thus, two reading positions are being suggested: one of the reader and one of the reading, as it were, and the author's efforts are oriented towards the incipient but never guaranteed transition between these positions, with the language of the work taking up its themes from this ongoing tension.

In 1940 Blanchot had remarked that the form of Lautréamont's work was such that, in relation to the problems of meaning it poses, 'a long study would be useful' (not 'useless', as the translator of this volume has put it) [FP: 201/175]. So, in 1949 he published an essay that was almost as long as *Les Chants de Maldoror* itself and would be the longest single piece of critical writing he would produce. The necessity of writing such an extensive work arises not only from the need to follow Lautréamont's writing as closely as possible in order to grasp the scale of its challenge but also from the need to raise the stakes of the critical engagement with his writing, to demonstrate its seriousness. In response to these points, Blanchot decides to follow Lautréamont's work as it proceeds so as to find those points where it goes astray, in order to understand how and when a prose that appears to be so clear can become so suddenly and intangibly obscure. This is not a search for meaning but an attempt 'to prove to what extent one can follow a text and at the same time lose it', and it is not the least of the problems facing any reader that it is often when Lautréamont is at his most self-critical that the apparent lucidity of the text becomes most unfathomable [LS: 251/48]. What is found is that the commentary within the text itself does not define or explain it but only modifies it further, provoking more changes that strip it of the power to illuminate itself or to reveal any kind of final judgement on it. The 'clarifications' that the work seems to provide about itself show themselves to be simply further aspects of its movements, such that Lautréamont's thought must be understood to be apparent in all these moments, however obscure or contradictory, which only places more pressure on the interpretive gaze of the reader. If everything is to be explained, as Blanchot writes, then this must include the fact and the problem that not everything can be explained, since this is also part of what is at stake [LS: 253/50].

Hence Blanchot begins with a lengthy methodological preface, for with a work like Lautréamont's it is not adequate to focus on one issue in order to draw out the sense of the whole, nor is it any better to seek to organize all of the latent themes of the work. In both cases the work is treated in abstraction to its actual development, which indicates above all that *Les Chants de Maldoror* is written in and with time, to such a degree that neither the writer nor the reader is at any moment apprised of a finished work from which such evaluative judgements could be made [LS: 276/70]. This temporal pressure asserts itself partly through the long meandering sentences and digressive sequences, which feel as though they are developing unexpectedly each time they are read, and partly through the rapid and sudden changes, the ruptures that cause each strophe and song to begin again as if without precedent. In each situation there is a sense of time opening without certainty, and thus of the text unfolding (upon) a future whose reason is unknown. Consequently, as the text itself comes to take up these contradictions and inversions its own reason and status becomes far from clear, and the apparent lucidity of its writing is now anything but reassuring as it is not clear what constitutes it. Instead, the work seems to pursue its own thought, as it were, to discover the mind that it itself constitutes, its own form of reason [LS: 283/77]. To some extent this insight is trivial, as it merely indicates that this is the work in progress of a young writer, but Blanchot also wants to make a stronger case: that the very thought of the work, the mind that would make it possible, has not yet come about and will do so only by way of the development of the work, through its experience. On a textual level this point is reflected by the absence of any author's name on the first version of the first song, since 'Lautréamont' literally does not yet exist, not just as an authorial marker but as the name around which the work will find its meaning. Indeed, Blanchot follows the writing of the two versions of the first song very carefully to show how they develop the writer's voice and are in turn changed by it.[7] As he makes clear, the metaphorical manoeuvres by which the later songs become so distinctive is only weakly imagined in the first song, but what is apparent is the way their early appearance comes to affect the writer's thought, the way the opening up of metaphor changes the relation to time and language, and that the very possibility of pursuing the time of change, as it will later emerge, manifests itself only as the writer unravels the force of metaphor.

If we say that in metaphor something is *like* something else, then it is the very question of this 'likeness' (*pareil aux*) that becomes opened up in Lautréamont's prose and, in particular, its temporal mode or duration, its time of inertia and transformation, a time that is also a space apart, an opening without a given end that leads into the unknown as such [LS: 293/86]. 'Lautréamont', as a name, comes to be the marker of this interval and its extended leap into the void, a launch into an indeterminate element that is staged thematically in the strophe on the ocean and elsewhere, and formally in the pervasive metamorphoses of irony, which perpetually resist stabilization [LS: 290/83]. The constant emphasis on movement, speed, or change might suggest that all these metaphors are to be understood collectively as metaphors of metaphor, underlining the persistent transformations that mark the text, but Blanchot is quite clear on the deficiencies of this approach, which assumes that the various images in a work are to be understood in general by what they seemingly lead towards or what appears to support their individual efforts. Although much of Lautréamont's work is oriented towards the discussion of different forces of change and their open-ended possibilities, these images also expose the peculiar time of their expressions, which is not wholly organized around such apparently centralizing themes. Key to many of the transformations undergone in *Les Chants de Maldoror* is not simply an eccentric trajectory but also the inertia or impassiveness that underlies such changes, the stagnation that exposes and withdraws from change, and the insomnia and fatigue that dulls language and thought and draws its movements into a decay of time and meaning [LS: 312/103]. These aspects may be part of the movement of change, but what they emphasize is the illegibility of change, its resistance to time and thought, and the impossibility that is to be overcome only by the rupture of form and the sudden bursts of violence that move the text from transition to transition, which is marked so explicitly by the persistent broaching and retreat from the exit to the preface of the work. In this regard much has been made of the image of flocking starlings that appears in the penultimate song, for in this image Lautréamont brings together the two apparently distinct movements of the text, its onward trajectory and its swarming and never-completed collapse:

> Flocks of starlings have a way of flying that is theirs alone, and seems as governed by uniform and regular tactics as a disciplined regiment would be obeying the

voice of a single leader with precision. It is the voice of instinct that the starlings obey, and their instinct always leads them to draw closer to the centre of the group, while the speed of their flight bears them unceasingly beyond; so that this multitude of birds, thus united by a common tendency towards the same magnetic point, unceasingly coming and going, circulating and crisscrossing in all directions, forms a kind of highly agitated whirlpool whose whole mass, without following a fixed course, seems to have a general wheeling movement around itself resulting from the particular circulatory motions appropriate to each of its parts, and whose centre, perpetually tending to expand but unceasingly compressed, pushed back by the contrary stress of the surrounding lines bearing upon it, is constantly denser than any of these lines, which are themselves more so the nearer they are to the centre. Despite this strange way of swirling, the starlings cleave through the ambient air with no less rare a speed, and at each second tangibly gain precious ground towards the end of their labours and the goal of their pilgrimage. Likewise, reader, pay no attention to the bizarre way that I sing each of these strophes. But, be convinced that the fundamental accents of poetry nonetheless maintain their intrinsic claim upon my intelligence. Let us not generalise upon exceptional facts, I'm happy to oblige: however my character is in the order of possible things.

CM: 249–50/159–60

It has been known for some time that the details of this passage were copied almost entirely from the entry on birds in Jean-Charles Chenu's *Encyclopédie d'histoire naturelle* (1850–61), a work that was the source for many of the descriptions in Lautréamont's bestiary.[8] Blanchot had noted earlier, in reference to the poetic practice of Baudelaire and Lautréamont, that 'poetry can completely cease to be new without ceasing to be original, that its efficacy, its purity, its original force are not necessarily broken in the vice of reminiscences and under the weight of what has already been said and that a poet sometimes succeeds in expressing himself, and in a way that is unique to him, by expressing himself as another' [FP: 186/162]. While repetition can be a source of originality, as Ducasse's later practice of plagiarism emphasized, it is also apparent how well Chenu's description fits into Lautréamont's own writing, and not just in terms of its thematics. This flocking among starlings, which is known as murmuration, is understood to be a type of emergent phenomenon that arises out of the local behaviour of each bird as it tries to stay at a certain distance from its neighbours. But the tensions that are drawn out by Chenu and Lautréamont are nevertheless still manifested at this emergent level by the onward movement of the flock towards its goal and its swirling about itself as its internal and external pressures alternate, leading to a form of perpetual revolution that keeps falling outside itself as it proceeds, without it being possible to settle or decide the differences between these tensions. The same tension is found in the writing in the undecidable forwards and backwards movement of citation and repetition, but it is important to note Lautréamont's own words here, as his approach depends on 'an eminently philosophical conception, which ceases to be rational as soon as it is no longer comprehended as it has been imagined, that is to say, expansively' [CM: 250/160]. In reading Lautréamont, we are engaged with a different form of rational conception, one that is to be understood according to its generalized speculative possibilities rather than as determined *a priori*.

Reading must submit to Lautréamont's text in both its expansive and immersive aspects in order to grasp its transformations in their trajectories as well as in their inertia, and to do so means not extracting a panoply of keys from the narrative to decipher its images but to find that reason itself becomes changed in engaging with its eccentric logic. Thought is not to remain safely exterior to the work in reading it but to find (and lose) itself in its movements and thus experience itself in and through its transformations. In relation to this point, it is possible to examine how Lautréamont's sense of experience converges on or diverges from Hegel's own understanding of experience, as it is discussed in the Introduction to the *Phänomenologie*. As Hegel describes it, consciousness finds itself transformed as its awareness of the object changes; that is, in knowing an object, consciousness discovers that the object is not what it took it to be, such that what changes is not only knowledge but also the form of the object, which reveals itself to be different as consciousness comes to know it. In discovering that the object is not as it first appeared, consciousness is then led into a new form of knowledge, unfolding a dialectical process that gradually reveals the truth of the object as it shows itself not to be what it seemed but something else, a process that Hegel calls 'experience' (*Erfahrung*) [PG: 60/54–5].[9] Knowledge thereby develops necessarily and immanently through an engagement with objects as they progressively reveal themselves, which is also the strategy of reading and thinking in the course of the *Phänomenologie* as a whole.

Lautréamont's response to this account would be eccentric, as for him the course of experience does not converge on absolute knowing as the unity of subject and object but finds that the transformation of thought occurs through the phenomena of literature without ever settling. The nature of the literary image is at the heart of this experience, for by way of the unfolding space and time of the image in its transformations there is an opening up of new dimensions of thinking. This is not to limit the impact of Lautréamont's writing to literature, as literature is that area in which thought and language are able to explore their mutual stabilizations and destabilizations through the movements of figures and metaphors: the elusive material significations and obscure conceptual expressions of thought as it experiences its relation to language. The image is at the far reaches of this experience of thinking; as Lautréamont stated, it is in the realm of possibilities, of what is to come. And, as Blanchot has emphasized, this experience is concerned not solely with the development of knowledge but also with the deterioration of thought as it endures these transformations. In revealing itself in diverse ways, the object of literature does not always lead to a thought of the unity inherent in each metaphor but can also find (or lose) itself in the obscurities of that which does not reveal itself, that which bears out a sense of formless, pointless change, a metaphoricity without metaphorical form. A form of life, of sorts, that is not differentiated from death but finds its own larval duration and so cannot be formulated within the framework of a dialectical process of subject and object as it indicates instead a ceaseless turmoil. *Les Chants de Maldoror* would then seem like a blind inversion of the *Phänomenologie*'s *Bildungsroman*, with just as much rigour as it has speculation:

> it is also to no avail that Maldoror seeks to abolish consciousness [*conscience*]. Terrible struggle. Certainly, he overcame his enemy, he reduced her to nothing, he "chased her from his house", he drowned her, gnawed her skull, but he must always annihilate her further. With the intention of shattering her, he throws himself, with her, from the top of a tower: profound dream fall. Then he "gathers" her up, withdraws her from the abyss, resuscitates her in some way because he still wants to make her the witness of his crimes. Infinite contradiction: the freedom of crime demands the disappearance of such a witness, but the possibility of crime demands its survival. Necessarily, the death of consciousness has for its horizon the consciousness, always revived, of death.
>
> LS: 315/106

Blanchot's description makes it apparent that the inescapability of the thought of death cannot be thought with any clarity because of its immersion in this death, which Lautréamont has demonstrated so remorselessly: Maldoror has taken his *conscience* (consciousness and conscience) and sought to destroy it, but this destruction must be witnessed if it is to be complete, which means that it will never be complete, as consciousness needs to be both present and absent at its own destruction [CM: 186–7/104–5]. In this way, Lautréamont is also marking his own relation to a text that he can neither complete nor expunge, neither void nor avoid. And throughout, just as in the last part of Blanchot's *L'Arrêt de mort*, the presence of consciousness is personified (in French it is *la conscience*, in the feminine) in a way that does not make it any clearer, for while this personification renders its destruction more painful, its excessive distortion only voids the way that figuration may make the analogy more concrete, since the figuration is understood through its rupture of form, rather than the reverse. The shape of consciousness itself, in Hegel's terms, is never innocuous; the very figuration of thought bears its own fatefulness (or lack thereof).

Consciousness as its own light is also necessarily that which obscures itself in its self-relation, whether in thought or in writing, and so the search for clarity and rigour is partly a struggle against consciousness itself, the futile struggle against the sources of its own darkness, which only leads it further into obscurity in a manoeuvre that cannot be decided as either success or failure. The marks of this darkness can be found in those passages of the work that deal with the sudden arrival of childhood alienation as well as in those that are concerned with the long-running struggles between Maldoror and the Creator (so-called), but it is in the way that language is drawn into the world of the subhuman, of the animal and the filthy, of bodily decay and estrangement, that the effects of this darkness become most profound. There is 'a feeling of horror, inspired by the human body, and the one who experiences it sees himself changed, through the disgust that he feels, within the object of his disgust, becomes viscous like this thing, becomes this thing'. Viscosity lends a different sense to any unity of thought and object, one that lacks clear differentiation and is liable to unpredictable change, making the boundaries between language and materiality uncertain, by which the work of writing becomes changed, as Blanchot goes on to specify: 'It is at this moment that language also succumbs to a new vertigo' [LS: 323/113]. What takes place then is a movement in which language enters a labyrinth of its own materiality, with its own logic and significations, a different form of language that is another kind of existence, outside any arrangement of appearance and disappearance in which meaning comes to light; a singular mutation of language that is its own impossible thought and experience but is also a monstrous singularity, since it implies a search for a novel communication that is less about meaning than infection, the decomposing delirium of another transformation.

The duplicity of this experience – which perversely parallels that of Hegel's understanding of the relation between consciousness of the object and consciousness itself, between what is taken to be the object in-itself and what is found to be the being-for-consciousness of the object – is that out of which a new object emerges, 'which presents itself to consciousness without it knowing how this happens to it, which for us, as it were, goes on behind its back [*hinter seinem Rücken vorgeht*]'. Hence the experience in which a new object comes about does so 'through a *reversal of consciousness* itself', a reversal for us as the readers or phenomenologists of this experience, who come to perceive how this new shape emerges not through will or desire but through a more or less accidental discovery that brings about a new configuration of knowledge alongside a new perception [PG: 61/55–6]. Thus, there is not so much a progression of consciousness in a conscious and explicit manner as a series of reversals into new forms. It is this other side of experience, its lining or inverse, that Lautréamont seems to be exploring in the ruptures and contradictions of his writing, for

> if the paroxysm of furious violence, in provoking a rupture, can tear him from himself, the power [*puissance*] of an infinite passivity, in suppressing time, is no less capable of encountering the undecided [*indécis*] moment between life and death when the same disappears and the other approaches – a double possibility the progressive ordeal [*épreuve*] of which is the profound experience of *Maldoror*.
> LS: 328/117

Consequently, what becomes contaminated in this experience of the endless passivity of transformation is not just time or reason but also the nature and possibility of will and desire.

The comparison between Lautréamont and Hegel becomes halted at this point, as *Les Chants de Maldoror* purports to be neither a systematic nor a progressive study of the shapes of experience. To some extent, both are addressing the model of the *Bildungsroman* as a philosophical problem, but Lautréamont is also pursuing an extensive and subtle exploration of the transformations of experience in literature, which enables a greater examination of the textual disfigurations and aporias of experience. Equally, in Blanchot's repeated studies of Lautréamont through the 1940s, it becomes apparent that the interplay between philosophy and literature is the means by which the status and nature of the work as such can be rethought, first from Blanchot's early thoughts on the novel and then to his rethinking of the possibilities and impossibilities of literature in the *récit*. The essay that he publishes in 1949 tracks these transitions, which is why it is so patient and thorough, for as the issues of genre in Lautréamont's work become more pressing, they lead to the point where the experience of transformation (which these issues have exposed) draws the work into new formal demands. This is the labyrinth of language and experience that

Blanchot had noted, in which both are transformed into new figures, as the eccentric movement of phrases and sentences draws reading into a movement in which it is persistently displaced and contested. As has been noted, the writing of *Les Chants de Maldoror* brings about its own changes, as the figure of Lautréamont is first found through it, which leads to the work changing into the form of the novel, only for this move to be displaced again by the appearance of Ducasse and the *Poésies* as entirely new configurations. There is thus a complex interchange between the form and status of the work that emerges as its nature changes in being written, which enables Blanchot to draw his own practice into focus as an open-ended exploration in which all its terms and forms are put in question. Indeed, in a remarkable transition that occurs at the beginning of the last song, Lautréamont tells us that what we have read so far is merely a preface that has led us to a point from which the actual project, the novel, will then commence. Hence, in a strange echo of Hegel's method in the *Phänomenologie*, *Les Chants de Maldoror* is an exercise in bringing readers to a certain point of thinking so that they can approach what has (already) been placed before them, but the contrast with the *Phänomenologie* could then not be greater, as will be shown.[10]

The nature of this exploration is indicative of its orientation towards the future, like the magnetic point towards which the starlings are drawn, as the transformations are continually being pulled into ever new forms. This is why Maldoror must overcome his memories and physical form as much as his moral and social habits, for the development of reason is such that it extends not simply into a new mode of thought but also into a new form of existence. It is from this reading that Blanchot can link Lautréamont to Sade, as both are writing towards a transformation of the possible structures of reason and of the existence that would pertain to these structures, by enabling readers to 'modify the conditions of all understanding' [LS: 49/41]. The persistent ruptures and repetitions that mark the text of *Les Chants de Maldoror* are part of its approach to this horizon, in relation to which it can only be a series of prefaces opening (onto) its future. At the level of the sentences, as was seen in the image of the flocking starlings, 'this movement through which the motifs are always brought closer to the centre – while also pushing the centre back towards the outside' is not simply virtuosity but demonstrates how language 'turns back on itself and projects towards the surface the point designating the extremity of the gyration and the gulf' of its variations, by which this singularity itself becomes reason, the emergent sense of the work, just as its clarity becomes obscure, as it is its own (idiomatic) sense [LS: 337/124]. It is by way of this cyclone or whirlpool of language that the reader can become 'as fierce as what he reads', as the opening sentence of the work had pronounced, a fierceness that has no goal or purpose but is just the ferocity of transformation. For if everything must be said, then there can be no end to this work, except for the peremptory interruption of death or illegibility, which lies latent in each of its changes as the lining of its impossible finality:

> if *Les Chants* are truly the dreams of an abyss, this abyss is firstly that of Lautréamont, and its narratives [*récits*] do not form a simple mystical, lyrical meditation without connection to their author, they also touch on his existence, and it is the torment of this existence and the depths of his peculiar past that they try to bring to the light of day [*au jour*] through the extended effort of a work at the heart of which the images, the imaginary powers and the real memories of life, take shape, are developed, feel their energy, then, from one metamorphosis to the next, having discovered the ground of obscure things, in this obscure *discovered* ground attain the deliverance of daylight. It is enough, in truth, when we read *Les Chants*, to be obedient [*docile*] to this movement of images, to their course and their transformations, in order to recognise, within this disordered procession and capricious tumult of words, the most obstinate labour and the most extraordinarily pursued experience that exists: one of a work resolved to attain, at a remove [*à la écart*] from logical unity, a coherence however absolute and, this coherence realised, to make it equally the greatest clarity and the greatest obscurity, the lowest *point*, the furthest from lucidity and the moment wherein lucidity, penetrating this point, is again found and liberated.
>
> LS: 356–7/141–2

Such is the basis for the constant struggle with sleep, in which 'it is not because feelings become pure and clear that awakening happens [*se produit*], but this purity and clarity is the very transparency of the day that arises' [LS: 354/139]. The struggle for reason in language is the struggle for transparency in which the emergence from narrative into reality is aligned with an awakening that is also death. For the pure transparency marked in every metaphor is obscured by the persistence of evasion in every moment, which is thus not the mark of the real in its transparency but the endless instability and dissembling of its metaphoricity, no matter how slender or absurd the translation involved. Reality thereby emerges through its failure to be grasped in these relations, just as the strangeness of the narrative is sustained by its inability to be explained. The aporia of these reflections is the mark of their reality as the obscure transparency onto which they abut.

It is apparently from this realization that Lautréamont can emerge in the last song as the writer of a novel: 'We are no longer in the narrative', we are told, and the announcement then comes that the prefatory part of the work has been completed; so this ground that, as Blanchot has described, will henceforth be the obscure foundation of Lautréamont's 'future poetics', is merely 'the synthetic part' from which the analysis will now proceed [CM: 275/182, 284/189]. In leading into the end of his work, Lautréamont has reversed the traditional path of thought from analysis to synthesis, reversing out of the synthetic miasma of images in his preceding *récits* into the analysis that will be his future novel. For Blanchot, however, it is apparent that the novel that emerges in the final song is a step back from the subtlety and intensity of the work so far, although in saying as much, he is able to specify more clearly how radical the preceding writing had become. In particular, he singles out the use of irony and eroticism, both of which give expression to the force of metamorphosis that Lautréamont has been pursuing in his furious struggle for sovereignty that became a sovereignty of fury. Irony, as Blanchot emphasizes, is the very experience of metamorphosis in language, for through its extreme and pervasive use the nature and status of meaning is placed in doubt, such that 'words would no longer be words, or the things that they mean, or this meaning, but *another* thing, a thing always other'. It is significant that he also places eroticism in this context, as a material exploration of what irony has explored on a linguistic level – the possibility of transformations without goal or stability and the violence and senselessness that comes with this instability – since this sheds light on his own attempts to explore a similar notion of eroticism in *Le Très-Haut*. Furthermore, Blanchot suggests that in this displacement of the reader by the text, in which the reader becomes more and more stupefied, the text begins to be conscious of itself, and this impending change insists in the text as its duration or interval so that any reading of *Les Chants de Maldoror*, 'due to this suspense [*à force de l'attendre*], is already experiencing this change' [LS: 361/146, cf. 338/125].

So it is that, in moving away from the viscous complexity of irony and eroticism, Lautréamont finds that his writing can no longer sustain itself and as a result the last song ends somewhat abruptly and unexpectedly, its images completing and destroying themselves in the extraordinary perfection of Mervyn's trajectory as he is flung from the top of the column in the place Vendôme and crashes into the dome of the Panthéon (a distance of about 1.5 miles). After this apotheosis of the image, in Blanchot's words, which realizes itself in the transparency of an act that also extinguishes it, there is nothing more for Lautréamont to write, and thus for 'Lautréamont' to be at all. It is perhaps for this reason that the *Poésies* will be so different, as if the insight that opened *Les Chants de Maldoror*, and that effectively culminated in the discovery of its generic change at the beginning of the last song, were to be grasped only when the relation between genre and generation was opened up to its never-ending transformation so that it remained persistently singular and *sui generis*.

It is important to be clear about the claim that the text becomes conscious of itself, for it does not mean that the work itself begins to think, as if it were some kind of artificial mind. Instead, what Blanchot is drawing our attention to is the process whereby the function of reader or writer is slowly and subtly displaced by a text that appears to come to an awareness of itself in experiencing itself. This point has been elaborated and emphasized in the readings of Marcelin Pleynet and Philippe Sollers, who align it with the post-structuralist manoeuvre in which the human is erased in favour of the text as it becomes autonomous, whether this is understood in semiotic, psychoanalytic, or political terms.[11] The situation of Lautréamont seems to lend itself almost paradigmatically to this reading, especially considering the brief extent of his biography in comparison to the work he produced. But the point Blanchot is raising is more closely attuned to the way that, temporally and metaphorically, the movement of the text opens up a space and time, a duration, in which it can experience its own transitions and thereby consider both its onwards movements and its self-consuming involutions. It is as such that the text begins to pursue its own burgeoning awareness in the form of this unfolding reflexivity, which, as Blanchot underlines, is never complete, either in terms of the text's self-awareness or the loss of the subject position of the reader or writer. There is a tension and tropism between the two, but it is never finalized, for what is uncovered in this duration, which is the form of the image in the text, is both its stagnation and its violence. This dilation in the midst of each transformation is the deviation in which the reader and the text find a mutual estrangement, which is also the form of the impending life or thought that arises.

Consider how the text frames itself, from the first sentence to the last lines of the preface before the novel that completes it. First: 'May it please heaven that the reader, emboldened and become momentarily as fierce as what he reads, find, without loss of bearings, his wild and abrupt way across the desolate swamps of these sombre and poison-filled pages' [CM: 99/27]. Traditionally, in the epic form, the work begins with an address to the muse with thanks and commemoration for the ability to proceed with the work itself. Lautréamont has inverted this gesture by beginning his work with an address that concerns not the recitation of his songs but their reading; that is, what is risky is not the production of the work but its reception. Moreover, the opening address is not so much directed to the reader as it is about the very possibility of it being read, so it is addressed to the heavens (*plût au ciel*) with no small irony, given the place of the transcendent in what will follow. In reading this phrase we are reading about reading, about the possibility of our own reading in relation to a text with which we are already engaged and whose possibility is only questioned further by the irony with which its celestial grounding is configured. For if it will be thanks to heaven that readers can make their way safely across the pages of this work, then this chance is undermined in advance by the framing of this belief. And, by casting doubt on this belief, the possibility of reading is left without any grounding, so that reading's only hope, if it can be called one, is for it to become like the text itself. The ambiguous resemblance is then borne out by the alternation between the fierceness of the text and that of the reader, of the chance that the latter will not become disoriented but will instead find a 'wild and abrupt way' across a work that is dark, toxic, and without hope. The nature of this resemblance is evident in this opening sentence through its digressive syntax and exaggerated phrasing: as readers, we have already become complicit, even if we are not aware of it. The poison has started to take its disorienting effect if it has not repelled us entirely.

The staging of this opening is not gratuitous, as if it were simply a Gothic cliché; rather, it deliberately inducts readers into its experience by first making them confront the problematic status of reading as such. As the sentence goes on, the stakes of this incipient transition become all too apparent, 'for, unless he brings to his reading a rigorous logic and a concentration [*tension d'esprit*] at least as equal to his distrust, the deadly emanations of this book will soak up his soul as water does sugar'. The last phrase is slightly odd, as it might ordinarily be thought that the emanations of the book would be soaked up by the soul, rather than the reverse; but in saying as much, the reversal of book and reader comes up against the very distinction that Hegel had stated in his understanding of the movement of reading. The process of reading is a key example for how Hegel understands the movement of spirit between materiality and ideality, subjectivity and objectivity, and interiority and exteriority, and as a result it becomes a metaphor of itself as it bears a movement between the literal and metaphorical and their sublation. Thought 'in the written word becomes a thing', which then 'recaptures its subjectivity out of a dead thing [*einem todten*], an object, in reading'. This notion is an early version of the dialectic and appears in Hegel's writings on Christianity from 1799 as a way to understand the movement of spirit in the transubstantiation of bread and wine. But even though it is developed in this context, it is apparent that Hegel is focusing on the metaphorical nature of this relation and the difficulty of grasping its movement, for which the analysis of reading is not simply an example, and perhaps not even a metaphor, if by the latter we seek to distinguish its understanding from 'literal' transubstantiation. This complexity, as we have seen, comes to be reflected in Lautréamont's own version of this movement, but it is just as significantly reversed. As Hegel notes, the comparison between transubstantiation and reading 'would be more striking if the written word were read away [*auf-gelesen*], if by being understood it vanished as a thing', but of course it is not; there is, as Derrida emphasizes, always a remainder.[12] Furthermore, in Lautréamont's revision, there is perhaps only the remainder, only the *partes extra partes*, since it is the soul that risks being read away by the text while remaining foreign to it. As a result, this uncertain relation of the reader to the text (and thus of the text to the world) can already be seen to be at work in the opening sentence through the appearance of the adverb *comme* (as) in the phrases 'as fierce as what he reads' and 'as water does sugar', which explicitly (trans)figures this relation as the elusive problem and chance of our reading.[13]

However, if we now turn to the opening pages of the last song, we find that in Lautréamont's understanding of the preface, as was noted earlier, this challenge to the possibility of reading has not been satisfied but has only been deferred further, or displaced altogether and perhaps indefinitely:

> This hybrid preface has been set out in a way that perhaps may not appear natural enough, in the sense that it, so to speak, surprises the reader, who does not see very well where he is at first being led; but, this feeling of remarkable stupefaction, from which one generally seeks to shield those who pass their time reading books or pamphlets, I have made every effort to produce. Indeed, it was impossible for me to do less, despite my goodwill: only later, when a few novels have appeared, will you better understand the preface of the renegade with the dusky face.
>
> CM: 285/190

In the last phrase Lautréamont aligns himself with Maldoror, blurring their narrative positions such that it would seem we have been reading not only the work of Lautréamont but also that of Maldoror, who has now come to emerge in the voice of the work. In Hegelian terms, the observed figure and the observing figure have realized their identity, not as a completeness, however, but as a movement whereby Maldoror discovers himself in Lautréamont, and vice versa, by way of the phenomenology of (literary) experience that Lautréamont has been following. Although, if the first sentence of the work is also directed towards himself as the work's first reader, then it must be considered that 'Lautréamont' and 'Maldoror' may have both lost themselves in crossing the desolate swamps of its pages, so that the two names would be non-identical markers of this estrangement. The Hegelian assumption that self-reflection leads to return is thereby voided, for the aspect confronted at the end of this series of investigations, as throughout, only exhibits an obscure, smoky (*fuligineuse*) face, rather than one in which its image is clearly beheld.[14] Hence what is of equal importance is the revelation that readers may not have managed to find their way across the pages of the work but may have been led astray, if not deliberately stupefied. The hybrid preface, which has been the work so far, is only partly a preface, perhaps because it must necessarily lead into what it purports only to introduce, or perhaps because it does not do so but rather leads elsewhere, ever further into its desolate swamps; the decision over its hybridity is suspended, and only later, if at all, will this be understood. Thus, the text has neither fulfilled its initial challenge nor avoided its risks but remains stranded across the interval or hiatus of its opening as its 'own' anomalous form and experience.

In a letter to his father's banker in Montevideo, which Ducasse sent just before the publication of the *Poésies*, he spoke of his feelings in regard to *Les Chants de Maldoror*. Aside from the fact that the publisher had refused to distribute it, Ducasse wrote that for him the whole work had still 'gone down the drain' (*tombé dans l'eau*) and that this event had opened his eyes [CM: 382/261]. The transition from this work to the *Poésies* is, as Blanchot remarks, both a rupture and a continuity, for the obvious and extensive break with the former work only repeats the rupture marked by the transition in the last song, and this means that the appearance of the *Poésies* is implicit in *Les Chants de Maldoror*. As a result, the later work cannot be seen as a refutation or denial of what had gone before, even as it seems to express this position, for it instead expresses its truth (almost in Hegelian terms) as its rupture and continuation. In Blanchot's words, the failure of the earlier work 'seems to have been the jolt from which the new state, the other choice, implied in the evolution of *Chants de Maldoror* (as its truth), is abruptly crystallised'. He can then specify the *experience* of Lautréamont that he has been pursuing: 'It is upon this incident that he became conscious of himself as changed and, doubtless, changed thanks to this work, but also by this work, rendered completely different from it' [LS: 371/156]. What takes place is not a convergence of progressively unifying moments but a shattering evasion of both work and author, for from each moment to the next the ruptures and continuities of the work leave its parts, as Derrida writes, as 'exteriorities heterogeneous to each other' [D: 50/43]. In this transformation it is not a question of putting aside the earlier nightmarish investigations but of understanding how their severity remains and is recapitulated in a different form in the severity of the *Poésies*, which is what allows for the regeneration of the work.

These considerations are not without relevance for Blanchot's own career, as Christophe Bident has suggested, but the reflections contained in both studies of *Lautréamont et Sade* are also a detailed and extensive excursus on the discussions first raised in 'La littérature et le droit à la mort' on the relation between the writer and their work (understood as both noun and verb), and the concomitant struggle for sovereignty and its effects on reason.[15] In this earlier essay, the Hegelian dimensions are explicit and lead in the article on Sade to a Kantian orientation towards the conditions of possibility for the transformation of reason, but the Lautréamont piece is more concerned with the deviations that emerge from the slow exploration of the eccentricities of experience in literature. As such, the conundrum Blanchot is left with is indicative of the move that his own work is coming to address: on the one hand 'writing well is impossible, because writing is always brooding [*broyer du noir*], is being on the side of evil' [LS: 376/161]. But on the other hand, before his always future book, the birth of Lautréamont 'is an infinite event', an unlimited aspiration 'where, ceasing to be himself, he can become, outside of himself, completely himself, coming finally and forever into the world at the ultimate instant that makes him disappear from it' [LS: 379/163–4]. On both sides of this undecided aporia Blanchot avoids a reading that would allow Lautréamont easy passage, for in each case, without dissolving their pressure, they slide into each other, resolving neither themselves nor their undecidable instability. If birth is endless, and leads only to its own alienation and disappearance, that is because it is an opening that never ends, and as such it is also the hiatus of transition into which the brooding writer sinks, for with writing there is only transition, without satisfaction. Evil is always to be found in the time between, the time of formlessness and its fury, but it is by way of this time that an opening towards futurity is possible and, as prefatory, impossible.

As such, the tension involved in the absorption of the mind by the text needs to be explored further. It is apparent that the text bears a risk of consuming the mind and that this is an unavoidable aspect of its reading, yet it is apparent that this is not sufficient either, that it would also be necessary for thought to remain separate from the text even as it is absorbed. The constant construction and destruction of figures in the text brings reading face to face with the substrate of meaninglessness in language and its endless capacity for generating its own meanings outside any reference to anything else, putative or otherwise, which is the illusion of 'meaning' as such, and the inhuman emptiness of language itself, as it is so called. With the exposure to this implicit illegibility, the text is no longer simply language or a text; we are now 'reading' what cannot simply be read, and as such there is an absorption of the mind. The text stages its own reading but also its undoing. It is thus that we can understand the mind or thinking of the text as the interplay between the apparently automatic generation of images and their catachrestic disintegration. What becomes significant about Lautréamont's text is that there is almost no distinction between its perfect syntactic formulation and the endless misuse and abuse of its figures, so that every sentence both forms and deforms the work, is both its inside and its outside. Thus, as Derrida pointed out, catachresis becomes the form and basis of this general metaphoricity and also its material exteriorization, the sites and figures by which it touches on what it is not.[16] If the figurality of language does not derive from a naturalist ideology, then all figures are necessarily catachrestic, and when we come across points of evasive and resistant materiality in a text, we come across exactly those points where catachresis reveals itself in its material instances, and vice versa, as the text is ruptured by this opacity, from outside.

Lautréamont only refers to a risk that the reader's soul might be absorbed by the text, but it is apparent that if this were not present, then it would not be possible for reading to take place. Hence, insofar as it does occur, there will be a movement in which the text comes to its own form of life as readers lose their own; not that the reader dies but that the text brings about both the life and death of the reader as a subject, and, as a result, that reading involves a relation of life death between the text and its reader. It is this intermediary movement that constitutes reading and is its own form of materiality. In referring to the materiality of language we are to some degree speaking metaphorically, since what is at issue is not just the actual form of the words and the text but also their aporetic resistance to comprehension. However, it is also the case that in speaking of the materiality that is encountered in the world, the same sense of materiality is at work. At this point what we mean by materiality becomes stranded between the literal and the metaphorical and between language and the world.[17] In this way 'materiality' becomes paradoxically primary and, in this catachrestic sense, can be considered the form of our sense of language. And, when it is impossible to distinguish the literal from the metaphorical sense of language, then this illegibility becomes what could be called speculative, the forms and stakes of which will be explored next.

2

Derrida: infinite outline

In order to understand how Derrida comes to consider metaphor to be catachrestic, and of the points of relation that this thought bears with that of Hegel, it is necessary to step back to consider Derrida's relation to Hegel more generally. For in this thought lies the condition of understanding the relation of language and the world, and thus the very possibility of what could be called speculative thinking. In 1967 Derrida registered the intention of pursuing a thesis on Hegel under the direction of Jean Hyppolite. This decision marked a change in direction in his thinking as Hegel had not thus far been a significant focus of his work, and for the previous ten years he had seemingly been working towards a thesis on the 'ideality of the literary object', also under Hyppolite (which would have derived from the problems exposed by Husserl's understanding of 'the idea in the Kantian sense').[1] While an article on 'the Hegelian theory of the sign, of speech and writing in Hegel's semiology', as he had described the thesis project, would emerge, the thesis itself would not be written, although its focus would be further developed in 'Hors livre' and *Glas*. The reasons why this change in direction occurred have been made clear by Derrida himself, but to understand how it manifested itself, and thus to essay the significance of this change, it is necessary to examine how the notion of *différance* took shape in his thought and especially how it came to be articulated in reference to Hegel's notion of *aufheben* and the relation of the finite and the infinite. By doing so it then becomes possible to understand how Derrida develops his thinking in relation to that of Hegel, and how he comes to take his distance from the latter.

Through this discussion it also becomes possible to assess the difference between Derrida's reading of Hegel and Blanchot's, which reveals that Blanchot has his own approach to Hegel that is in some ways more thorough, albeit less explicit. This point is perhaps provocative but, as the following pages will demonstrate, although Derrida is an incisive reader of Hegel and is very sensitive to the nuances of his thinking, he nevertheless comes to Hegel's works from a perspective that primarily considers his place (however privileged) within the history of metaphysics, rather than as an ordeal for thinking. The reading developed here is thus an exercise in seeking to ascertain the points of distinction between Derrida, Hegel, and Blanchot, and as such it does not seek to promote one perspective over another. Instead, it is more pertinent to find the difficulties that are unique to each and follow through on their implications in order to be apprised of the still unthought possibilities that each has left behind. Uncovering what has been passed over in these readings leads to a rethinking of Hegel and Blanchot that yields a renewed understanding of the problems posed to thinking by the infinity of literary language.

It is helpful to sketch out the trajectory of the pieces that Derrida wrote on Hegel, which are perhaps less widespread than might be thought. Aside from *Glas*, there are five articles that deal with Hegel substantively from 'De l'économie restreinte à l'économie générale' in 1967 to 'L'age de Hegel' ten years later, including 'Le puits et la pyramide', 'Hors livre', and 'Le parergon'. In addition, there are significant discussions in 'Violence et métaphysique', 'Ousia et grammē', 'La "différance"', and 'Les fins de l'homme', as well as critical mentions in *La Voix et le phénomène*, *De la grammatologie*, 'La double séance', and 'La mythologie blanche', along with the 1971 interview 'Positions'. There are other mentions elsewhere, but these are the main texts and they appear to come in two waves: setting aside 'Violence et métaphysique', it can be seen that there is an initial burst of activity from around 1966–9 that covers most of the texts above, and then a second wave from about 1971–4 that includes 'Positions', 'La mythologie blanche', 'Hors livre', and 'Le parergon', and, of course, *Glas*. As I am concerned with how Derrida approaches Hegel, I will be tracing the emergence of the thought of *différance* and its relation to Hegel's thinking through this first wave of writings, with a glance to the 1971 interview for indications of how Derrida's position develops (as such I will not be examining *Glas*, however the current work is preparatory for an extended reading of that text). This division is naturally somewhat arbitrary, especially as the lecture courses that Derrida gave in these years have not yet been published, but as a sketch I hope to show its value as a means to begin an understanding of Derrida's readings.[2]

Blanchot's writings on Hegel are less easy to specify, for while he is the focus of 'La littérature et le droit à la mort' (and to a lesser extent, 'Le langage de la fiction', also in *La Part du feu*), the effects of reading Hegel can be found throughout Blanchot's works, both critical and fictional, for example, discussions of Hölderlin or Mallarmé cannot but pass by way of Hegel at some point. Nevertheless, it is evident that there is a renewed interest in the 1960s, which coincides with his reading of Derrida and becomes apparent in many of the essays in *L'Entretien infini*, and later, *Le Pas au-delà* and *L'Écriture du désastre*. What is of note here is the way that Blanchot seeks to take account of Derrida's readings while continuing to pursue the lines of his own thinking, so that the readings of Hegel that emerge in these later writings tend to oscillate between taking up the points raised by Derrida and reaffirming his own perspective in light of Derrida's works.[3] Central to this last point is the role of the *neutre*, towards which Derrida is initially sceptical but that Blanchot slowly develops, so that by the time Derrida comes to write 'Pas' in 1976 he is more willing to consider its unique significance. This overview is again rather crude and only serves to indicate the main lines of inquiry, but although many of the notions that Blanchot considers (the *neutre*, the fragmentary, the outside, the disaster, the other night, and so on) can be understood as forms of rethinking key aspects of Hegel's thought, this is clearly not their sole source or basis. However, part of what I want to stress here is the effects of the widespread interrogation that Blanchot pursues, which insistently if indirectly questions the role and nature of the system, dialectics, mediation, sublation, and the absolute, etc. And it is as a result of this critical milieu that he is able to bring about a far-reaching rethinking of Hegel's ideas. Stated even more crudely, there is a feeling that as Hegel's works provide the environment of Blanchot's thinking (much more so than those of Heidegger or Nietzsche, for instance) this gives rise to a more thorough critique than that given in Derrida's writings, for whom, by contrast, it is the works of Husserl and Heidegger that provide the key environment.

As will be seen, Derrida's starting point in thinking relates to the question of the sign and the concomitant issues that arise from this, such as the relation between materiality and ideality, word and concept, metaphor and metaphysics, and so on. However, this is not the only way to approach the underlying concern with the status and borders of philosophy and literature, as Blanchot's writings indicate, which focus instead on the spatiality and temporality of the image and the experience of the textual field. The interest in the sign is a properly philosophical interest, insofar as it concerns the nature and structure of meaning, but it inevitably carries an emphasis on the distinction between signification and reference, and, perhaps more critically, sense and non-sense. Moreover, in its extension this emphasis creates a concern with reading in a strong sense. To clarify the implications and stakes of this approach it is helpful to look to a very different but parallel concern, that which arises in some forms of paranoia. When it becomes particularly severe, paranoia can give rise to a state in which meaning is felt to be present in all phenomena, however slight or contingent. This is not just a feeling that everything bears a meaning that directly impinges on the individual but one in which everything can become a vehicle for meaning. Thus, there is a persistent need to monitor and regulate this border of legibility, to determine the content of that which seems to be meaningful and to clarify that which is not readily readable. In such cases, paranoia leaves no room for that which is simply meaningless, so items that cannot be subsumed into the networks of significance become a further source of irritation until they are rendered into signs. This level of negotiation of the borders of legibility is a constant struggle with the accidental and merely empty and suggests something of the underlying imperative of the philosophical gaze.

Derrida clearly does not fall into this trap as his concern is with the way that this notion of meaning works and unworks itself and thereby generates the structures of thought that we know as metaphysics. But the emphasis on the urgency of reading in its relation to the demand to make meaning sets out the preliminary dimensions of his approach, which leaves it with an interest in the dissonance between sense and non-sense that is then drawn out in relation to the thought of Plato, Husserl, Freud, Lévi-Strauss, Foucault, Saussure, and so on. Hegel becomes an anomaly in these readings, for the more that Derrida examines his thinking the more Hegel seems to become a kind of simulacrum of his own thought, and, as such, the smaller the distance becomes between Hegel's works and those of writers like Artaud, Mallarmé, or Bataille. As will become apparent, the movement of *aufheben* is as much a 'metaphor' of metaphor, and thus of everything this entails, as *différance* in its own singular and non-substitutable manner. It is perhaps for this reason that *Glas* represents the culmination or exhaustion of this first period of his writings, as well as the bridge into his later concerns with issues of ethics and politics.

The aim of this inquiry is thus not to claim that Blanchot is in some way a better reader of Hegel than Derrida, for such a claim is clearly meaningless, especially as it is obvious that the terms in which we now approach Blanchot or Hegel are unavoidably indebted to Derrida's thinking. Instead, it is to explore the possibility that the peculiar form of writing that Blanchot develops may offer avenues of rethinking that Derrida did not pursue and that, consequently, the possibility of rethinking Hegel may also require such an alternative, which has considerable implications for the kind of thinking that Hegel has left to us to interrogate. Blanchot's writings provide one of the most extensive and important discussions of Hegel's thought in the last century, and to some extent this is precisely because it remains an implicit analysis. And it is perhaps only by way of this reading that we can come to a better understanding of the subtlety of Derrida's response to Hegel.

I The sovereignty of *différance*

Derrida's first important comments on Hegel come in his 1964 article on Levinas, where Levinas's works are persistently put in question by testing his claims to have moved beyond phenomenology. Thus, Derrida reads Levinas by way of Husserl and Heidegger but also, and especially, Hegel, whose thought indicates the difficulty of determining any position beyond or after metaphysics by way of the border thereby posited and the violence of the movement essayed. In particular, the ethical thought of Levinas – of the face, the gaze, desire, the other, and so on, all of which are formulated in terms of their infinity – is placed in contrast to Hegel's thinking of the infinite and its critique of transcendence, and metaphysics as such [e.g. ED: 175–6/119–20]. Hegel's role in Derrida's thinking is thereby designated by this question of the infinite as an interrogation of the border, which in this article is repeatedly but also provisionally marked as a question that remains to be addressed, and perhaps remains pressing to a greater extent than the issues arising from the works of Husserl and Heidegger. This early assessment is extensively modified in the winter of 1964–5, when he lectures on Heidegger and to a large degree seems to take up the criticisms of Hegel that Heidegger promotes; that Hegel remains a thinker of fulfilled presence, teleology, and rationality.[4] However, during this same winter, Derrida also writes an essay on Artaud that features the first appearance of the idea and term *différance*, which takes up this complex relation of the borders of language. In his earlier works, this relation was articulated in response to Husserl and his thinking of the idea in the Kantian sense, but the development of *différance* in 1964 seems to mark a different sense that perhaps owes something to the (infinite, immanent) Hegelian critique of transcendence.

After 'La parole soufflée', *différance* reappears (briefly) a year later in the second article on grammatology, and then again in the lecture on Freud and the scene of writing in March 1966.[5] In this way its development seems to take place by way of a triangulation of concerns from literature, psychoanalysis, and linguistics, which is to say, as a critique of philosophy from outside philosophy, as it were. Provisionally, we might say that the anomalies found in literature are given form in the sense of difference that occurs in linguistic and psychic differentiation (as drawn from Saussure and Freud) however, from the beginning, Derrida makes the ambivalence of this thought very clear. For example, in Artaud's letters to Rivière there is mention of something furtive (*quelque chose de furtif*) that haunts thinking and language, which, as Artaud explained, eroded his thoughts and robbed him of words so that, as Derrida writes: 'The furtive would thus be the dispossessing power [*vertu*] that always hollows out speech in the evasion of self [*dérobement de soi*]' [ED: 264/177]. That is, furtiveness is a double power of eroding and eroding (it)self, so that it takes place through this duplicity, which has considerable consequences: 'To let speech be spirited away [*souffler*] is, like writing itself, the archi-phenomenon of the *reserve*: the abandoning of the self to the furtive, to discretion, to separation and at the same time accumulation, capitalization, the security of the delegated or deferred decision. To leave speech to the furtive is to be reassured into différance, that is to say, into economy' [ED: 285/189–90]. This would appear to be the first mention of *différance*, and it is of note that it is marked in relation to a thought of economy as its necessary other, which will have a stronger bearing in the reading of Bataille, but for the moment it sets up the difference of *différance*: its inner distance and deferral that both conditions and destabilizes it.

What is important for present purposes is the way that Derrida comes to parse this difference, which indicates the stakes and the dimensions of his reading. It should be recalled first that, in reading Artaud, Derrida is seeking to take the measure of a form of speech that appears without measure, which appears to be the singular speech of madness in contradistinction to the measured and framed language of metaphysics. But, as this division is itself made from within the perspective of metaphysics, it cannot tell us what is ongoing when speech is spirited away (or stolen, whisked, or blown away; *souffler* refers to all these senses, which indicates the difficulty of assigning its agency or direction) from any such limits. Hence

> difference – or différance, with all the modifications that are laid bare in Artaud – can only be thought as such beyond metaphysics, towards the Difference – or Duplicity – of which Heidegger speaks. It could be thought that the latter, opening and at the same time concealing truth, distinguishing nothing in fact – the invisible accomplice of all speech – is the furtive power itself, if this were not to confuse the metaphysical and metaphorical category of the furtive with that which makes it possible.
>
> ED: 290–1/193–4

It thus becomes clear that the equivocation of *différance* is operating in relation to the ontological difference sketched out by Heidegger, and yet does so from its other side, as it were. This point will become very important in regards to Derrida's relations to Hegel and Blanchot, for whom the ontological difference is less definitive. In regards to Artaud, however, the reading that *différance* offers is such that it allows us to pass from one side of its limit to the other, in Derrida's words, that is, to see how Artaud operates both within and without the metaphysical, and particularly the metaphysical notion of madness. This also means that its reading allows for an understanding of the closure of presence within which metaphysics treats madness, and therefore of that which seemingly escapes it, while at the same time exposing the ineluctable tendency towards presence that this language comprises. This framework resembles the model of the history of metaphysics developed by Heidegger as that which cannot simply be overcome but retains its own oblivion. But it should also be remarked that this approach to reading difference comes with its own framework of posing these questions, and a thematics of inescapable closure and division. These aspects will have a decisive effect on Derrida's readings of Hegel, as will be seen, but will also make it possible to grasp the ways in which Blanchot, for instance, does not pursue such a thematics and thereby exposes a different way of relating to Hegel.

Consequently, in *De la grammatologie* the first mention of *différance* is in relation to Heidegger's sense of ontological difference, as if its first designation required a negotiation of its most immediate philosophical forebear. As Derrida explains, the sense or meaning of being is not a transcendental signified but 'a determined signifying trace', which means that in relation to the ontico-ontological difference both the ontic and the ontological are '*derivative* in regard to difference; and in relation to what we will later call *différance*, an economic concept designating the production of differing/deferring [*production du différer, au double sens de ce mot*]' [DG: 38/23]. To say that the ontic and the ontological are derivative of *différance* does not mean that the latter is their origin or ground, unless we rethink these terms under erasure, as that which is erased under the determination of that which follows from it; in this case, the difference of being and beings, between what is and the sense of what is. Nevertheless, the differentiation of *différance* is phrased in terms of this ontological difference, and moreover is explicitly marked as an economic concept designating the production of its differing and deferring (although Derrida will later insist that *différance* is neither a word nor a concept, hence the current definition should be seen as only partial). The import of this designation comes from the way that difference itself is primarily understood in terms of the differentiation of being and beings, a distinction specific to Heidegger's thought but one that he would later find wanting. However, by defining the meaning of being, as that which arises from and as this ontological difference, as a determined signifying trace, Derrida is sketching out quite densely the overlapping vectors or bearings that this meaning will take.

The ontological difference is only partially relevant to understanding the manifold of difference; there is also the question of its relation to linguistic and psychic differentiation, for can the latter also be phrased in terms of an ontological difference, and if so, what would be the necessity of this move? These distinguishing marks in the development of the thought of *différance* are important as they indicate how the thought arises in relation to its concerns, and it is significant that after introducing the term in this way Derrida explicitly turns to the question of its relation to the tradition, which is the point at which Hegel is introduced. As he explains, the hesitation of these thoughts about *différance* arise from the fact that the perspective of deconstruction always arises within the structures of previous thinking, specifically post-Hegelian thinking, and in doing so it borrows 'all the strategic and economic resources of subversion from the old structure', which of course carries its own risks and limits. A point emphasized by the fact that Hegel himself 'was already caught up in this game', as is found in his readings of Kant and Fichte where his thinking emerges precisely as that of an immanent and dialectical critique. Hence the results of this approach are always problematized by the necessity of inhabiting old structures, so when Derrida spells out how Hegel was caught up in this game, we should understand that his own thinking (and especially that of *différance*) will necessarily also suffer under the same constraints: On the one hand, Hegel 'undoubtedly *summed up* [résumé] the entire philosophy of the logos. He determined ontology as absolute logic; he assembled all the delimitations of being as presence; he assigned to presence the eschatology of parousia, of the self-proximity of infinite subjectivity. And for these same reasons he had to debase or subordinate writing' [DG: 39/24]. But equally, 'all that Hegel thought within this horizon, all, that is, except eschatology, can be reread as a meditation on writing. Hegel is *also* the thinker of irreducible difference. He rehabilitated thought as the *memory productive* of signs. And he reintroduced, as we will try to show elsewhere, the essential necessity of the written trace in a philosophical – that is to say, Socratic – discourse that had always believed it was able to ignore it' [DG: 41/26].

Unfortunately, the latter promise is not fulfilled as the discussions in 'Le puits et la pyramide' and 'Hors livre' do not go as far as demonstrating this essential necessity. Nevertheless, it is noteworthy that Hegel is described as the one who provides a model of thought as productive of signs, just as *différance* was said to be a concept designating the production of differing and deferring. More critically, however, the problem of a model that says that Hegel is this but also that, is that it leaves its equivocal aporia unexamined; whence arises this difference, and is it genuinely balanced? If what is said in the second account is true, then surely it unsettles the possibility of the first account, and if both are true, then their mutual unsettling would lead to a model that could not be so parsed without simplification. In Derrida's own terms, both aspects are derivative of a more originary thought, which would need to be approached first if an understanding of Hegel's thought in its actuality is to be obtained. Thus, the binary image that emerges from this equivocation is precisely that which emerges from an exterior perspective, not that which arises when one approaches Hegel's thought from within, which would have shown how this apparent duplicity necessarily arises out of the matter of his thinking, and is thereby anything but a simple duplicity. The limits of Derrida's approach here have come from the fact that he is attempting to approach the thought of *différance* from both within and without the tradition, across the borders of its economy.

It is in Derrida's last study of Husserl, which was written in 1966 as an introduction to the problem of the sign, that this equivocation starts to receive a more substantial focus, as it begins to take in the relation to time and to death, and Derrida crucially marks this transition in the conclusion where he explicitly turns from Husserl to Hegel. To some extent, Derrida is repeating the critique of phenomenology that had occurred in his essay on Levinas, but this time the rethinking of transcendence comes by way of the complex iteration of temporality as *différance*. As a result, *La Voix et le phénomène* draws together the elements of this critique through an analysis of the notion of the living present, so that it becomes a discussion that involves time and consciousness, memory and signification, and life and presence, and in doing so *différance* becomes articulated to a more profound degree. Through a discussion of Husserl's writings on time-consciousness, the notion of the present, the now, is distended and destabilized so that, as Derrida writes, it is constituted 'through the very movement of *différance* it introduces', where *différance* is understood as the 'originary' trace that makes possible the very structure of repeatability, of the moment as that which can be the now of life and meaning [VP: 75/58]. To elaborate, Husserl's study of the temporality of the present moment showed that its experience is constituted by protentions and retentions, traces of anticipation and memory, which undermine its possibility of existing as a single point. However, this model counters the understanding of representation he had developed in relation to primary and secondary memory, which would insist that the former is not contaminated by the latter. Hence the thought that Derrida introduces is to say that both retentions and representations derive from a more originary trace:

> The ideality of the form (*Form*) of presence itself implies in effect that it is repeatable ad infinitum [*à l'infini*], that its re-turn, as a return of the same, is necessary ad infinitum and is inscribed in presence as such; that the re-turn is the return of a present that will be retained in a *finite* movement or retention; that there is originary truth, in the phenomenological sense, only as it is rooted in the finitude of this retention; that finally the relation to infinity can be instituted only in the opening of the form of presence to ideality, as the possibility of a re-turn ad infinitum.
>
> VP: 75–6/58

Here is the basis of the later understanding that infinite *différance* is finite, but what is evident is the closeness of this model to Hegel's thinking of the now, and, more pertinently, that the aporia over Husserl's apparently differing aspects is worked out in terms of an equivalent tension within Hegel's thought. That is, the trace that is meant to be that from which the disparity of retention and representation is derived is developed in Hegelian terms as an implication of the finite and infinite, as Derrida will later make explicit, but without registering the resonance that this has for the equivalent tension in Hegel's thought. For if the trace of *différance* can be found to be what underlies and undermines Husserl's thinking, then can not the same be said in terms of the tensions within Hegel's thinking, especially when the trace is itself worked out in Hegelian terms? In which case are not these apparent tensions illusory and merely effects of a more originary and yet to be explicated thought?

Indeed, Derrida seems to allude to this by saying, 'does not this "dialectic" – in all senses of the word and before any speculative resumption [*reprise*] of this concept – open living up to différance'? [VP: 77/59] To think dialectics without speculation is not the same as to think it without relief (*relève*), although by terming this a speculative resumption Derrida is perhaps suggesting an isomorphism, but this would only be the case if one were to concern oneself with the ends of speculation rather than its results, as Hegel made clear. This point is brought out in the concern with a movement to infinity, and what it might mean to think the *différance* of the present moment to infinity, in all its repetitions and returns, especially, as Derrida writes, as it is this auto-affection of the present through *différance* that constitutes the subject. However, it does not do so in relation to 'a being that would already be itself (*autos*). It produces sameness as self-relation within self-difference, sameness as the non-identical' [VP: 92/71]. Hence the dialectic, of sorts, of this movement does not disrupt the possibility of the subject but is its basis, as that which constitutes the form in which it actualizes itself in both its identity and its difference. Difference is not originary but is rather a mode in which this originary trace assumes and relieves itself, thereby appearing as nothing but its own erasure and instability. Thus, parallel to the description in *De la grammatologie* we find the following lines where *différance* is said to be 'the operation of differing/deferring that at the same time fissures and retards presence, submitting it at once to an originary division and delay'. It is 'the active labour [*travail*] of difference' [VP: 98/75]. But the earlier point should not be forgotten, since this effect is ongoing to infinity; the presence of the living present, the moment of the now, and the very return to same of the subject in its identity and difference is that which takes place *ad infinitum*.

Before this is seen as the point by which *différance* distinguishes itself from Hegelian thought – by way of the passage to the infinite of subjectivity in its endless return, or repetition without end – Derrida makes very clear that this is exactly the thinking of the infinite in its genuine form that Hegel proposes, and in doing so goes much further than Husserl: 'Within this schema Hegelianism seems more radical: especially at the point where it makes it apparent that the positive infinite must be thought (which is possible only if it thinks *itself*) in order that the indefiniteness of différance appear *as such*'. That is, it is only through the implication of the infinite within the finite that the originary indeterminacy, from which identity and difference as such are derived, can be thought. The point of distinction does not lie in infinite repeatability but elsewhere:

> this appearing of the Ideal as infinite différance can only be produced in a relation to death in general. Only a relation to my-death [*ma-mort*] can make the infinite différance of presence appear. At the same time, compared to the ideality of the positive infinity, this relation to my-death becomes an accident of empirical finitude. The appearing of infinite différance is itself finite.
> VP: 114/87

Infinite *différance*, as that which constitutes the living present as the now (in whatever infinitely repeated and deferred form) of consciousness, can only be made to appear at the loss of this moment, which is to say that it is beyond experience, and in appearing it thereby punctures experience with an irretrievable, irresolvable finitude. So, if the dialectic is to open up the living to *différance*, then it can only do so by way of death, but death in general is not the same as my own death; it is rather that which occurs in my death as that which is anonymous and senseless, infinitely so, it is my death not as mine but as the death of all propriety or identity: my-death. It cannot be assumed or assimilated; there is no possibility of existential heroics here but only its endless evacuation as sheer meaninglessness, which is in effect what the experience, without experience, of *différance* would be. Thus, as this finitude of life, *différance* 'can no longer be thought within the opposition of finitude and infinitude, absence and presence, negation and affirmation' [VP: 114/87].

This relation to death as the loss of all sense is perhaps more critical to Derrida's reading than the distance he wants to take from a thought of experience (or negativity or contradiction). For a question is opened up in the thought of *différance* 'that opens neither upon knowledge nor upon some non-knowledge that is a knowledge to come. In the opening of this question *we no longer know*'. This is not to say that we know nothing, rather, it is necessary to understand this question 'as no longer belonging to the system of meaning [*vouloir-dire*]' [VP: 115–16/88]. Nor is this simply nonsense, for the lack of meaning as *vouloir-dire* is precisely that of intended meaning (*Bedeutung*), which is thus to undermine the possibility of completely satisfied intentions. This was, in part, suggested by Hegel when he wrote that in experience we learn 'that there is meant something other than what we meant' (*daß es anders gemeint ist, als sie meinte*), which is what is underway in the thinking of the speculative sentence, and of speculation as such, despite Derrida's reservations about this term [PG: 44/39]. However, Derrida has in mind a more severe aporia than that of emptied intentions, as the non-experience of death that punctuates life is a profound void of sense that cannot be articulated or appropriated in any form, and yet it subtends the very movement of such an assumption. But even here, when Hegel discusses the life and death struggle in the *Phänomenologie*, he makes clear that it is not simply death as the loss of life that is at issue but death as absolute negativity, which in its 'absolute melting-away of everything stable, is the simple essence of self-consciousness' [PG: 114/117]. As is evident, Derrida is pushing at the very possibility of distinguishing his thought from that of Hegel by testing his thought against it at every point, and what arises from this attempt are the innumerable nuances of emphasis that he makes in which there is found – to some extent by virtue of the mere fact that these nuances have been made – that which (out) lines the movement of *aufheben*.

It is from this position that it becomes possible to approach Derrida's 1967 essay on Bataille more clearly, since the difficulty of this essay is that Derrida is seeking, by way of his reading of Bataille, to essay the stakes and the possibility of extricating any thought from that of Hegel. While it might seem possible to dismiss Bataille's works from a philosophical point of view, doing so does not address the significance of their impact, for which it is necessary to proceed in a different manner. Consequently, Derrida does not deal directly with the flaws in Bataille's readings of Hegel, but rather focuses on the manner in which his thinking and writing sketch out challenges for the very form of Hegel's thought, which is at once a more important but more intangible question. For example, in the first part of his essay Derrida seeks to examine the laughter that Bataille raises in response to Hegel's analysis of the life and death struggle in the *Phänomenologie*, which marks his understanding of sovereignty in contrast to Hegel's own thinking of mastery or lordship. To understand what this distinction entails and what subtends it, Derrida describes laughter as that which 'alone exceeds dialectics and the dialectician: it bursts out only from [*depuis*] the absolute renunciation of meaning, from the absolute risk of death', which is to inscribe it in the movements of Hegel's thought at the same time as it exceeds them, since laughter does not really appear, for in its absence of meaning it is removed from the sphere of phenomenality and the very order of presence. Laughter is thus not a negativity, which would still leave it within the sphere of Hegel's thinking, but a simulacrum of phenomenality, that which, trait for trait, resembles a figure of appearance but alters all of them absolutely. As such, it is not abstract but rather the unbounded field of play, 'the almost-nothing into which meaning sinks absolutely' [ED: 376–7/256].

In providing this set of descriptions Derrida goes much further than Bataille in clarifying the import of his ideas, but in doing so he also raises the stakes for his own analysis as it is now a question of remaining faithful to this absolute renunciation of meaning, which is not simply madness or stupidity. The challenge that these ideas present to Hegel is considerable, but it is also a challenge to the nature of philosophical discourse in general, and even discourse as such, for it is a challenge to any attempt to find or express meaning. Thus, the problems begin to arise when Derrida seeks to pursue the relation of Bataille's ideas to Hegel's thinking, as this approach inevitably runs the risk of positioning each of the two, however delicately he tries to avoid it. Although Derrida makes it clear that Bataille is not working against Hegel, anymore than he is working with him, and precisely to the degree that he does not work in any kind of relation to Hegel, in his own reading there are nevertheless unhelpful statements – as when he makes comments about totality and presence, for instance, following the received image of Hegel as a thinker of systems.[6] However, insofar as Derrida is not discussing Hegel, but Bataille, it is perhaps not relevant to counter these mis-readings, but instead to pass through them to what Bataille was seeking to articulate by way of them, despite their generalizations. This problem only emphasizes the difficulties inherent in any attempt to present Bataille's thoughts, since the problems of his formulations are symptomatic of the fact that he was unable to find a form for his thinking that would be sensitive to their profound resistance to formulation. As a result, when they are introduced as part of an essay that seeks to assess their philosophical impact, however sensitively, they risk becoming bathetic, merely meaningless.

This is the risk that Bataille's thinking constantly skirted, and which he was not afraid to admit, but if such a thinking is to avoid the dialectic of meaning absolutely, then it is not sufficient for it to remain merely meaningless, it must bring about a disaster of meaning as such. But when Derrida goes on to write that 'the conscientious suspension of play [...] was itself a phase of play', and that 'sovereignty provides the economy of reason with its element, its milieu', these inversions do not seem to go far enough in their critique of Hegel's apparently totalizing thought [ED: 381–2/260–1]. Certainly, non-sense in its profoundest occurrence is unbounded, which is an aspect of its absence of reason, but the positioning that this economic reading draws out suggests that there is still a relation of (non-)grounding between reason and sovereignty. In Derrida's words, Hegel blinds himself 'to the baselessness [*sans-fond*] of non-meaning from which the basis of meaning is drawn and withdrawn [*se puise et s'épuise*]' [ED: 378/257]. (*Épuiser* means to exhaust, so this phrase could also be rendered as that which inspires and expires the ground of sense, like *souffler*, which is particularly resonant in relation to the discussion of laughter. It should also be recalled that Saint-Fond was one of the major characters in Sade's *Juliette*, a reference never far from Bataille's thought.) However, Derrida is making another distinction here that is exposed but left unmarked by the (economic) designation of grounding, which is that meaninglessness does not interrupt discourse like a caesura but occurs as an irruption of unboundedness.

Consider these lines: 'the sovereign operation, the *point of non-reserve*, is neither positive nor negative, it cannot be inscribed in discourse, except by crossing out predicates or by practicing a contradictory superimpression that then exceeds the logic of philosophy' [ED: 380/259].[7] And again, 'sovereign speech is not *another* discourse, another chain unwound alongside significative discourse. There is only one discourse, it is significative, and here one cannot get around Hegel [*Hegel est ici incontournable*]. The poetic or the ecstatic is that *in every discourse* that can open itself to the absolute loss of its sense, to the (non) basis [*(sans) fond*] of the sacred, of non-meaning, of un-knowledge or of play' [ED: 383/261]. These points are exactly what is at issue (as Blanchot would confirm in his 1971 essay on Merleau-Ponty), and it is not clear how Derrida will take them up, but it is worth noting that Hegel's discourse itself raises the issue of whether it is *incontournable* in that speculative language is exactly that which unwinds itself. The problem is made more acute in the lines following the last quotation, where Bataille is quoted as saying that sovereignty announces itself *in* the renunciation of theme and meaning, which is almost an apophatic claim. For if, as he wrote, poetry were simply play without rules it would become subordinated, instead, it must be 'accompanied by an affirmation of sovereignty (giving the commentary on its absence of meaning)'.[8] This is a challenging thought, as Derrida notes, for it outlines 'an admirable, untenable formulation, which could serve as the heading for everything that we are attempting to reassemble here as the form and torment of his writing', since its attempt to be a thought of experience and non-experience would appear almost impossible to deliver [ED: 383–4/261]. But this is the sense of a key aspect of Bataille's thought that he worked out in conversation with Blanchot: that sovereignty is the experience *of* non-experience, to the point of contesting itself, such that it only exists insofar as it expiates itself.

Despite Bataille's atheism, it is hard not to see such a thought as being some kind of mysticism (which he has however reconceived in an entirely different manner that separates it from both rationality and irrationality), and this is because it is primarily a thought to be explored in the sphere of experience, rather than in language and thought, as might be said to take place for Blanchot or Derrida. And, as if to confirm this point, Derrida moves into a discussion of Bataille's interest in sliding words, words that (like Artaud's thought of the furtive) appear to silence themselves, like the word 'silence' itself, which can only renounce itself in its annunciation, and thus opens onto meaninglessness. For the word, in so sliding, leads to an experience of a continuum that is, in a certain way, as Derrida insists, foreign to difference as it transgresses the limit of discursive difference, of articulated language.

> But – here we are touching upon, as concerns the movement of sovereignty, the point of greatest ambiguity and of greatest instability – this *continuum* is not the

plenitude of meaning or of presence such as it is *envisaged* by metaphysics. Pushing itself towards the non-basis of negativity and of expenditure, the experience of the *continuum* is also the experience of absolute difference, of a difference that would no longer be that which Hegel had thought more profoundly than anyone else: the difference in the service of presence, at work in (the) history (of meaning) [*au travail dans l'histoire (du sens)*]. The difference between Hegel and Bataille is the difference between these two differences.

ED: 386–7/263

As was found with Artaud, the subtle ambivalence of this point is such that it is difficult to imagine how it could be explicated and, as before, this would seem to be precisely the problem since, as an experience, it cannot be discursively explicated, and so its philosophical demands remain to some degree intractable. For, if the experience of this continuum is to be found through certain words that slide towards meaninglessness, then

> what must be found, no less than the word, is the point, the *place in a pattern* [lieu dans un tracé], at which a word drawn from the old language will start, by virtue of having being placed there and of having received such an impulsion, to slide and to make the entire discourse slide. A certain strategic twist must be imprinted upon language; which, in a violent and sliding, furtive movement, must inflect the old corpus in order to relate its syntax and lexicon to major silence.

ED: 387/264

No one who has studied the movements of Hegel's use of *aufheben* would be in any doubt as to the pertinence of this description, outside the mentions of sliding and silence, but the exact nature of the difference between the two approaches remains unclear. If the move towards silence is to be understood as that of meaninglessness, then the risk of erasing difference remains unaddressed. There may be a possibility of discourse being unsettled by such disruptions, but this would need to be shown so that difference can be found to persist in such moments of sliding. At this point there is no reason to suppose that what Bataille is doing is anything but a mystical (experiential) inversion of Hegel's thought, and the necessity of this move remains obscure.

If the sovereign operation is one in which the move towards non-sense is accompanied by its commentary, then it is necessary for the non-relation exposed in this sliding to be rigorously related to its discourse. This would be a language that relates to that which bears no relation, but that would not participate in the relation of relation and non-relation, in Hegelian terms. Thus, Bataille's task is to uncover this relation of non-relation, but as a sovereign operation it is unconcerned with results and possesses no authority; so there can be no assessment of its operation, no ability to determine whether it is successful or accurate. It is as such that Bataille is more oriented towards the experience, rather than its exploration through writing or thinking, even as he insists on developing its accompanying commentary. This is a double bind that seems insurmountable and yet he remains convinced as to its necessity, and it is here that we come to an understanding of his distance from Hegel. For if sovereignty seeks neither to subordinate nor to be subordinated, then it cannot assert itself over its own loss of experience and attempt, by whatever means, to recoup its failure as a higher meaning. Instead, it is a movement of sheer loss, without return and without reserve, a meaninglessness that cannot be converted into meaning in any form. So, the form of writing that arises to accompany sovereignty must be one that does not seek to maintain or assert itself but loses itself from the beginning, absolutely, and thereby puts at stake the very *space* of writing. In doing so, Bataille's thought becomes indistinguishable from that of philosophy, necessarily, insofar as it is concerned with the limits of experience, but at the same time everything in it is twisted out of shape so that what we read may appear to be the same as what is found in Hegel, for example, yet it finds itself becoming meaningless, exposed to an unbinding of its relations and an undoing of sense. Such writing would have expiated its links to knowledge and history, and any kind of identity or status, which then raises the question of the impact of these moments of sovereignty – in their necessary (non-)relation to Hegel – on Hegel's own thoughts.

It is important to realize that in the reversal that Derrida has drawn out, the inflection granted to Bataille's writing is such that it is now impossible to think of Hegel's discourse as operating within the simple circularity of a restricted economy, as the title of the essay makes clear. If the writing that is associated with sovereignty twists its terms out of their relation to meaning and exposes them to a non-relation to non-meaning, then this writing, which is seemingly indistinguishable from Hegel's, must be considered in terms of its effects on the latter, in terms of how it is read and experienced in reading. If non-meaning is the non-ground of meaning, then even if this does not mean that it is its source per se, it does mean that 'such a rupture of symmetry must propagate its effects throughout the entire chain of discourse' [ED: 399/272]. This point is crucial, since it means that the movement of *aufheben* itself 'is forced in writing to designate a movement that properly constitutes the excess of every possible philosopheme' [ED: 406/275]. What has been found in the multiplying series of inconclusive substitutions that characterize Bataille's thought is a series of mutual erasures that unground Hegel's thought of the transitions of determinacy, not entirely, but nevertheless inevitably. Instead of finding that Bataille's movement beyond Hegel merely confirms Hegelianism by virtue of this step beyond, the reverse takes place; everything that has been passed over is brought to the point of unsettling itself.

In writing this essay Derrida appears to take up a position in relation to Bataille that in part echoes the latter's own relation to Hegel. This is not just a result of the requirements of a sensitive reading but also allows for a better understanding of the language with which Bataille approaches Hegel, which despite its obscurity demonstrates a strategic displacement of Hegel's text. As Derrida had remarked earlier in relation to Artaud's writings, it is not enough simply to reverse the standard interpretative procedure – moving from the singularity of a text to its generalities – by seeking to preserve the singular on its 'own' terms (however this is construed, and Derrida is explicitly criticizing Blanchot's readings of Artaud and Hölderlin on this point) as this will not prevent it from being reduced in turn. Instead, what is needed is a reading that allows the singular to emerge within it in such a way that it comes to 'destroy itself as commentary' [ED: 260/174]. Thus, whenever we are told that Hegel's thought operates with a systematic circularity of meaning, where every purported loss is recouped as a higher meaning, so that nothing is ever allowed to escape, these statements are designed to indicate the sites and the stakes of a thinking that will necessarily undo itself. This point is made clearer when it is realized that Derrida has taken up Bataille's suggestion in the development of *différance* itself, which is an extension of the implications of *aufheben* as a rewriting of this speculative notion without relief.[9] However, questions still remain about the way that non-sense is said to be the ground or outside of sense, as this would seem to imply a certain relation or order of necessity, even as we are told that this must also be thought as a non-relation. While this is a variation of the thought of the conditions of possibility and impossibility of relation, it also indicates a further question about the relation of the finite and the infinite, which pertains to any kind of border or system.

II The spacing of *Aufhebung*

Taking up Bataille's suggestion, Derrida's readings focus on the economy of Hegel's thought, which is to say that they concern the systemic movements by which his thought takes place, with particular emphasis on the economic notions of use and value, profit and loss. At first, there seems little in Hegel's thought that would justify such an approach, but economy is a word used by Derrida across many contexts and its significance is twofold, insofar as it moves critique away from a discussion of whether a body of thought is meaningful or correct and towards a greater awareness of the dynamics of its thought, and secondly, a study that takes this economic point of view is obliged to address the decisions by which certain choices are made about what is included or excluded, what is valued or devalued in any body of thought. But there are disadvantages to this approach, in that its concern with evaluating the usage of concepts and terms and assessing the movements of the system as a whole bears its own assumptions. Moreover, by adopting this approach, critique is inevitably led into a (quasi-) transcendental enquiry into the conditions of possibility or impossibility of any thought, which is then, in Derrida's early writings, coordinated with a consideration of ontological difference, of the ground of being, which again carries assumptions about the nature and status of such conditions or grounds. This is not a problem in all of Derrida's readings of Hegel, but occasionally his approach seems to indicate a presupposition about the apparently onto-theological and onto-teleological dimensions of Hegel's thinking, which is likely to be derived from Heidegger's readings of Hegel but unfortunately bears little accuracy in terms of the detail of Hegel's thought.[10] It can be seen that assessing Hegel's thought as a teleological system that seeks to subsume all meaning into the self-realization of absolute knowing adopts this economic approach of modelling large-scale dynamics and their overall outcome. But it does not follow from the immanent working-out of the contradictions of the negative that it is inherently teleological, such would be a presupposition that Hegel's approach would disallow, as with any kind of assertion about the pre-existing or inevitable circularity or totality of the dialectic, as will be shown.

Heidegger's readings of Hegel (although criticized by Derrida in 'Ousia et grammē') carry an interpretation of his thought as that of presence and teleology that severely distorts his understanding of logic and history. These readings are found in *Sein und Zeit* and *Holzwege* and are taken up by Derrida in the 1964–5 lecture course on the question of being and history, which is the kernel for much of his works of the late 1960s, and it is clear that they are for the most part followed by Derrida, despite their evident limitations. Both these terms (presence and teleology, and their variants) act as models that frame Hegel's thought according to certain ontological suppositions about its movements and how these are organized into a system. But, as Hegel makes clear, his approach is not primarily ontological but logical, and as a result it is concerned with pursuing an immanent critique and development of thought that unfolds solely according to its own contradictions. This is not to say that Derrida's criticisms are invalid, since the question of the remainder and its relation to the movement of *aufheben* is of key importance, but this reading needs to develop from within the unfolding of the dialectic, rather than by assuming in advance that sublation is always teleological and totalizing.

Hegel begins from the point of wanting to develop thinking critically without presuppositions, so his thought cannot rely on a pre-existing external goal, or *telos*, which would act as a kind of magnetic pole, orienting the argument and drawing it towards its complete and final summation. Instead, without this presupposition, the argument can only emerge immanently and dialectically by working through the contradictions of the material as it presents itself to thought. Thus, one of the key points about the *Phänomenologie* is that each of its transitions is distinctive to its context, since each arises out of a loss of the certainty attached to its previous shape, which is the sense of experience that was discussed in the last chapter. So, for consciousness, the progress of this path involves a loss of a sense of self and of truth, alongside its reformulation into new shapes. This point drives Hegel in *Wissenschaft der Logik* to focus on the movement of the negative more closely, but the logic is also a work of pedagogy in that it seeks to teach us how to follow this movement and thereby assess whether its determinations are both accurate and necessary. In this way there is no suggestion that this logic is the only form in which the absolute comes to know itself, otherwise the extensive studies of history, religion, politics, and aesthetics would have no pertinence. Each determination that arises in the course of the unfolding of these contradictions is specific and implicitly directs us to what has been lost, for such is the labour of the negative. Furthermore, the place of the dialectic is to be understood solely in terms of these concrete scenarios; there is no abstract *aufheben* as such that can be extracted from its situations. As a result, Derrida is following in the path of Hegel in his own thinking of *différance, pharmakon, hymen*, and so on, but what he has brought to it is a much greater awareness of the internal displacements that occur as part of the movements of *aufheben*; not distorting it beyond measure but exposing it to its own singular mutations and ruptures. Thus, the problem of the nature and extent of this distortion then emerges, insofar as it forces us to address whether that which is discussed under the name of logic is fatally affected by its course or not, and what such blind spots would imply, if they can be said to imply anything at all if they lie outside the remit of logic, and hence what this will say about logic itself.

It is as such, and following Bataille, that Derrida will draw out other varying instances of such disturbance, which cannot be translated or substituted for each other as they are in each case singular differential marks. *Différance*, inevitably, plays a more pivotal role, not because it is in some ways the most basic or preliminary of these notions but because of its almost accidentally significant character, its appearance as a kind of textual pun, which evidently provoked as much delight for Derrida as the discovery of *aufheben* had for Hegel. So, the most helpful description comes when he writes that through *différance* 'the *Aufhebung* – the *relève* – is constrained into writing itself otherwise. Perhaps, very simply, into writing itself. Better, into taking account of its consumption of writing' [MP: 21/19; cf. D: 12/6–7]. The last point refers to the economic discussion of Bataille and Hegel, but also to Hegel's understanding of the communion of the Last Supper in terms of reading. In doing so, it raises the question not just of the material inscription that writing brings about but also of the syntactical *spacing* of sense, which then leads to the interest in forms of phrasing in which this spacing becomes apparent, and in which the association with (and deviation from) a kind of speculative sentence becomes most critical. Thus, the way that the notion of *aufheben* is oriented towards issues of temporality, memory, and metaphor undermines the straightforward association with the realization of sense in the sign, and indicates that the understanding of identity that occurs through the speculative sentence exposes a more scattered and divided thought. This understanding is developed in the first few essays of *Marges de la philosophie*, beginning with some remarks in 'Ousia et grammē', which discusses Heidegger's critique of Hegel's thinking of time and was based on a seminar from the winter of 1966–7, thereby making it contemporary with the Bataille essay.

In the *Naturphilosophie* Hegel elaborates a model of space and time in which space, which exists as 'self-externality' (*Außersichsein*), negates itself through the successive development of point and line, until time emerges as the truth of space [ENZ: §254, 243/28]. As Derrida writes, summarizing this account, time 'is thus thought in the wake of or in view of the point; the point in the wake of or in view of time. Point and time are thought in this circularity that relates them one to the other. And the very concept of *speculative* negativity (the *Aufhebung*) is possible only by means of this correlation or this infinite *reflection*' [MP: 47/43]. In Hegel's thinking, space, by way of its determinate difference, immediately negates itself into the point, which then negates itself into the line, which in turn negates itself into the plane, and thence to the geometrical body, thereby giving rise to the dimensionality of an affirmative space. It is thus that this negation (and negation of negation) is also a sublation in which each stage absorbs, overcomes, and expresses its internal difference into further forms as the progressive unfolding of the reason (self-difference) that animates space. But as dimensionality reveals an affirmative space, the negativity inherent to space itself has still to reveal itself, and it does so as a negation of this formation of spatiality as such, and it is thus that the negation of space emerges as time.

Derrida works through these stages but insists that time is present from the beginning of this series of negations, in that the movement by which the point becomes the line necessarily involves time, but this seems to miss Hegel's argument that the negation of space into the point and the line is immediate and evanescent, to such a degree that the point does not actually exist. Indeed, it is only with the emergence of time out of the negation of spatiality that the point achieves actuality [ENZ: §257 Z, 34]. By combining space and time together in the point Derrida also misses the possibility of accounting for the relation between them and hence for the emergence of time. (Perhaps this is because Derrida is seeking to draw out the flaws in Heidegger's reading of Hegel, since Heidegger had claimed that Hegel thought time as a form of space, whereas, in Derrida's reading, space for Hegel always already involves a temporality.[11]) Nevertheless, by stating that time is thought in the wake of or in view of the point, and vice versa, he remains true to Hegel if we understand that the point passes from non-actual to actual by way of time. It is this movement that Derrida emphasizes when he writes that the very concept of the *Aufhebung* is only possible by way of an infinite reflection, which is thus to mark speculative sublation with the delay and dilation of *différance*. For the 'concept' of the *Aufhebung* is impossible to the degree that it only appears by way of an *infinite* reflection, and there is therefore a profound and seemingly unbridgeable disparity between the word and the thought of *aufheben*. What is marked in this finite inscription is the infinity of an endless oscillation and correlation to which thought can only submit, without any hope of mastering it, as its concept remains on the other side of this reflection. And, insofar as the circularity and reflection that is mentioned here is that of temporality as it emerges, then this is in no way a circle or reflection that can entirely return to itself.

This point is expanded in a footnote where Derrida refers to passages from the ends of *Wissenschaft der Logik* and the *Phänomenologie* to explicate how, in his words, time 'is the *existence* of the circle', and is thus 'that which, in the movement of the circle, dissimulates circularity', losing the unity of its beginning and end and hiding its totality from itself.[12] There are two aspects to this circle, for on the one hand this sense of circularity means that any enquiry into the meaning of time in general will give rise to a suppression of time, which will struggle to distinguish itself from an onto-theo-teleology; but, on the other hand, as Derrida points out, this erasure of time is also 'a writing that gives time to be read', thereby maintaining it in suppressing it, such that this erasure is also an *Aufheben* [MP: 60/52–3]. In deleting time through thinking its meaning in general, it is thus realized in its deletion, just as the circle discovers and obliterates itself in its actualization, passing over its own course as both its existence and its concept. The passage thereby becomes ineradicable even as it dissimulates itself, which suggests that in this thought Hegel has perhaps come close to Klossowski's reading of Nietzsche (or even Bataille's understanding of sovereignty), and has not succumbed to a *parousia* of timelessness, for this thought of time is only insofar as its determinate existence is erased and thereby inscribed in finitude. As Derrida had concluded elsewhere, in thinking this 'trace' of temporality Hegel is therefore both the 'last philosopher of the book and the first thinker of writing' [DG: 41/26; cf. D: 27/20].

This ambivalent situation is of critical importance because the next essay in *Marges de la philosophie*, which comes from the same year as 'Ousia et grammē', 'La pharmacie de Platon', and 'La "différance"', is an extended analysis of Hegel's 'semiology'. In this discussion of the theory of the sign in Hegel's *Philosophie des Geistes* Derrida makes it clear that 'the process of the sign is an *Aufhebung*' [MP: 102/88]. While his analysis of this theory is developed through a study of the contradictory relations between imagination and memory in the production of signs, my focus is more specifically on the way that the sign is configured in the thought of *aufheben* as a trace, and thus as a form of spacing, as well as time. The process of signification, in which an intuition becomes a sign, occurs not only across time through its memorization but also across space, since, in Hegel's words, an intuition 'acquires, insofar as it is used as a sign, the essential determination of occurring only as sublated [*aufgehobene*]', that is, it occurs as a passage across its own interiorization and exteriorization.[13] As Derrida explains, intelligence produces the sign by negating its sensible spatiality, in a manner that echoes the movement by which time appears as the negation and sublation of space. This indicates the movement of time in the process of the sign, but also its trace of finitude, for if the sign is the truth of the intuition then, as Hegel writes, this also means that 'the truer shape of the intuition that is a sign is a reality [*Dasein*] in *time* – a disappearance of the reality as soon as it is' [ENZ: §459, 453/194].¹⁴ It is this combined existence as disappearance and truth that then comprises the sign, which is marked out in the movement of both memory as interiorization (*Erinnerung*) and its expression as sound and thereby language.

But, as Derrida recalls, the fact that the sign also occurs in the form of sound has its own implications, for in the *Naturphilosophie* sound is integral to the movement whereby material spatiality becomes material temporality in the form of vibration. There is thus, alongside the disappearing movement of the sign as trace, a double movement of materiality in which the mutual externality of the material parts of a body is negated, as the parts come together and interact, and then, as this negation is further negated, they separate again and begin to resonate, which leads to an inner oscillation that takes shape as sound. Or, in Hegel's words, 'through the momentary negation of its parts and, equally, the negation of their negation, the two being so linked that the one evokes the other, and so, through an oscillation between the subsistence and negation of specific gravity and cohesion, the material body as this *ideality* is the simple form *existing for itself* and arises as this mechanical animation [*Seelenhaftigkeit*] of appearance' [ENZ: §300, 297–8/137].¹⁵ Hegel terms this transmissibility (*Mitteilbarkeit*) of sound an ideal sublation, as it only takes account of the abstract materiality of bodies, insofar as it does not depend on their specific determinations and does not lead to any actual changes, unlike heat. Hence, just as there is a sublation of space into time, and a sublation of material spatiality into material temporality (in sound, but also in music and voice), so there is a sublation of sensible space into represented time in the move from intuition to sign to language (by way of memory).

Therefore, in the development of language that follows, there is a twofold aspect, for on the one hand there is the sublation of sound into the voice, in which its material element is displaced in favour of the expression of the idea, and on the other hand, in the sublation of the idea into the voice, the idea is made real. And so for Derrida the analysis of sound, and in particular the concept of vibration, reveals that

> it always marks the passage through the operation of negativity, of space into time, of the material into the ideal passing through "abstract materiality" (*abstrakte Materialität*). This teleological concept of sound as the movement of idealisation, the *Aufhebung* of natural exteriority, the *relève* of the visible into the audible, is, along with the entire philosophy of nature, the fundamental presupposition of the

Hegelian interpretation of language [...] and also its articulation with the more general system and the more ample chain of logocentrism.

MP: 109/93–4; cf. ED: 148/100

This reading is accurate except for the references to teleology and logocentrism, as the accounts in both the *Ästhetik* and the *Enzyklopädie* emphasize the alternation in the modes of sublation between materiality and ideality, while Derrida reads the negation of negation that occurs in sound as a double displacement of materiality, rather than its resonance or resounding by way of its material and ideal alternation.[16] Sound thus becomes a key mode of spatiotemporal configuration and orientation, but insofar as it always involves a passage through negativity, it is also a mode of disfiguration and disorientation. Such a distinction is important for what it indicates about the issue of writing, for if there is this double sublation in the voice (of the sign and language), the movement of idealization and materialization in writing is such that it renders this unity complex and evasive by way of its (re)introduction of the element of spacing.

Although the relation to materiality is intrinsic to the process of signification, by which it involves the experience of that which is without meaning and thus a relation of the proper to the improper, it also directs the question of meaning towards the relation of the finite and the infinite, to the very borders of the known, and hence to the nature of the border as such. The sublation of this opposition occurs within a renewed thinking of space as difference, as spacing, which begins to convey the sense of what Hegel discusses as the true infinite. This sense of immanent but non-present pervasion of the limited by the limitless, the proper by the improper, life by death, is also conversely the punctuation of the infinite by the finite, which is indicated in the way that the analysis of texts as negotiations of meaning becomes modified when they are instead seen as fields. It is in Derrida's 1969 reading of Mallarmé that this change of approach becomes most evident, as it examines the way that the text constitutes itself as a field of blanks and folds. The blank is not only the space between words, and between the text and the seemingly endless field of the page, but it is also to be found within the words themselves in their phonic or textual form as the whiteness or emptiness (*blancheur*) of their spacing, alongside the curves and seams of their *plis*, with all their thematic and lexical variations. As such, the space of the text is rendered infinite as it has no inner or outer border: the margin only has an arbitrary outer limit, and there is no inner point at which the distinction between page and word is grounded as the interplay between words and spaces undermines their position and formation. Hence Derrida can go on to state that the search for meaning and the analysis of themes becomes undone in Mallarmé's writings, so that critique as such becomes disoriented.

This notion of inner destabilization had already been marked in *différance*, insofar as it is both more and less than a simple word and not simply relatable to a concept. Instead, it is undermined by an undecidable oscillation between being a mark and a remark as it remarks its own literality, which is also its own rhetoricity, and as a result indefinitely displaces any precise grounding of its sense. Such corrosion provokes an eternal return of reading as it continually seeks (and fails) to determine its meaning and so move on, thereby creating a spacing and deferral of the text, an opening onto its own limitlessness. The effects of this disruption on thought are not simply to nullify it but rather to render it speculative in Hegel's sense: to enable it to experience its own transformation. This strategy can also be found in the syntax of 'without' in Blanchot's writings, and in the use of *pas* (which will be discussed later), both of which focus on the nature of the border and its metaphysical corruption. As a result, it is critically important to examine the speculative possibilities of phrases like *pas sans pas*, or *sans sans sans*, given the displacements already effected on the movements of *aufheben* by the use of *différance*. Since, in their undecidability, these phrases have neither beginning nor end, neither grounding nor identity, but seem to entail an exposure to the infinite and its thought. Syntax has to do with the articulation of sense, and thus bears a form of violence in its gathering and binding of expression, but in the openings found in these phrases used by Blanchot there is less a form of articulation than a vertigo [ED: 219/147–8; EL: 22/31; EI: 65–6/46].[17] For this reason, thought finds itself unmoored from the scope of economy, of the circulation of values and their management, which is to say that it is not quite metaphysical any longer, but rather speculative. In his review of Derrida's reading of Rousseau, de Man observed that this problem arises in relation to texts that we call 'literary', which is to say; 'any text that implicitly or explicitly signifies its own rhetorical mode and prefigures its own misunderstanding as the correlative of its rhetorical nature'. And, as he goes on to say: 'it follows from the rhetorical nature of literary language that the cognitive function resides in the language and not in the subject'.[18] It is precisely this thought, and its cognitive aporia, that is at issue in Hegel's writings as much as it is in Derrida's.

Hence rather than focusing on the themes of a text – which reduces it to being no more than a form of expression, a 'representative psychologism', in which there is a conventional dialectics of appearance, a phenomenology, wherein the text seeks to bring forth a pre-existing idea – it is necessary, as Derrida explains in reference to Mallarmé's writings, to examine both the destabilization of this approach and the *diacritical* appearance of another kind of reading: the lateral, differential variation that is marked by the spacings and openings of the text. These are not variations from an established or potential centre or culmination, for as Derrida makes clear the diacritical expanse cannot be gathered up into a final or total meaning, not because there is an ever-receding horizon of significations granted by the overflowing richness of sense in the text, but because its limit is reconfigured 'through the angle and the intersection of a re-mark folding the text upon itself without any possibility of its fitting back over or into itself [*de recouvrement ou d'adéquation*], without reduction of its spacing' [D: 282/251]. It is apparent that this is a reconfiguring of the thought of the infinite and its intersection with the finite, in which the non-themes of the blank and the fold prevent us from asserting any kind of transcendental meaning that would exist in a realm beyond the text.

This assertion is the basis for Hegel's rejection of the problems inherent to the bad infinite, which in its limitation by the finite becomes a transcendent sphere outside finitude, and whose limitations are only overcome in the true infinite, which takes place through the finite as its endless turning in and of itself. Derrida is aware of this account but he feels that his own thought of the fold goes against that of the Hegelian infinite, for even though infinity takes place in the text through this immanent pervasion there remains a lining of non-sense that is not recouped in its movements, as will be seen. But in showing how this sense of the infinite occurs in the text, we are given a much greater awareness of how its implications and inversions unfold according to a non-totalizing, non-teleological eccentric expanse, even within the Hegelian model. Although Hegel uses an image of a circle to describe the true infinite, this is to call our attention to its lack of beginning or end, and in stating that this circle is closed and wholly present, he is not so much claiming any sense of *parousia* as directing us to its lack of exteriority or transcendence. In the return to itself of the finite and the infinite, the true infinite is both being and its determination (negation), that which *is* and *is there*, as he writes, and it is thus that it is also becoming [WL2: 136/149].[19] Hence the true infinite is not static and complete but is the continual alternation of the infinite and the finite in their dialectical inter-relation, as they each negate and sublate themselves into the other, and it is as such that it is infinite. The finite, as that which passes away, and the infinite, as that which goes on, are brought together as moments of a process that endures even as it transforms itself. The image of the circle should then be understood speculatively, in much the same way that we need to extend our understanding of the notion of the sphere (as finite but unlimited) as an image of the large-scale structure of the universe in contemporary cosmology. Derrida is not countering Hegel's thought on this point as much as he is marking out the undefined limits of its movements and their implications.[20] Thus, the resonance between Derrida's reading of Mallarmé and Hegel's account of the true infinite comes from the way that the unfolding in Mallarmé's text is not that of an abundance, but rather 'a very singular and very regular monotony', and that the variety of apparent themes is actually no more than an endless disappearing, which is its finitude.

Let us take the fan (*éventail*), which draws out many of the issues of the fold for Mallarmé. To do so, as Derrida spells out, involves not only an inventory of its occurrences, and a description of its phenomenological structure, but also an awareness that the fan remarks itself (and is thus more, or less, than either a word or an idea). Alongside the object that it names, it indicates all the units of meaning that take up this movement of opening and closing, and further, 'inscribes *above and beyond* [de surcroît] it the movement and structure of the fan as text, the explication and implication of all its valences, spacing, fold, and hymen *between* all these effects of sense, writing setting them up in relations of difference and resemblance'. Between the book, the page, the text, the phrase, the word, and the space that permeates through the opening and closing of this writing, there is no possibility of finding a grounding, or starting, or culminating point or sense, as each continues to reflect and inflect the other through 'a scattered [*eparsé*] infinite' [D: 283/251]. In this remarking the mark is never just a mark but that which leads beyond itself, marking both its limits and its negation, such that it is not transcendent but infinite: it is that which reflects the finitude of the mark as that which not only ends but leads into its other as its negative, which is the realization of its (im)possibility. It is thus that this surplus appears in the form of metaphor, even though it is not one, as it 'marks the structurally necessary position of a supplementary inscription that can always be subtracted from or added to the series' [D: 283/252]. So, despite these manifold changes and complex inversions, the sense of their still being an 'it' to which these transformations refer is not lost; the fan remains or endures even if it is no longer possible to delimit its identity or position.

The same can then be said in regard to the blanks, with even more intricacy and convolution, in that they directly implicate the nothingness intrinsic to the movement of the surplus (in a way that resembles but also extends the parenthetical openings in Roussel's works). The blanks in Mallarmé's writings may appear to carry the weight of a meaning that bring all his works together; however, they not only mark themselves in their multiple valences but, as blanks, also mark the spaces between the valences. 'Hence the *blanc* (is) the totality, however infinite, of the polysemic series, *plus* the partly opened [*entr'ouverture*] spacing, the fan in the form of the text' [D: 284/252]. It is important to note that *plus* can mean both 'more' and 'no more', and Derrida is making use of both aspects to underline the supplementary and syntactical nature of the mark [D: 50/43]. Thus, the surplus is not just one extra mark but nor does it become the one mark that organizes and grounds the whole. Instead, the blank becomes an emptying of meaning that nevertheless explicates itself, without thereby constituting (itself as) meaning or signifiers. It therefore becomes non-sense, precisely, relating the different meanings to each other while keeping them distinct and thus falling outside the possibilities of being defined or circumscribed. There are no descriptions of the blanks in Mallarmé's writings, and so no scope for critique to adopt a similar approach in relation to them; there is only the spacing of their diacritics as 'a readability without a signified' [D: 284/253]. Reading encounters a polysemy that in being infinite has no beginning or end since it is not a differentiation of meaning from or to a particular sense. It is as such that Derrida will prefer the term dissemination, as the text bears no centre or order and, as infinite, is pervaded by finitude, as its blanks remark themselves in their disappearance as erasure and non-sense. 'Finitude then becomes infinitude', as Derrida writes, but 'according to a non-Hegelian identity', even in its speculative sense, which is explicated in following way, reiterating the argument thus far: 'through an interruption that suspends the equation of the mark and the meaning, the "*blanc*" marks every white [. . .] *plus* the blank that allows for the mark in ensuring the space of reception and production. This "last" blank (or just as well, this "first" blank) is neither before nor after the series' [D: 285/253]. The blank thus takes up the role of negativity as mediation in Hegel's thought, but suspends its determination, which means that the identity of finite and infinite is neither completed nor guaranteed but is exposed to the endless convolutions of its aporia. And, as Derrida then states, because the blank is not limited to the spacing of the white but is to be found within and between all series of meanings, it prevents seriality as such from being constituted while yet liberating 'the effects of a series, in marking itself out it *makes us take* agglomerates – for substances' [D: 285/254]. It becomes productive, that is, of difference in both its Hegelian and Derridean senses.

Thus, this reading does not undermine the appearance of the Hegelian sense of identity, but places a stronger emphasis on the possibility of its fulfilment by indicating the degree to which negativity takes place within the dialectic when it is released from an erroneous belief in teleology or totality. This sense of negativity, or non-sense, is what remains of the *Aufhebung* when it is understood that the dialectic takes on a myriad of specific forms according to its context, and that in these contextual contingencies there is always that which is not part of the transformation of contradiction but instead remains (preserved as) strictly meaningless. There is no *aufheben* as such; it is always to be understood by way of its finite occurrence as it is the passage of the finite as it negates itself, which reveals what was negated and what arises out of it, as well as the spacing that enables this movement to take place, which only appears afterwards as its hollow. In his attempts to delineate the difference between *différance* and *aufheben* Derrida makes much of the irreducibly written aspect of the former, its material inscription, as well as its deviation from a thought of resolved contradiction. But it is important to remember that *aufheben* is not just an idealist thought but a word, and a word that is not identical to itself; moreover, despite gathering up the senses of cancellation, elevation, and preservation, *aufheben* is still an anomaly as the word marks itself as an inability to clearly distinguish and coordinate these phases.[21] Conversely, the significance of the word for Hegel is this quality of combining contradictory meanings without dissolving them: resolution does not mean the loss of difference but the resolve to hold to its inescapability; to recognize the truth of contradiction by rendering it absolute. In particular, as Adorno emphasizes, the role of the dialectic is to resolve contradictions only in the sense of rendering them fluid again by re-solving their reified forms.[22] The thought of *aufheben* is thus irreducible to the word even as the word itself remains irreplaceable and non-negligible, and we can grasp a sense of this in the profound difficulties that have arisen in trying to translate it.

In this regard it is distracting when Derrida refers to the *Aufhebung* as 'the decisive target', or when he states that 'it goes without saying that the double meaning of *Aufhebung* could be written otherwise' [D: 280/248; P: 55–6/41].[23] For on other occasions he is sensitive to the peculiar manner of its appearance, as when he asks, in relation to contradictory senses of *aufheben*, whether it is by chance that 'these "words" that escape philosophical mastery have, in widely differing historical contexts, a very singular relation to writing' [D: 250/221]. Indeed, some years earlier, he had gone as far as to say that 'one would have to do for each concept what Hegel does for the German notion of *Aufhebung*' [ED:

167/113–14]. Interestingly, this last point is revised in 'La double séance', just before the remark about the evasion of mastery mentioned above, when Derrida states that 'it is not a case here of repeating in relation to *hymen* what Hegel undertook to do with German words like *Aufhebung*', and in saying this he provides a more helpful characterization of the distinction that separates his thinking from that of Hegel, since what counts is not the lexical richness of a term that bears contradictory meanings but 'the formal or syntactic practice that composes and decomposes it' [D: 249/220]. In saying as much Derrida is emphasizing the diacritical importance of *hymen*, in that the word is not significant in itself, unlike *aufheben*; instead, its importance arises more as a result of its syntactical role, its placing and displacing within the writing of thought, than through any content that it may bear.

III *Aufheben* with and without relief

With these points in mind it is worth looking more closely at Derrida's 1971 interview with the Marxist-Leninist critics Jean-Louis Houdebine and Guy Scarpetta, as it gave rise to some of his most emphatic descriptions of his thought and its distinctions from Hegel. These points have been addressed by others, but largely in passing and, as is often the case, merely as confirmatory statements. This lack of critical engagement is problematic because what Derrida says here is complex and sometimes appears at odds with his more nuanced statements elsewhere.

> If there were a definition of différance, it would be precisely the limit, the interruption, the destruction of the Hegelian relève *wherever* it operates. The stakes here are enormous. I emphasise the Hegelian *Aufhebung*, such as it is interpreted by a certain Hegelian discourse, for it goes without saying that the double meaning of *Aufhebung* could be written otherwise. Whence its proximity to all the operations conducted *against* Hegel's dialectical speculation.
>
> P: 55–6/40–1

Read in context the comment about the writing of *Aufhebung* now appears quite differently: not as a dismissive gesture but rather as a recognition that *différance* itself might be a form in which *Aufhebung* could appear, if it were written otherwise. Such is the import of the qualification that *Aufhebung* exists at the borders of Hegel's text, insofar as it can both support a certain kind of Hegelian discourse and appear alongside those operations conducted against it. This point then leads into a discussion of the necessity of differentiating between

Hegelianism in its traditional forms – as idealism, as dialectical materialism, as rationalism, as eschatology – and the word and thought of Hegel's texts, which leaves the following issue:

> I have attempted to distinguish différance (where the *a* marks, among other things, its productive and conflictual character) from Hegelian difference. And have done so precisely at the point where Hegel, in the greater *Logic*, determines difference as contradiction only in order to resolve it, to interiorise it, to relieve it [*relever*], according to the syllogistic process of speculative dialectics, into the self-presence of an onto-theological or onto-teleological synthesis. Différance must signify (at a point of almost absolute proximity with Hegel, as I have emphasised, I think, in the lecture and elsewhere: everything, and what is most decisive, is played out here in what Husserl called "subtle nuances", or Marx, "micrologies") the point of rupture with the system of the *Aufhebung* and speculative dialectics. This conflictuality of différance, which can only be called contradiction if one demarcates it by means of a long work on Hegel's concept of contradiction, never lets itself be totally resolved, it marks its effects in what I call the text in general, in a text that is not reduced to a book or a library and that can never be governed by a referent in the classical sense, by a thing or a transcendental signified that would regulate all its movements.
>
> P: 59–61/43–4

Derrida adds a note to the point about Hegel's *Wissenschaft der Logik* to specify the section he is referring to [WL2: 279/431]:

> "Difference in general is already contradiction *in itself*" (*Der Unterschied überhaupt ist schon der Widerspruch* an sich). As it can no longer simply be subsumed under the generality of *logical* contradiction, différance (the *process* of differentiation) permits a differentiated accounting for heterogeneous modes of conflictuality or, if you will, for contradictions. If I have more often spoken of conflicts of force than of contradiction, this is first of all due to a critical wariness as concerns the Hegelian concept of contradiction (*Widerspruch*), which, in addition, as its name indicates, is constructed in order to be resolved within dialectical *discourse*, in the immanence of a concept capable of its own exteriority, and of having what is outside it right next to it. To reduce différance to difference is to stay far behind in this debate [...] Thus defined, the "undecidable", which is not contradiction in the Hegelian form of contradiction, situates, in a rigorously Freudian sense, the *unconscious* of philosophical contradiction, the unconscious that ignores contradiction to the extent that it belongs to the logic of speech, discourse, consciousness, presence, truth, etc.
>
> P: 60/101

Despite the lack of subtlety in some of Derrida's statements, as when he refers to 'the self-presence of an onto-theological or onto-teleological synthesis', the basis of the distinction he is drawing lies in the diminished role that Hegel grants to difference, which is explicitly redressed in the transition and translation to *différance*. It is unfortunate that Derrida does not recall Hyppolite here, as his book shows why difference is displaced by contradiction, by demonstrating that difference as such remains an aspect of the (empirical) understanding insofar as it only views it from the outside, rather than speculatively seeing difference within objects and thought as their own inescapable contradiction, their own difference and opposition to themselves [LE: 145–57/113–21].[24] Nevertheless, this transformation still takes place for Derrida in the way that difference is, in effect, 'translated' into *différance* on one side of the *Aufhebung* just as is the contradiction that lies on the other side. For, in going on to refer to Freud, Derrida shows that the undecidability at issue is not a contradiction to the degree that it operates as the unconscious of discourse, which allows for a further rereading of the stakes of the translation of *aufheben* (which is perhaps taken up more thoroughly in Lyotard's *Discours, figure*).

Thus, for *différance* to be 'the limit, the interruption, the destruction of the Hegelian relève *wherever* it operates' is to follow the detail of Hegel's (translated) thought of *aufheben* along each of its dimensions of elevation, preservation, and cancellation, such that it may not ever be possible at all, or rather, that its possibility is always measured against its concomitant impossibility. As a result, the thought of *différance* can only be fully understood to the degree that the same occurs to that of *aufheben*, as it is only by realizing the manifold difficulties of *aufheben* that the significance of Derrida's intervention can be gauged. And the same can be said in relation to contradiction and difference, for despite the displacements that Derrida provides there still arises a problem when it is claimed, for instance, that contradiction, 'as its name indicates, is constructed in order to be resolved within [*est fait pour être résolu à l'intérieur du*] dialectical discourse', as this risks imposing a tautological and teleological order on Hegel's thinking (there is no necessary link between contradiction and discourse; contradiction is not limited to speech but is primarily a logical form for Hegel, and thus is the concrete form of life and all the social, cultural, and historical forms that arise from it) and also puts in place the possibility of an opposition between the voice of language in its self-presence and the differentiating and deferring disruptions of textuality, an opposition that in its simplicity has done much to reduce the subtlety of Derrida's thinking. Equally, while it would indeed be a misreading to reduce *différance* to difference, it is also necessarily the case that the thought of difference is partly that from which *différance* arises and so difference is never simply difference, as is evidenced by the fact that *différance* is paraphrased as the '*process* of differentiation', just as, in the lecture that he refers to, the active sense of differentiation apparent in Hegel's phrase '*differente Beziehung*' is also paraphrased as *différance*.[25]

The situation is, then, more complicated than it first appears. And, as the interview progresses, Houdebine in particular presses Derrida over the relation between his thinking and that of dialectical materialism, and in doing so the questions of materiality and contradiction become more critical. While Derrida has much to say about the history of materialism and the concept of materiality, the issue of contradiction is one that he appears to equivocate over, perhaps inevitably. Although he reaffirms his earlier reluctance to use the term, he also concedes that contradiction could be rethought, with the necessary critical precautions and negotiations with the Hegelian text, and even paraphrases *différance* as an effect of contradiction [P: 102/76]. This is not to draw out a flaw or inconsistency in Derrida's position but rather to emphasize the peculiar difficulty of coming to any kind of definitive relation to Hegel's thought. As such, the equivocation found in this interview is representative of this problem, for in seeking to explain his own thinking Derrida is led to make some strong statements about its distance from Hegel's thought, but when he is pushed into discussing Marx and Lenin he comes to make some more nuanced statements about the lack of unity to Hegel's text:

> In effect I believe that Hegel's text is necessarily fissured; that it is something more and other than the circular closure of its representation. It is not reduced to a content of philosophemes, it also necessarily produces a powerful writing operation, a remainder of writing, so it is necessary to re-examine the strange relation that it maintains with philosophical content, the movement by which it exceeds its intended meaning, lets itself be turned away from, returned to, and repeated outside of its self-identity.
>
> P: 103–4/77–8

The distinction over the differing readings of contradiction and difference, which is at the heart of the difference between Derrida and Hegel, is partly drawn from Hyppolite's *Logique et existence*. The key significance of this book lies in the fact that Hyppolite moved from Hegel's phenomenology to his logic by way of language, which united both aspects of his thought and introduced the notion of difference as such, insofar as it realized the double-sidedness of language as active contradiction, or differentiation. It is from this reading that Derrida's early thinking emerged, in that he took up the ambivalence of sense and signification in language, as well as the relation between thought and memory, in his concerns with the problem of the sign in Husserl's thought, which in turn laid the ground for his readings of Hegel.[26] However, as he has indicated, Derrida leaves this understanding of contradiction behind to emphasize the role of difference, at least partly because his readings of Heidegger and Saussure (and Freud) focus on their understandings of difference, and also because his studies of Husserl yield a critique of presence that leads to the distinction between writing and the voice that appears to underlie the forms of *différance* and contradiction (it can also be seen that he is unwilling to let his thought be aligned to the thinking of contradiction found in contemporary Maoism). Understanding Hyppolite's account is thus of crucial importance for ascertaining how it might be possible to read Hegel's works otherwise: with less of a view to their significative teleology and more in terms of the ambivalence already at stake in the experience of language, as is the case in Blanchot's understanding of the work of literature and the negativity of language. This ambivalence is perhaps more trenchant in its critique than the thought of *différance* on its own, which, as has been shown, to some degree still equivocates in an oppositional reference to *aufheben*.

Thus, even if some of Derrida's general comments are occasionally unhelpful, his conclusion in 'Le puits et la pyramide' remains significant for its manner of posing the possibility of evading the limits of Hegel's thinking: 'what might a "negative" be that could not be relieved?' Such a negative, which would not appear or make itself present, and so would not take part in meaning, would still 'get on' (*réussirait*, in the sense of doing well, thriving, succeeding) but would do so as pure loss, a kind of functioning without utility or result. This pure functioning would be unthinkable insofar as it has no meaning and so could not be relieved; it is instead a non-work (*non-travail*) and yet it proceeds (*marche*). 'Alone. Outside.' (*Tout seul. Dehors.*) [MP: 126/107] This somewhat odd use of language takes up the point raised in the Bataille essay, where the attempt to avoid the sphere of Hegelian thought must first proceed by undermining its linguistic tone and form. And so, as he had said in the *différance* lecture, the main virtue of this word is the translation that it effects, for 'despite the relations of very profound affinity that *différance* as it is so written maintains with Hegelian discourse (such as it must be read) up to a certain point it cannot break with it (which has no kind of meaning or chance) but it can operate a kind of displacement that is at once infinitesimal and radical' [MP: 15/14]. However, one of the key points of Hegel's dialectic is that it discounts any sense of purity, so there cannot be any possibility of pure loss, a point Derrida would probably also maintain. Equally, in light of the essay on Bataille, where the thought of Hegel is contrasted with the disruptions of laughter, eroticism, poetry, sacrifice, and drunkenness, it is apparent that these notions of what evades the dialectic are too simplistic, as none of these instances can be counted as occasions of entirely meaningless loss [ED: 405/275]. In this way, it is perhaps to the degree that Bataille's thought is (strictly) unsatisfactory that Derrida's readings of Hegel are also unsatisfactory, which is not a mere sophism but a marker of the difficulty of putting into philosophical discourse that which contests the very basis of a language that aims to bring about satisfactory resolutions.

Nevertheless, the point remains about the possible status of a negativity that could not be relieved, and the displacement that this will imply for the operation of *aufheben*. Such negativity means nothing and plays no role, not by virtue of some purity that keeps it removed but by its weakness and emptiness. If it is the fact of contradiction that leads to the *Aufhebung*, then this negativity would evade it, not because it lacked contradiction, but because it could not be mediated, because it somehow fell short of it. The word that Bataille uses here, as does Blanchot, is *neutre*, which Derrida rejects as still being tied to the form of the negative as not-this (*ne-uter*), but this criticism does not take account of the way that the *neutre* persists in being neither this nor that, in a manner that Bataille and Blanchot would call sovereign.[27] Bataille's examples are unconvincing, he says as much himself, so are his attempts to criticize Hegel, and yet there remains something elusive in his writings, something that by virtue of their genuine untenability suggests points of loss that in doing so mark their evasion of relief, precisely to the degree that they also evade satisfaction. Blanchot's writings perhaps appear more persistently challenging to the extent that they distort philosophical discourse in favour of literature, which is exactly that which remains too weak to be relieved and too contradictory to be resolved. The thought of *aufheben* cannot be avoided by avoiding its passage through negativity, as Derrida himself concludes in his postscript to the interview above, 'the Aufhebung is always there' (l'Aufhebung, *y en a toujours*) [P: 130/94]. Thus, to understand its limits, *aufheben* must first be understood in detail, without presupposing that it is teleological or totalizing, but instead by tracking its negativity and its possible points of deterioration.

3

Hegel: uneasy infinite

I *Aufheben* in sense-certainty

To understand Hegel's thought of *aufheben* it is essential to grasp how it is developed, and the way that its complexity is articulated, as this tells us much about its specificity and the difficulty of generalizing it. The term is first used in the *Phänomenologie* in the discussion of sense-certainty and specifically in the analysis of the 'now', which in being pointed out ceases to be. Consequently, the now that *is*, is not the one pointed to but another one, so that the now is no more when it is pointed out but is rather what has been (*ein gewesenes*). The truth of the now is thus that it *is* not, it has no essence. Hence in this pointing out there is a three-fold movement that is the first appearance of sublation: Firstly, I point out the now and assert its truth, but in doing so the now reveals itself to be what has been, which is thus what has been superseded (*ein Aufgehobenes*).[1] Secondly, I assert as true that the now has been, and that it has been superseded. The third move is more complicated as it involves a double realization that what has been asserted as true cannot be true as it is an assertion of what is not, therefore the negation of the now, as it is found to be what is not, is itself negated in turning back from the assertion of the sublated now into a more nuanced position in which the now is asserted as what is in both its coming to be and its ceasing to be. The now is neither what is pointed to in simple indication, nor is it what has been, nor that which comes to supersede it as the new now. Instead, the now is the combination of these modes as that which is not simply indicated and asserted as either present or absent. The now as a moment is instead enlarged to become one in which there is a manifold of nows and their absences, this now and this and this, and so on, along with their non-existence as that which has been and thus is no more. This is the moment in which the now realizes its universality as more than a mere sensible particular, a mere point.

This argument is repeated in relation to the designation of here, with the same results that it is not simple but involves many other not heres, and so reveals the universality of the here that is latent within it. But the realization of this universality is not a consequence of the elimination of the here that is there but rather presents itself alongside it. There is the here, and there is also the here there and there, and so on, and also what is not here, and thence also what is here in the fuller sense of what is realized as here in this combination of here and not here as a manifold of negativity and complexity that is marked by this 'also'. The heres and not heres are not dissolved or suppressed but remain together in a movement that presents a universal 'here' as an intrinsic aspect of what was here and what is here, but is only revealed as they come together to indicate what has not been accounted for in these simple designations. The universal thus revealed is part of sensible experience as the universal of its particularity, and so cannot be separated from it as it is what constitutes its experience as more than just sense-certainty. As a result, these transformations in the pointing out of the now and the here mark the transition from sense-certainty to perception in the next paragraphs of the *Phänomenologie*, where the significance of the movement of *aufheben* is explicitly marked for the first time. But it should be noted that this is merely a term for the movement implicit to consciousness as it attends to the objects of its experience, in which they reveal themselves as otherwise and so mark the transformation of consciousness. What is important is not the generalized form of this movement as a shorthand for thought but the actual and ongoing experience of negativity and contradiction and their continuing transformations. *Aufhebung* is useful as a term as it bears multiple meanings and thus shows that these transformations are never simple, but what is undergone in its experience is not reducible to a word or concept unless these are also transformed in being thought speculatively.

The spatiotemporal disruption encountered in the distension and negation of the here and the now leaves the experience of this basic intuition marked by a differential non-presence, as the apparent purity and simplicity of now and here are shown to be pervaded by what is not and what has been, what passes away and what appears as other than what is not. Moreover, 'the now and pointing out of the now are thus so constituted that neither the now nor the pointing out of the now is an immediate simplicity but a movement that has various moments in it', and so it has some moments that do not have their truth in being as they *are* not. This does not yield a mere dissolution of the now but something more complex: experience as a movement of return that refers to and reflects on itself, although in this manifold of various moments there can be no simple return to self. Instead, there is an explication of what is and what is not, what was and what is otherwise:

> *this* is posited, but it is rather *an other* that is posited, or this is superseded: and this *otherness*, or the superseding of the first, is itself *again superseded*, and so has returned into the first. But this first, reflected into itself, is not wholly and exactly the same as it was in the first, that is, an *immediacy*; on the contrary, it is *something reflected in itself*, or a *simplicity* that in its otherness remains what it is: a now that is absolutely many nows, and this is the true now.
>
> PG: 67–8/63–4

The movement of sublation therefore contains many moments of sublation, such that the designation of first or last loses pertinence; instead, there is a passing away of immediacy, which in itself never was, and an unfolding of negativity that is never lost. Simplicity is thereby understood speculatively as that which remains what it is in its otherness from itself, not as an assimilation or identity, but as the explicating implication of itself.

As such, the multiple renderings of *aufheben* are given greater resonance, since it is precisely because this term bears differing translations, while inhibiting one simple equivalent, that it is able to mark the variety of movements encountered while never being reducible to one form on its own, or in itself. The specificity of what is ongoing is better marked by the different meanings of the word, since what is superseded, elevated, suspended, sublated, or relieved involves a countervailing movement between and across what has been left behind and what has been brought out, in which neither of these moments can be eliminated nor made into the single ground to which the movement as a 'whole' can be reduced. The fact that it exists as a single word in German should not suggest any form of essentiality, as this is just the simple form in which it remains what it is in its otherness in the idiomatic rendering of its thought, which is singular to its language but marks the universality of its multiplicity as the unfolding of this singularity. By comparison, acedia is not the same as melancholy, ennui, boredom, désœuvrement, sloth, saudade, and so on, even though all mark an experience of loss or absence, which is particularly relevant to the movement of *aufheben*. Each term marks a specificity that can be rendered into a universal without erasing the singularity of its concreteness, even as this is undercut by the movement of translation. Consequently, melancholia is never that which the word names, it is always removed from its own experience, leaving the word as a hollow *aufheben* and necessarily marking the possibility and impossibility of its discourse as a universal whose completeness is never available. This problem is the other side of *aufheben*, which must be considered if it is to be thought speculatively.

Hegel makes this point clear when he goes on to write that the dialectic of sense-certainty is nothing but the history of its movement or experience, so that sense-certainty itself is nothing other than this history, for in it 'natural consciousness also reaches this result, which is the truth of it, but equally it always forgets it again and starts the movement again'. Thus, there is no possibility of remaining with the position of asserting as universal experience 'that the reality or being of external things as *thises* or sense-objects has absolute truth for consciousness'. Instead, consciousness is involved in the supersession of such truth as it explicates the negativity of sense and supersedes this again in negating this negativity. Interestingly, Hegel returns to an argument he had developed a few years earlier in saying that the assertion of truth of a 'this' of sense as a universal experience is undone by 'the secret of the eating of bread and the drinking of wine: for the one who is initiated into these secrets not only comes to doubt [*Zweifel*] the being of sensuous things, but to despair [*Verzweiflung*] of it; in part he brings about their nothingness, and in part he sees them bring this about themselves' [PG: 69/64–5]. Although delivered with irony this point is important as it refers to the first model of the dialectic that appeared in Hegel's thought: when he attempted to consider the movement of spirit in the Last Supper, and in doing so compared the consuming of bread and wine with the act of reading in which sense or spirit is first made objective in the writing or food and then made subjective in its consumption. As these examples make clear, the dialectic never reaches a point of immaculate resolution, no more than the assertions of sense-certainty are able to sustain the truth of its experience as universal:

> They mean *this* piece of paper on which I am writing *this*, or rather have written; but what they mean is not what they say. If they actually wanted to *say* this piece of paper that they mean, and wanted to *say* it, this is impossible, because the sensuous this that is meant is *unreachable* by language, which belongs to consciousness, which in itself is universal. In the actual attempt to say it, it would therefore crumble away [*vermodern*]; those who started to describe it could not complete it, but would be compelled to leave it to others, who would themselves finally have to admit to speaking about a thing that *is* not.

The dialectic of *aufheben* never catches up with itself in this movement of sense-certainty, since what is involved is not just the negativity of the object but also that of its indication, which is taken up in the elusiveness of the linguistic relation in such a way that, as in his earlier discussion of the Last Supper, it is not simply a metaphor of the relation to objects in general. For, as Hegel significantly notes, language 'has the divine nature of immediately inverting [*verkehren*] meaning, of making it into something else, and thus not letting it *get into words* at all [*und so sie gar nicht* zum Worte kommen *zu lassen*]' [PG: 70/66].

The movement covered thus far is that in which sense-certainty transforms itself into perception, by realizing the universal in the dialectic of negation and supersession in the thisness of objects and their designations as now and here, and therefore realizes itself as taking the truth of experience, or perception (*Wahrnehmung*). It is here that Hegel explicitly refers to the linguistic aspect of this development in his thinking, just after this pun over perception, in which '*Aufhebung* exhibits its truly doubled meaning, which we have seen in the negative; it is at once a *negating* and a *preserving*' [PG: 72/68]. This preliminary designation marks its own specificity in that this explanation is not as detailed as the later remark in *Wissenschaft der Logik*. At this point in the *Phänomenologie*, the relevance of *aufheben* lies in the manner in which it has not only elucidated the transition of sense-certainty into perception but has also acted alongside this dialectic by showing how language instantiates the same relation with its objects, which should thereby give us pause before we consider the status of Hegel's prose in its own dialectical relation of negativity and supersession. As he had noted, the dialectic of sense-certainty is nothing but the history of its movement or experience, which is to say that the subject of this experience (in thought and in language) is itself to be understood through this dialectic, that is, speculatively. The 'example' (*Beispiel*) of writing and reading here is thus not simply an example, as it shows the manifold nature of the negativity at issue, in which 'this' occurs alongside 'that' as that which *also* occurs in the object:

> Since its principle, the universal, is in its simplicity *mediated*, it must express this in itself as its nature; it thereby shows itself as *the thing of many properties*. The wealth of sense knowledge belongs to perception, not to immediate certainty for which it was only the by-product [*Beiherspielende*], for only this contains *negation*, difference or manifoldness, in its essence.
>
> PG: 71/67

It is this facility of the example (of writing) that is drawn out in the pointing out of the 'this' and its distribution across the here and now, and gives an early indication of the implication of the sign into the experience of negativity. Two further points are worth emphasizing: since the transition from sense-certainty to perception is the first transition in the *Phänomenologie* its manner of development is of key importance, both in general and in particular. Equally, the way that *aufheben* occurs in this section highlights its universality (as per the experience of sense-certainty) and its particularity, in that language, like perception, is able to pick out both the particular and the universal in the object, which the use of *aufheben* itself demonstrates in its (paradoxically) idiomatic conceptuality. Hence what the *Aufhebung* does, as it is experienced and thought, is to provide an understanding of mediation, rather than assimilation, and a mediation that takes place across difference and recurrence as a thinking through and of negativity. For what mediation tells us is that there is no purity or origin of sense, everything occurs by way of something else, with which it is always in relation and is thus without possible conclusion. It is therefore apparent how much this transition foreshadows the movement between being and nothing in the opening sections of *Wissenschaft der Logik*, and the intimate relation this alternation has with language as it seeks and fails to approach any relation to being, any ontology.

The word *Beiherspielende* is not just related to *Beispiel* but is the term used in scholasticism to translate Aristotle's notion of accident (as opposed to substance), hence it is that which is incidental or contingent, a mere by-product rather than an essence.[2] That Hegel uses this term to refer to the knowledge of the universal in the experience of perception implies an inversion, in which the particular is prioritized and the universal occurs as a by-product of the experience of the sense-object. This means that the universal cannot occur without the particular, just as the experience of the latter gives rise to the former. Particularity exists not as punctiform but as that which is mediated by its differential negation as well as its universality, so it appears as a manifold of aspects or properties that interpenetrate but remain indifferent to each other as (lacking essentiality) these determinacies relate only to themselves. As a result, to understand the *Aufhebung* that takes place in perception, it is necessary to understand that each of these aspects are only really properties by way of further determinations that are always to come (*durch eine ferner hinzukommende Bestimmung*), and that they occur indifferently alongside each other only by way of the universal in which they participate [PG: 72/68]. There is thus a double mediation at play in the experience of the sense-object, which is never completely satisfied. Looking to find a way to discuss this abstract universal medium in which the object reveals its thinghood or essence, Hegel can only conclude that its plurality exists by virtue of the indifferent 'Also' that holds it together, so that this Also is the universal itself, which is perpetually incomplete. The Also is not a synthesis but the barest and most minimal form of gathering in which the properties of an object occur next to each other without integration or assimilation. The absolute, as Hyppolite says, is mediation, which has to be understood in both directions [LE: 74/61].

Thus, the *Aufhebung* reveals itself through the way that an object appears *as* it is: as itself and also as its own example. This leads to the final moment in the perception of the object since the medium, insofar as it excludes another object, just as properties do in relation to each other, becomes not just an Also that loosely holds them together but a unity or one, a moment of negation that determines the thinghood of the object as a thing: 'Negation is inherent in a property as *determinacy* that is immediately one with the immediacy of being, which through this unity with negation is universality; however as *one* it is set free from this unity with its opposite and exists in and for itself' [PG: 73/69]. Sense-certainty negates itself as it attempts to validate itself and in doing so it becomes transformed into perception, which thereby brings about a different experience of the object, as well as a different way of knowing, with its own contradictions – for perception in turn will struggle to validate itself in trying to negotiate the tension between the two aspects of the object as a mass of properties and as an ungrounded universal. This tension will gradually reveal itself to be illusory, as the two aspects of the thing become equally essential and inessential and in doing so indicate that the examination of this issue has become speculative, in that it involves an oscillation between identity and predication in relation to what the thing *is*, in which each is understood by way of the other, by way of its negation.

Such is the first appearance of the *Aufhebung*, and I have gone through this sequence slowly to show the care with which Hegel develops its thought, but it is also evident that the thought itself remains to be developed. To some degree this is evidence of the form of negation occurring at this basic level of sensory awareness, as the subtlety of its movements will only become apparent in the experience of more complex phenomena. However, this rudimentary form is significant for the way that it indicates how the *Aufhebung* develops immanently out of the contradictions of experience, and in doing so provides a concrete and specific expression. And, as it emerges from the material of experience in later developments of the *Phänomenologie* rather than being imposed across its forms as a Procrustean synthesis, the *Aufhebung* will become more complex but will not become entirely universal and abstract.

II *Aufheben* in logic

As is apparent, I have not been reading this section of Hegel's work for its ostensible argument but have been focusing on the way that the notion of *aufheben* is used and developed. Several years later it would receive its canonical definition in *Wissenschaft der Logik*, but even here this definition will only occur after the fact, as it were, after it has already been taken up in the discussion of becoming, which is the first moment of transition in the logic, and proceeds as follows: Being as pure being is found to be indistinguishable from pure nothing, for in its indeterminate immediacy there is nothing to it, but insofar as this nothing is, then it is being in its emptiness. In this flickering transition between being and nothing there is only the transition from one to the other, since each is no more than an indeterminate emptiness. As such they are not the same, for each is the distinct movement from being to nothing, or nothing to being; even though they are inseparable they form distinct moments in the immediate vanishing of the one into the other: 'The truth is neither being nor nothing, but that being does not pass over but has passed over [*nicht übergeht, sondern übergegangen ist*] into nothing, and nothing into being'. It is thus that being and nothing reveal themselves as becoming, 'a movement in which both are distinguished, but through a distinction [*Unterschied*] that has equally immediately dissolved [*aufgelöst*] itself' [WL2: 69–70/82–3]. This point marks the appearance of the *Aufhebung* in the form of dissolution, as difference appears and disappears, which will give rise to the stronger readings of sublation as the dissolution of difference *tout court*. But it is apparent that this dissolving only takes place in the constant movement of becoming that arises through the alternation between pure being and pure nothing: as there is nothing here but pure indeterminacy, there is nothing to prevent it from being dissolved as easily as it arises.

(It is worth pausing for a moment on this thought, for in stating that there is a distinction in this transition that dissolves itself, Hegel presents an image of *aufheben* that runs in the opposite direction from that which he had mentioned earlier in stating that *aufheben* was a negation that preserved itself [PG: 72/68]. This is not an inconsiderable difference but nor is it a conflict; instead, Hegel has shown up the differential tenor of each of the directions of *aufheben*. It is necessary to think through these transitions carefully in order to understand what it would mean for there to be a negation that preserves, which is a kind of suspension, as against a distinction that is dissolved, which is a kind of transience. For if both these movements mark the space of *aufheben* then they work in different registers by both downplaying and highlighting the manoeuvre.)

This point is made clearer when Hegel goes on to state that becoming is not a unity that abstracts from being and nothing but is the unity *of* being and nothing, in which they are only as vanishing, sublated (*Aufgehobene*) moments. The tense of this phrase is crucial, just as is its combination. The self-subsistence of being and nothing is merely imagined; instead, they are only moments that are distinct at the same time as they are sublated [WL2: 92–3/105]. So sublation occurs not as the erasure of difference but as that which preserves it even as it transforms it. The situation is actually more complex, as these moments of being and nothing are themselves unities of being and nothing, for insofar as being is not, it is nothing, and insofar as nothing is, it is being. Therefore, there is no being and nothing as such, only being as becoming nothing, and nothing as becoming being. It is thus that becoming arises from being and nothing and leads to a unity in which their distinction is unequally determined as ceasing to be (*Vergehen*) and coming to be (*Entstehen*). Hence, rather than sublating each other externally, 'each sublates itself in itself and is in its own self the opposite of itself' [WL2: 93/106]. The combination of ceasing to be and coming to be just is becoming, so that becoming only is through the distinction of each of these vanishing moments: their vanishing is thus the vanishing of becoming, as well as the vanishing of vanishing, in which becoming in turn changes or collapses into the settling of this ceaseless unrest. This happens because becoming is inherently contradictory, as it is constituted by both the vanishing and the distinction of its moments, so in the settling of this contradiction, becoming itself vanishes as it realizes itself as being, but now as determinate being (*Dasein*). Thus, as Hegel notes at the beginning of his following remark on *aufheben*, the nominal form of the verb, the sublated (*das Aufgehobene*), is only as ideal (*das Ideelle*).

This remark begins by claiming that *aufheben* constitutes one of the most important concepts in philosophy, which occurs repeatedly throughout it, and as a result it is a term whose meaning must be grasped carefully, particularly in its difference from nothing. The last point reinforces the fact that its thought has arisen from the analysis of being and nothing, as a difference from nothing in which nothing is immediate and the sublated is that which is mediated. The sublated is thus nonbeing (*das Nichtseiende*) that has arisen from a being, so that it still bears the 'determinacy' of that which produces it: 'Thus the sublated is at the same time preserved, it has only lost its immediacy, but is on no account annihilated' [WL2: 94/107]. As a result, the two meanings Hegel has used, to preserve (*aufbewahren*) and to allow to cease (*aufhören lassen*), are combined in their speculative meaning as sublation, for each meaning has united with its opposite in just the manner in which being and nothing have been shown to occur as moments of becoming. The latter discussion is exactly the careful understanding of meaning that he had indicated, which in turn demonstrates the same implication of language and thought that had been noted in regards to perception in the *Phänomenologie*, especially because this is a concept that occurs as a moment arising out of the negativity of becoming.

There is much that is difficult in these analyses and Hegel recognizes this point to some degree, for in the equivalent passage in the *Enzyklopädie Logik* he admits that the statement that 'being and nothing are the same' seems paradoxical or absurd, so that it might not appear to be meant seriously. But he reaffirms its significance by saying that it is one of the hardest propositions that thinking dares to formulate; whatever is meant by this statement is clearly not to be dismissed. This claim is made doubly hard in that the statement repeats itself in the opposite form, that being and nothing are not the same, which may seem unremarkable on its own but, coming after the earlier statement, it becomes vertiginous, as the two statements are obviously contradictory and yet are both said to be true. Hegel makes it clear that he is only speaking of being and nothing in their purity as indeterminate immediacies, but it nevertheless seems impossible to make sense of his account when being and nothing are said to be both the same and not the same. Plainly, what is at issue in this problem is the status of sameness and its relation to being, which is to say that it is a question of identity. As was pointed out before, being is nothing just as nothing is being, so contrary to first impressions the statement about their sameness is at this point more acceptable than their lack of sameness. Consequently, Hegel emphasizes that 'this distinction has here not yet determined itself, precisely because being and nothing are still the immediate; it is, as belonging to them, the *unsayable*, mere *meaning* [*bloße* Meinung]' [ENZ: §88, 125/141]. On the one hand, being and nothing are the same, but on the other hand, being and nothing are not the same, and the latter distinction has not yet been realized. This is not a temporal elaboration but logical, as determination as such is yet to appear, and will do so only in the move by which becoming collapses into determinacy. In this way, the contradiction between the two statements is made part of the immanent unfolding of the negativity of being, which is revealed in the movement from indistinction to distinction as it determines itself.

Nevertheless, this movement of determination is not entirely stable or given, and so far only its logical necessity has been demonstrated. Hence the statement that being and nothing are the same remains challenging in its relation of thought to language. As being and nothing are not, at first glance, the same, understanding this sentence is not only a question of the logic of being that Hegel is spelling out but also of the language of thought in which the notion of sameness and identity is at issue. The thinking of being is not just of being but also of its thought, so that the language with which this thought is to proceed must participate in that which is ongoing, which thus affects the nature of its grammar and syntax. The limits of thought are to be found in the one-sided perspective of the understanding, as the thought of becoming (in which the sameness and non-sameness of being and nothing take place) can only be grasped by reason in its speculative capacity:

> what has to be grasped is the unity *in* the diversity that is *given* and *posited* at the same time. As their unity, *becoming* is the true expression of the result of being and nothing; it is not just the *unity* of being and nothing but it is inward *unrest* – a unity that in its self-relation is not merely motionless but through the diversity of being and nothing that it contains is inwardly turned against itself.
>
> ENZ: §88, 127–8/143

It is this movement that will need to be carried into language if it is to say what is meant in the sameness of being and nothing, a sameness that, if it is to be both given and posited, must find its expression in a sentence that is its own example. The notion of the *Aufhebung* itself is partly an answer to this speculative demand, for in combining a positive and negative meaning in the same word we discover 'the speculative spirit of our language, which transcends the either/or of mere understanding' [ENZ: §96 Z, 154].

In consequence, by thinking what is at stake in the sentence 'being is nothing' we are forced to reconsider the nature of the copula, and its ontological claims, for this is no longer a statement of predication but nor is it one of simple identity (as the problems with perception had indicated earlier), if by the latter we mean that which is simply the same. This problem leads us back to the thought of the speculative sentence that was raised in the Preface to the *Phänomenologie*, where the relation of predication must be rethought through speculation as that which does not lead from a subject to a predicate, as when we say that Canada is large, for example, but moves restlessly from subject to object and back again, since it cannot ground itself in either term as that which is apparently more fundamental. Instead of realizing itself in the object and thereby passing through it as its determination, the thought of the subject 'is checked in its progress, as that which has the form of a predicate in a proposition is the substance itself. It suffers, as we might put it, a counterthrust. Starting from the subject as though this was a permanent ground it finds that, since the predicate is the substance, the subject has passed over into the predicate and thereby becomes sublated'. In thus reconsidering the nature and role of the copula we come to understand the other parts of the relation, for the subject is no longer passive, it is not 'inertly supporting the accidents; it is on the contrary the self-moving concept that takes its determinations back into itself. In this movement the passive subject itself perishes; it enters into the differences and the content, and constitutes the determinacy, that is, the differentiated content and its movement, instead of remaining over against it' [PG: 42–3/37]. It is the movement itself that becomes the object, and in this state it is absolute, as it has no predicates and there is nothing beyond it that determines it and that it can pass beyond. The movement is absolute in its endless self-relation, its infinite passage through itself.

While this speculative relation can be seen in the movement between being and nothing, the status of the sentence itself takes on a stronger role if we recall the role of positing that took place in the earlier discussion of the now and the here. In these cases there was a movement of loss in which positing became negating, as that which was indicated passed over into that which was not or no longer, and this led to the experience, within perception and language, of this loss, as that which is exposed and brought about by this indication. This point provides a critical insight into the relation of being and language, since it means that the movement of positing and negating that occurs in language both arises from being (in its self-negating passing away of itself) and is reflected back into being by language as part of its infinite conceptual unfolding. Dialectical sublation occurs in two directions, or across two dimensions, as language and being both occur as self-positing, self-reflecting sublations. With this in mind it is now possible to read the following passage without immediately assuming that Hegel is totalizing thought: 'This process of determination is a *setting-forth* and thus an unfolding of the concept that is *in itself* and at the same time the *going-into-itself* of being, its own deepening into itself. The explication of the concept in the sphere of being becomes the totality of being, just as the immediacy of being or the form of being as such, is sublated by it' [ENZ: §84, 121/135]. Totality is not a term marking a systematic enclosure but rather emphasizes the lack of transcendence: there is nothing beyond; no other sphere to which we might turn, there is only the infinitude of this self-unfolding and self-enfolding complexity as it is thought.

The thought of infinity is key to understanding the *Aufhebung*, and in this way Hegel's thought is found to be closer to the dense reflexivity of Mallarmé's writings than was initially thought, and also to the notion of the *pas au-delà* that marks Blanchot's thinking as the reconfiguration of the beyond as that which is not. As Hegel insists, the sublation of the form of the speculative proposition must not only take place in an immediate manner through the content of the proposition, that is, it is not just a question of the inhibition (and emptying) of the movement of the subject. Instead, the return of the concept into itself must also be set forth in the movement that the proposition was initially supposed to accomplish. Hence speculation is only fully apparent when it is *actual* speculation; not just a proposition but the exposition of the dialectical movement of the proposition [PG: 45/39–40]. The step beyond is thus not beyond, but equally the not-beyond is a step-beyond, insofar as the finite remains endless as it sets itself forth in its own exposition of itself. Consequently, the beyond is a not-beyond in both its dialectical aspects: a not that is beyond, and a beyond that is not, in their mutually explicating and infinite sublation. So, what becomes of issue is the question of the circularity that this unveils – and of the return that this circularity implies – when the exposition of the dialectic of the proposition must take place in and through a new mode of writing, such that this thinking can be actual, since this is what Hegel is seeking through the text of the *Phänomenologie* itself.

In this regard, it is of considerable note that in his writings on Hegel, Derrida refers almost entirely to 'the Hegelian *Aufhebung*', even though Hegel himself very rarely uses the nominal form, preferring instead to use the verb *aufheben* in the infinitive, and its passive past participle, *aufgehoben*. Not only does Derrida thereby reify the term but in doing so he renders it unitary, as if all Hegel's thoughts on this issue can be reduced to this single noun, which would be its sum and goal. But, as Jean-Luc Nancy points out, the use of both *aufheben* and *aufgehoben* grants its movement an unstable duplicity as they name a movement that has already happened but is also yet to be completed.[3] This is exactly the manner in which the beginning of the logic is worked out, in which the movement from being and nothing to becoming is that which has already occurred, as Hegel had emphasized, being does not pass over into nothing, or vice versa, but has passed over, the transition has always already taken place as it happens immediately, that is, prior to or outside temporality. The logic begins, in effect, with becoming, 'the first concrete thought', which is thus both ongoing and already past, so the thought of *aufheben* reveals that the beginning is always marked after the fact; there is no pure origin, only its abstract indeterminacy, which is merely an empty thought that in its impurity explicates itself and thereby begins [ENZ: §88 Z, 144]. It is with this thought in mind that we should approach the fragmentary beginning of the logic, '*being, pure being,* – without any further determination', which, as has often been pointed out, is not a complete sentence as it lacks a verb, the ontological copula that would ground its statement.⁴ But, insofar as thought begins with this empty beginning, it does not so much leave it behind as it progresses but elaborates and preserves it as its own immanent development, and it is for this reason and in this way that the logic takes on a circular form [WL2: 58/71]. The circle is then a form in which thought returns to itself because it is at all times concerned with what is and what is not and is not diverted into some other sphere; there is only being and nothing and their becoming. This is not a circle as that which signifies completion and enclosure but as that which returns to itself in such a way that its beginning always already is and yet also is not [WL2: 60/74]. Hence this notion does not indicate full presence but the self-discovery of the immanence of being and nothing, and mediation and immediacy. Even as the empty word is elaborated into a concept, it remains an empty word (being, pure being) but one that now reflects its own determinations in their sublation: as what has already taken place and what is still to take place. It is only in absolute knowing that this circle is fully comprehended and actualized; for the philosopher or writer, by contrast, its thinking is always to come, its concreteness incomplete. Hegel refers to *aufheben* as a concept, but it is perhaps more like a word due to its linguistic intractability and lack of self-identity, and in recognition of this point, and recalling Bataille, Nancy refers to it as a sliding word. The meaning of *aufheben* does not present itself easily, for as a word it only offers a sense of that which it conveys, the sense of discovering something through its mediation and sublation.

As Hegel had stated, the movement of *aufheben* does not annihilate things but removes them from their immediacy, but as he had also stated, 'there is nothing in heaven or nature or mind or anywhere else that does not contain both immediacy and mediation' [WL2: 54/68]. Therefore, the movement of *aufheben* has always already taken effect and is also yet to be completed, but insofar as this effect needs to be discovered to be actualized, then it must be found in the same way that the word itself occurs in language: as that which has brought together opposing meanings and has thereby acted as an example for thought. And the example he gives is the following: 'Something is sublated only insofar as it has entered into unity with its opposite; in this closer definition as something reflected it may fittingly be called a *moment*'. Such had already been the term used when he had written that being and nothing take place as vanishing, sublated moments, but two pages later the point is reinforced in this way: 'In the case of the lever, *weight* and *distance* from a point are called mechanical *moments* on account of the *sameness* of their effect, in spite of the contrast between something real, such as a weight, and something ideal, such as a mere spatial determination, a line' [WL2: 95/107].⁵ Moment, as the more approximate rendering of *aufheben*, is not simply a temporal or logical passage but an impulse, that which carries an effect, and it is as such that it is thought, and in doing so its effects remain to be felt. Perhaps this is why it is a fundamental determination that purely and simply recurs throughout all of philosophy, a thought that is not just a word but a way of forming them, which is to say that it opens the question of syntax, of the sentence itself as actually speculative. As Werner Hamacher recalls, this point was already sketched out in the dialectic of sense-certainty, in which the now was written down and in doing so was removed from its immediacy and preserved, but then, on rereading, it was found to have become lost, and so writing is forced to develop itself through rewriting so as to attempt to re-articulate this passage of moments.⁶ All that is found is what has been sublated, the now as past, but in its place a new form has emerged as writing becomes the universal now, which contains all moments, but only insofar as it persists, insofar as it carries on the movement of sublation by writing more, which is then only actualized in a reading that can realize this speculative combination of what is and is not.

It is thus that the form of writing, especially that of the sentence, comes into question in its relational structure and limits. In a fragment like, '*being, pure being,* – without any further determination', there is not only a lack of structure, insofar as there is no subject-object relation, but there is also a strange tension brought about by the fact that the only term of syntax is negative. The syntax of 'without' has been taken up extensively by Blanchot, but here the focus of the phrase alternates between form and content, as they are called, because of the critical imperative of not beginning with any presuppositions that guides Hegel's thought. Hence the form of the phrase cannot assert a proposition but must arise from its matter in its pure impurity, or impure purity, of beginning. Thus, negativity occurs through the use of without, but then affects the form of the phrase, which in turn affects the manner in which its content appears in its combination of what is and is not, what is posited and what is negated, which is the form of its appearance. That is, the beginning appears in this form and thereby marks itself as such; it is its own positing and negating and so conveys its content through its form and its form through its content. This breakdown in the subject-object relation leaves the phrase with an uncertainty in both its syntax and its limits, which can be compared with the speculative sentence 'being is nothing'. While this sentence bears a copula, its form is transformed by the fact that being and nothing move into each other, rendering the subject-object relation null and thereby granting the copula a different form as the *moment* of its transition, and in which there is a relation of both identity and non-identity. However, this is still a sentence, whereas the earlier phrase-fragment of being without determination goes from its so-called subject outwards, without endpoint, even one from which it would be repulsed and recur throughout philosophy. Instead, the fragment exposes itself, in the sense of unravelling its positing through the negative, and thereby takes place. This alternative sense of the speculative in language is not necessarily fuller, as is apparent, but is more formally disruptive, and thus cannot be taken up so extensively when it is instead Hegel's concern to follow the path of the concept, of its reflection and self-actualization. It is perhaps in this sense that it can only be thought in absolute knowing, but it is not certain that the phrase of without that begins the logic can be thought to the same degree, or whether it can only be written, and in doing so releases something other that perhaps cannot simply be thought. As the remarks to these paragraphs indicate, the problem of this opening is profound, precisely because thought seems to have given rise to a thought that it cannot itself think. Or, rather, that in writing itself down thought exposes itself to a thinking that can only be thought by way of the logic as a whole, which is necessarily infinite. Does this mean that infinite *aufheben* is finite, that it is punctured or punctuated by the moment of its exposure? Furthermore, the distinction between finite and infinite is unravelled in this exposure, which is its reading, however this is actualized.

Hegel explains part of what is going on here by examining the statements just discussed, for in saying that 'being and nothing are the same' we are faced with a contradiction, as has been noted, for the two terms are distinct and yet are said to be the same, and so the sentence is both true and false. Thus, the sentence dissolves itself through this contradiction, but 'in thus vanishing, it is its proper content that comes to be in it, namely *becoming*'. This problem is repeated in the combination of this sentence and its opposite, 'being and nothing are not the same', for the two present their content in the form of an antinomy, even though their content refers to the same. Hence although the determinations expressed in the two sentences should be united, their appearance in a union 'can only be stated as an *unrest* of simultaneous *incompatibles*, as *a movement*' [WL2: 77–8/90–1]. The movement that had been marked as a becoming and thereby revealed as a form of *aufheben* is now rephrased, such that it can only be referred to as an unrest of incompatibilities. As Nancy explains, this significantly recasts our understanding of the movement of *aufheben* itself, making it restless, troubling its presence and identity:

One cannot therefore master what pertains to the modification of form, but on the other hand one cannot avoid being submitted to its singular alterations. In the repetition of reading a displacement or confusion is produced between the statements of Hegelian logic, between all the turnings of *aufheben*. And this displacement may consist above all in the way that *aufheben* is never made in the same way, is displaced from word to word, slides from text to text, forbids us from accomplishing the logic of the syllogism other than by returning, albeit in equivocation and unrest, to the proposition – whose concept from then on finds itself strangely confused, since one begins to fail to distinguish its relations to or deviations from speculative truth. But in fact it is the *aufheben* itself that confuses or mixes up its own concept in an ever stranger manner – as if, in search of the form of the speculative, of its own form, it was *deforming* itself: for must one *sublate* [relever] the proposition or *modify* it, must one suppress-and-preserve it or alter it? Or else, might there be an identity, but what singular misrecognisable identity might there be between *aufheben* and alteration, that is, between two terms that no dialectical sublation can articulate together?[7]

Nancy is extending the transformations of speculative reason beyond what the understanding can bear and in doing so opens up the possibilities of the plasticity of reason, which have been taken up by Catherine Malabou. But even if we do not follow this thought, the necessity of an antinomical restlessness (*Unruhe*, *inquiétude*) in the very form of the *aufheben* is remarked by Hegel when he writes that becoming is 'a ceaseless unrest that collapses into a quiescent result', as was noted earlier, and then again when he refers to 'the internal unrest of quality by which it produces and maintains itself only in conflict', or, in the discussion of the finitude of the something (*Etwas*), which is determined by 'the unrest of the something in its limit in which it is immanent, the *contradiction* that propels it beyond itself' [WL2: 93/106, 102/114, 115/128].[8] In all these cases, unrest is that of determinacy itself, which is to say of identity in its limits.

This unrest is intrinsic to the *form* of the proposition about being and nothing and thus to its thought, which is actualized in its reading, so while it will become less intransigent in more complex forms, where the place of being and nothing is not so trenchantly abstract, it will nevertheless cast an unavoidable distortion to its forms, which will leave open the question of how much this can still be termed an *Aufhebung* in the classical sense, if such can be said at all. For in its place comes another thought: of *aufheben* as an uneasy, disquieting combination of negativities that unravel themselves, in much the same way that the restless alternation between the finite and the bad infinite leads to a new form in the true infinite. Within the speculative proposition there is a reconfiguration of the relation between subject and object, as well as a transformation in the status of the terms, but this also means an emptying of the words themselves, as is shown in the fragmentary opening phrase of the logic. In the repetition of being, the sense of the word is flattened just as its movement is brought out, which is part of what takes place in the *Aufhebung* of language in memory, where iteration makes possible the opening of the word to its symbolic recapitulation but at the cost of its inner sense. This is to elucidate the meanings of *aufheben* as that which preserves as much as it cancels and elevates, for the 'sense' of the empty word is interiorized as it is lifted into a new sphere of meaning, which is to say, in reference to the opening of the logic, that being remains in its unanswerable emptiness alongside its transformation into becoming as that which bears both the possibility and impossibility of its *Aufhebung*. As Stephen Houlgate explains in reference to this repetition and emptying of words in memory, Hegel has shown that there must be a 'passage through *meaninglessness* for the emergence of self-consciousness and freedom', but this passage will necessarily remain as an infinite lining of non-sense.[9] Although Adorno is generally sympathetic to Hegel, it is in this passage that he finds what he calls the fallacy in his thinking, for while it is necessarily true to say that 'what is non-identical and unknown also becomes identical in being known, and through comprehension, the non-conceptual becomes the concept of the non-identical'. Nevertheless, the 'non-identical itself does not merely become a concept through the power of such reflection; rather it remains its content, distinct from it' [DS: 375/147]. It is thus that the dialectic remains true to its contradiction, since it is as important to emphasize the meaninglessness remaining in the passage of meaning as it is to recognize the sense that arises from senselessness, which then has implications for the nature and possibility of this passage in both its directions, as it means that one cannot simply pass from existence to logic, or vice versa: there is a disjunction and loss in any actualization, a moment of transition that is itself not sublated or mediated.

III *Aufheben* at the limits of language

This point returns the argument to the understanding of signification developed in Hyppolite's reading of Hegel, which was instrumental to Derrida's analysis in 'Le puits et la pyramide'. What is important about Hyppolite's reading is that it is an account of Hegel's logic that begins with his account of sense, and thereby demonstrates how the phenomenology leads into a logic of being, as is made clear in the chapter that Derrida refers to in his lecture. Here, Hyppolite focuses on the transition by which nature becomes *logos* in its explication, which is accompanied by the transition of thought as it becomes objective and external in language. The two movements are inseparable and intertwined and can be found in the way that the sensible becomes sense just as thought is alienated into language, which also bears its own transition of signification from symbol to sign. There is thus a double transition from nature to language, which in reflecting on itself becomes conceptual. The exact manner in which this double transition develops is the central focus of Hyppolite's work, which is to say that it concerns itself with the nature of the sublation that takes place in its double aspect and its reflective tension. In this sublation nature is both negated and preserved as it explicates itself as sense, and as such it is not eliminated but mediated in becoming thought and is thereby preserved as an echo, as Hyppolite will emphasize. By linking the account of sense-certainty to the discussion of memory and language in *Philosophie des Geistes*, Hyppolite can also speak of the way that the negation of the sensible allows the imagination to preserve it in its absence: 'it refers itself to what is not there in what is there, to what is there in what is not there'. And it is in this way that thought becomes symbolic, which means that 'this memory that interiorises the world only exists through the other memory that externalises the "I"', so that thought 'turns itself into a thing, a sensible being, a sound, while the thing itself is negated, interiorized into thought' [LE: 34–5/29]. It is important to note that these two movements do not come together in a perfect unity but revolve around each other without merging. Furthermore, there is always a tension and displacement formed by the internal echoes that are borne along with these movements, as the negativity that is preserved in its sublation. This would be like a form of *inframince*, as Duchamp describes it, 'when the tobacco smoke also smells of the mouth that exhales it', and is called a marginal sublation (*dépassement marginal*) by Hyppolite [LE: 33/28].[10] Also, the relation between the two layers is not reciprocally balanced: there may be a contradiction between what is there and what is not there but this does not involve a flattening out of the relation between identity and difference, since the movement from same to other is not equivalent to its reverse. While the sensible refers to the name by which it is determined, the name does not in turn refer to the sensible; instead, the name in its signification simply refers to other significations. In this way language transcends itself within language, it has no absolute exteriority, no other or beyond, only its own endless internal reflections and displacements, which become its infinite 'totality'.

Language thereby offers a first approach to how speculative thought is to arise, a thought that would avoid both empiricism and formalism, as well as mere ineffability, and would realize within itself the movement by which difference and identity is neither in things nor in thought separately (which encourages the pathways to empiricism and formalism, onto which the understanding takes hold) but takes place in both thought and things through the becoming and splitting apart of being. As Hegel describes it in an early work: 'The task of philosophy consists in uniting these presuppositions, to posit being in non-being – as becoming; diremption in the absolute – as its appearance; the finite in the infinite – as life'.[11] This is not to advert to the syllogistic understanding of the identity of identity and difference but to see how appearing and self-diremption are the same, as Hyppolite writes, which is also not to treat these perspectives as presuppositions, as this formulation has it (although Hegel clarifies this point by stating that a presupposition is merely the reflective form of the need of philosophy itself), but to realize that the forms of identity and difference give way by themselves to their own transformation [LE: 122/95]. Doing so reveals the contradiction in things and thoughts, their negativity and non-purity by which their identity and difference is both preserved and transformed. The study of language therefore exposes the way that the absolute distinguishes and sustains itself, and yet in doing so avoids becoming substantial as self-presence, but is sheer alienation, the restlessness of the negative. This transformation of thought and things leads to a new understanding of the whole that it constitutes and the finitude or infinitude of its form, so that the sense of totality or whole becomes transformed, in the same way that the genuine infinite surpasses the mere opposition of finite and bad infinite. Thus, insofar as the absolute is mediation, the passage of transformation, sublation is itself infinite unrest. As before, the transformation of thought and things is unequal, for 'insofar as it is conceived, we can say that [nature] is the logos, that it is its other; but insofar as it does not conceive itself, it preserves this proper opacity that turns it into the anti-idea' [LE: 132/103]. This lining of non-conception is borne along with every thought, and is the limit that literature seems to approach; in Blanchot's eyes, for instance, literature would not be a poetic creation and evocation of being but a non-thought, a material thinking in writing that seeks to avoid its own conceptualization the better to draw out its peculiar force, which animates and fractures thinking.

If we take the verb *aufheben* itself, then something of this movement can be made apparent, for at first we are presented with a word that has a meaning but, on closer inspection, also bears a second and seemingly opposed meaning. The word as such has now changed shape and a third form has emerged that is neither the first nor the second meaning, nor a *tertium quid* that combines or assimilates them, but a new form that is not reducible to either separate meaning or to both together. The word itself has now become a concept, a mode and form of thought in which these opposing meanings lead to a new kind of meaning, since *aufheben* is neither abolition nor preservation on their own but something that is different from both while yet remaining the same as them. The concept of *aufheben* remains linked to the word but is not the word, and is only to be understood through its reading in the text, through its variable contexts and across the whole of the work. The concept may actualize the word but the labour of doing so is extensive and, as we have seen, is pervaded by the negative, by the insistence of the neither/nor and the not yet/no longer, and it is only through this labour that there is *aufheben* in its fullest sense, even as this actualization is endlessly marked by its finite occasions. In bringing this idiomatic form to thought, the word is both mediated and determined, and thus rendered a concrete universal, but insofar as it finds no single, unified, or complete determination it remains without conclusion; it is not possible to say what *the* meaning of *aufheben* would be or to specify its translation finally and precisely. There remains an element of indeterminacy or negativity to the word that cannot be suppressed or surpassed and will destabilize thought the more that it focuses on it, as this is its exteriority to sense, the very medium of its mediation, which is perhaps language as such and in general, if there is or can be such a thing, insofar as it *is* not. From this thought comes the association of language with nothingness and death as absolute alienation, for in this experience (as Hofmannsthal's Chandos discovered) there arises in the reader or writer a sense of anxiety, 'not about this or that, or for this or that moment, but about their whole being; for they have felt the fear of death' [PG: 114/117]. This is not the experience of freedom that Hegel's bondsman finds but the experience of a language of empty words and words without syntax, and so without mediation or determinacy, a sheer spacing of thought without form or ground. And yet there is *aufheben*. Hence thought cannot safely and harmoniously adjudicate between these two slopes of word and thought, for they remain, and remain divergent.

In discussing how Marx developed the notion of alienation, Hyppolite claims that Hegel nevertheless 'went a lot further on this point than Marx', and in doing so 'opened perspectives that Marx neglected, and these perspectives bear precisely on the fact that for him every determinate objectification is an alienation. He discovered this dimension of pure subjectivity *that is nothingness*. The ground of self-consciousness is what, in nature, manifests itself as disappearance and death'. Bearing in mind the linguistic dimension of negativity that has just been mentioned, Hyppolite goes on to clarify the double-sidedness of this experience:

> Death is the revelation of absolute negativity because man, as pure self-consciousness, exists this nothingness [*existe ce néant*]. In apprehending death, man becomes the supreme abstraction that was nature's interiority, its nothingness, the detachment from all being-there [*être-là*], from every determination [...] This melting away of everything stable is the negation of negation, because everything stable is for man a negation, a self-limitation. In Marx, the proletariat is the comprehension of human alienation and this comprehension is its existence. In discovering the alienation of self-consciousness Hegel extends this term to every objectification.
>
> LE: 239–40/183–4

The experience of language is of the alienation involved in its objectification, an alienation that becomes in its most extreme form an 'experience' of nothingness, or rather a nothingness that is *existed* (not lived) and that is sheer abstraction. Each determination of language is a negation, as Blanchot and Mallarmé emphasized, but this is to say that it is both an abstraction and a disappearance, and when this negation is itself negated, as the writer seeks to go beyond what is negated to the negation itself, then language becomes what is not. Its existence is permeated by nothingness at every step, for each step is both a determination and its negation.

Not only does this show how closely Hyppolite's thought resonates with that of Blanchot but it also indicates how closely Blanchot is working in relation to Hegel's thought by extending its terms to the problematic of writing and language.[12] As will be shown in the next chapter in relation to Blanchot's essay 'La littérature et le droit à la mort', it is precisely in regards to this fear of death and the life of the spirit that maintains itself in it that his thinking of literature is articulated, and especially in terms of how it demonstrates the unexpected consequences for the Hegelian notion of the understanding in being the endless thought of this negativity. However, this point also shows the dimension of negativity that seems to be lacking in Derrida's response to Hegel, which may be because he is keen to move away from any existential thematic and its focusing on experience, which he sees as ineradicably associated with presence, or it may be because he is more persuaded by the discussions of difference and excess that arise in the works of Nietzsche and Freud, and by the descriptions of the Hegelian dialectic as totality and teleology that emerged in the writings of Heidegger and Kierkegaard. In doing so he appears to have missed the greater import of Hyppolite's reading, while Blanchot, by contrast, appears more aware in this instance of how negativity restructures the relation of and to language, and thus how thinking must proceed in its response to Hegel. What this will imply, as I have pointed out, is a reconfiguration of the finitude and infinitude of the text, which Blanchot pursues by way of his understanding of fragmentary writing, particularly as it develops in *L'Attente l'oubli* and *Le Pas au-delà*.

This problem enables an understanding of the dialectics of thinking, as Adorno points out, which addresses itself to the issue of where and how thinking is to start, that is, to its limits as that which is both finite and infinite. In approaching *aufheben* as a word, rather than trying to analyse it, we are able to grasp its sense as a whole, intuitively, as it were, but then in discussing it the thought becomes distinguished and torn apart into separate aspects. For in discussing the word it is expressed in propositions that alter its sense by determining it. But this process of determination is nothing external to the word as it arises from its explication, which is to say that the word considered in itself and on its own is nothing before this process of becoming determined, and yet in this process the truth of the word as a whole is lost, such that it can only be recaptured through the coming together of these differing aspects. The true, as Hegel wrote, is the whole, which is essentially a result, that is, not a final summative conclusion but the infinite (that is, endless) inter-relation of sense and mediation: 'whatever is more than just a word, even the transition to a mere proposition, is *a becoming-other* that must be taken back, a mediation' [PG: 19/11]. This is so because 'the subject matter is not exhausted in its *aims* [Zwecke], but in its *working-out* [Ausführung], nor is the *result* the *actual* whole, but it together with its becoming; the aim for itself is a lifeless universal' [PG: 10–11/2]. As Adorno explains, the working out of the sense of a matter still 'possesses the character of truth even if the absolute, as an all-embracing totality, cannot be given to us'. Thus, even though 'the infinite whole is not given, at least to the finite subject; or, in other words, because not everything that is can be resolved into the pure determinations of thought', nevertheless, 'in the negation of the individual concept, and in the compulsion to go beyond itself that the concept as such exerts, there lies a necessity, a moment, which already vouchsafes truth even if we cannot conceive of [*vorgestellt*] this whole, this totality, as something completely given to us'.[13] The word *aufheben* in its difficulty therefore presents an open-ended circularity of sense in which its initial uncertainty as a whole is determined and then rendered imperfectly united, which, in its working-out, however provisional, delivers a sense of its truth in the movement of thought. In stating that it is both of fundamental importance and intrinsically pervasive to thinking, Hegel thereby emphasizes the fact that its sense is made apparent in and as its infinite immanent transitions. The beginning of thought thus lies in the result only insofar as this is understood to be that which enables a perspective on its development, since it is only by considering thinking from the result that it can be released from a unitary and originary starting point, and can also be understood as that which is not pure or static but is always and everywhere involved in its own unfolding. It is from our perspective on this explication that its result, however partial, can be gleaned; the result is not the end but the issue of truth, it is our own merely arbitrary point of insertion into the movement of becoming.

It is important in this regard to understand something of Hegel's own development as a thinker, for in his early writings the notions of dialectics and *aufheben* were used negatively, as part of the critique of thinking, to enable the destruction or negation of concepts. It was only around the time of the Jena *Logik* in 1804–5 that these terms began to be used with a more nuanced understanding, in which *aufheben* came to be seen as that which preserved as well as negated, and dialectics became the method by which concepts could be shown to unveil their contradictions as part of the (finite-infinite) development of thinking. These thoughts arose as Hegel realized something of the limitations of his earlier thinking, particularly in relation to history, and were worked out rather obscurely and provisionally in the Jena *Logik* manuscript. It is partly because of this discovery that this manuscript was abandoned, as it led Hegel to rethink how he approached his philosophical project as a whole – as that which must take seriously the necessity of deriving its own beginning and unfolding – which is what would emerge in the *Phänomenologie*. But in these early thoughts on logic there is a complex and profound analysis of the notion of the limit that opens up the problems with the notion of the infinite, which in turn leads to the idea of the true infinite as that which overcomes the simple opposition of finite and infinite, and thereby exposes the immanence of circularity as its own endless development (*Entwicklung*, not *Bildung*), as will be shown. It thus becomes apparent that the meaning of *aufheben* as preserving and elevating is one that Hegel discovers as he comes to use and to further determine this concept; it is not that which orients its usage in advance but that which emerges from it.

For quality to emerge it must be defined, and it does so by distinguishing itself from what it is not. In doing so quality reveals that it is contradictory, not just because it *is* only according to what it is *not* but also because at its limit this distinction between what it is and the indeterminate amount (*Menge*) of what it is not is a combination of the defined and the undefined; the limit is itself both determinate and indeterminate. The determination of the concept, for instance, in which philosophy seeks to begin, comprises a simple connection to all other concepts, which enables it to exist as it is in itself and yet also displays it in its contraries, its connections to others. Quality thus reveals itself as quantity insofar as it is an individual reality that occurs indifferently in relation to what it is not. Quality thereby ceases to be what it is in itself and passes over into something else, which sublates the distinction between what it is and what it is not into the new form of quantity. On the other side, the indeterminate amount is revealed to be an infinite contradiction as it is both pure determinacy as quality as well as pure indeterminacy, just as quality was found to be a contradiction in that it is both an amount in its infinite connections to what it is not and a numerical one in that it is an individual in itself. The relation between the reality of quantity and its negation is then further sublated as this negation passes over into what it is not, leading to the formation of the new category of totality as the combination of unity and plurality. Through this the limit, as that which is the ground of determinacy as such, is found to be both finite and infinite, and thus leads to the discovery that this sense of the infinite is not the mere endlessness of the bad infinite but that which turns back on itself in its own infinite finitude. The mass of other qualities against which quality itself is defined is not simply an other, a beyond, which in its infinite expanse is merely the negative of quality's own finitude. Instead, the limit is that in which the reality and negation of quality sublates itself in the true infinite as the sublation of determinacy as such, that is, of the very nature of the limit as that which bears its own contradiction in itself.

The infinite 'is this absolute reflection into itself of the determinate', and as such it 'is the true nature of the finite: that it is infinite, that it sublates itself in its being'. This discovery has profound consequences, since it means that the 'determinate has as such no other essence than this absolute unrest: not to be what it is. It is not nothing, because it is the other itself, and this other, being just as much the contrary of itself, is again the first'. The reality of determinacy in the limit reveals this absolute contradiction as the nature of the infinite, which 'is thereby the sole reality of the determinate and is not a "beyond", but simple connection, pure absolute movement, being-outside-itself within being-within-itself'.[14] In this movement connection is itself transformed into relation, and the sense of this change can be understood in terms of the way that the subject-object relation is transformed in the speculative sentence, where the copula no longer expresses a simple external connection from one to the other but becomes the infinite relation in which the two are brought together in and through their endless alternation. Consequently, the nature of the subject as such is reformulated on the basis of this negativity in its absolute unrest and decentring, in that its projects are that in which it loses itself, and where any sense of a return or identity to this movement is reconstrued on the basis of its dissipation and its aporetic evasions.

It is in relation to this point that Alexandre Koyré develops his account of Hegel in 1934 – which would prove very influential for the readings of Kojève and Hyppolite and, later, Malabou – although he translates the understanding of unrest into an (anthropological) emphasis on futurity and incompleteness. This idea is then contrasted with the dialectical model of history, as that which resolves itself, to suggest that there is a tension between the two notions of time and history, which is ultimately decided in favour of history as that which is already over. In creating this contrast, drawn from the change in focus between Hegel's early and later thinking of time, and considering it by way of the anthropological concern with human projects, Koyré passes over the possibility of understanding time by first examining the notion of unrest in terms of its logical implications, as Hyppolite would later pursue. For, as we have seen, this unrest opens both the finite and the infinite onto a disruption of determinacy, which does not lead to a contradiction with the notion of the whole (of history) but rather to a moment in which each (the whole and the limit) becomes implicated in the other. As a result, in thinking this limit of (in)determination in and as the moment, thinking develops on the basis of this exposure, and it is as such that it becomes part of history, as that which is traversed by the border of the moment as both finite and infinite. Hence, in realizing the manner in which concepts unfold, each thinker is forced to confront their own relation to this unfolding, which is to say that they become situated in relation to a past that is both ongoing and, by virtue of the thinker's perspective, over (which repeats the doubled movement of *aufheben*), so that it is no longer the history of the past that is at issue, but thinking, which is always the result of thinking, its own (finite-infinite) issue. That which is past, for example, the philosophical tradition, is that upon which the thinker looks as a restless and contradictory mass of determinacies, for which the moment of its thinking is its issue as that from which it begins, as well as that which is discovered by way of its working-through.

The end is now, as it were, but as an end it is only to be discovered by way of its endless recapitulation, so that 'now' is not yet.[15]

In terms of the way that the *Phänomenologie* phrases its own situation on this point, the concrete existence of the past is reduced to a trace that appears externally to the individual as the inorganic or second nature of their culture, so that in running through this past, mechanically, as it were, the individual feeds off (*sich zehren*) these achievements – that make up what is inherited – so that they can be possessed in themselves and made one's own [PG: 24–5/16]. Thus, the first part of the *Phänomenologie*, which consists in the unfolding of the experience of consciousness, culminates in the discussion of the individual that takes itself to be real and its relation to the thing itself (*die Sache selbst*), where these concrete inheritances that have been made abstract through the development of thought become concrete again in being worked through in actions. But, as Blanchot showed in his reading of the *Phänomenologie* in 'La littérature et le droit à la mort', the way that thought is rendered complex in the concrete activities of reading and writing starts to unsettle the very possibility of this recapitulation realizing itself, since any consumption of the inorganic aspects of our culture would need to take account of how these acts void themselves, insofar as their status as acts becomes negated. While this instates the limit of historical indetermination in the ongoing experience of consciousness, it also marks the course of thinking with the meaninglessness of its tradition and the empty recapitulation of abstraction that is then played out in concrete action. In Derrida's words, thought is 'a perfectly neutral name, a textual blank, the necessarily indeterminate index of an epoch of différance to come. *In a certain way, 'thought' means nothing*. Like all openings, this index, by the face that lets it be seen [*se donne à voir*], belongs within a past epoch. This thought weighs nothing. It is, in the play of the system, that which never weighs anything' [DG: 142/93]. Thought as such, to whatever extent that it exists does so only as the passing vector of this temporal movement, as a mere function of its *différance*, and it is thus that it weighs nothing and means nothing but simply marks the receding point of this bearing. (It is significant that Derrida says that thought is *neutre* here, as this is not a term that he uses widely, and it also suggests how its existence as a textual blank demonstrates what happens when this passing vector is made concrete.) The dialectic of the infinite thereby realizes itself in the movement of history as that which reconstitutes the nature of the moment as both a limit and a relation in absolute unrest.

Koyré's own argument develops by suggesting that, in contradistinction to his reading of the resolution of history in the dialectic, the moment sublates itself into a future that is always to come (*à venir*, *zu-künftig*), which he believes is Hegel's most important and overlooked discovery, even by himself, a point that will only be taken up in detail in Malabou's thesis sixty years later. In contrast to this anthropological reading – which focuses on the historicity of existence and would lay the ground for Kojève's attempt to assimilate Hegel's and Heidegger's thinking – Hyppolite begins to focus on the more pressing logical question of how the dialectic of the infinite entails a passage to the limit, as has been shown, and what this means for the logic of the absolute. An issue that is to be understood in terms of the persistent unrest of its contradiction, rather than leading to the bad infinite of endless difference that would merely dissimulate contradiction [LE: 124–5/97–8].

IV *Aufheben* in the form of language

If we return to the sentence 'being and nothing are the same', Hegel offers a clarification that indicates much about the nature of the speculative sentence, for as he writes:

> insofar as the proposition "*being and nothing are the same*" asserts the identity of these determinations, but in fact equally contains them both as distinguished [*unterschieden*], it internally contradicts itself and dissolves [*auflöst*] itself. Bearing this in mind, and considering it more closely, what we have here is a proposition that has a movement through which it vanishes spontaneously. But in doing so, there takes place in it that which constitutes its own proper content, namely, *becoming*.
>
> WL2: 77/90

The sentence as such cannot simply be read as it no longer allows thought to remain abstracted from its sense. But, in becoming involved in its movements, thought loses itself and is transformed. This is not just the back and forth motion that was earlier found in relation to the inhibition of predication but something more profoundly unsettling. The subject does not pass from its own position to that of the object and back again but finds that the sense that is borne in this movement destabilizes even this unrest. For now, the back and forth motion results in the dissolution of the sentence, so that thought is left with only the echo of its indeterminacy as it fades. Hence thought can only think the indeterminate as such by way of losing itself, which is in part the speculative movement that brings the absolute knowing at the end of the *Phänomenologie* back to the simplicity of sense-certainty that can only say 'this'. However, just as was found in the discussion of sense-certainty, where the sense of this 'this' cannot be written, we now find that the speculative sentence can also not be read.

But this is not to abdicate from thinking in favour of a mystical intuition, as this vanishing of the sentence gives rise to its own thought, which 'is not itself *expressed* in the sentence; it is an external reflection that recognises it therein'. External reflection is thus meant in a double sense, which is the basis of how this thought differs from ordinary predicative judgement, for in the latter there is a relation of identity between subject and object, whereas in speculative thought both the identical and non-identical aspects of this relation take place. The latter are moments that are not expressed, as was emphasized, but occur in the form of the unrest of the sentence, where it is discerned that the sentence is not simply contradictory as a result of the fact that its form and content seem to belie each other. Instead, it is found that the sentence '*is just as false as it is correct*', and this is because it takes place as unrest, or becoming, a discovery that cannot be ascertained if one considers the sentence from only one side as its duplicity is intrinsic [WL2: 78/91]. While this thought gives rise to determination in the form of becoming, thinking itself has uncovered its infinity. For in the movement of the sentence, thought does not come up against a limit in its determination, but rather, this limit is taken up into itself inasmuch as thinking realizes itself in the thinking of the object. This is not because it finds mere identity and return in the object as other, but realizes its own non-identity and identity in the movement that arises out of its vanishing and reflection in the object, which is the move by which thought becomes speculative [ENZ: §28 Z, 67].

It is not the case that Hegel wants to replace predicative judgement by speculative thought, since the former has its role in developing the determinations of the understanding. Thus, the text of Hegel remains legible to that degree, but equally this means that it will be punctuated by moments of infinite illegibility (textual blanks) where speculation takes place. At these points thought becomes non-identical and restless, and punctuated by an indeterminacy that cannot be foreclosed. The text as a whole is marked by these punctures as experiences of negativity, which through its restlessness negates itself and negates this self-negation. But, as was noted, these experiences are accompanied by an external reflection, which recognizes the experience and indicates that it is not pure or simple. As a result, this reflection becomes a thought of infinity in its restless contradictions, which is the speculative move by which consciousness becomes aware of itself and its object in their mutually unfolding infinity. This transition is discussed in the *Phänomenologie* in relation to the problems of the inverted (*verkehrten*) world, where the endless appearance and disappearance of differences in the world is seen to be the form of infinity, and insofar as consciousness sees this form as a form, that is, as a unity of differences, it also recognizes itself in it and thereby realizes itself as self-consciousness:

> Infinity, or this absolute restlessness of pure self-movement, in which whatever is determined in one way, for example, as being, is rather the opposite of this determinacy, is, to be sure, already the soul of all that has gone before, but it is in the *inner* [*im* Innern] that it has itself first freely emerged. Appearance, or the play of forces, already exhibits it itself, but it first freely emerges as *explanation* [Erklären]; and insofar as it is finally an object for consciousness, *as that which it is*, so is consciousness *self-consciousness*.
>
> PG: 100/101

Nevertheless, the form of infinity, as one of absolute unrest, cannot be fully grasped by the understanding, which remains tied to the variety of differences, and so the transition to self-consciousness is not accomplished through a transformation in the understanding. Instead, self-consciousness arises as a new shape through the *movement* of the understanding as it passes between consciousness of the world and of its self, a movement that appears as desire (which, insofar as it remains desire, retains the form of infinity). The emergence of this self-consciousness thereby carries a recognition, however implicit, of the sameness between the form of infinity in life and that in desire. However, the emergence of this new shape can also be apprehended in the movement of the *Phänomenologie* itself, that is, within its reading/writing, through its linguistic sublation and external reflection of thought, in which the form of infinity is recognized. In doing so, infinity is realized (in life, as in the text) in the form of 'every difference as well as their sublatedness [*Aufgehobensein*]', which is also to say, as Hyppolite notes, that it is realized in the act of transcendence rather than transcendence itself [PG: 99/100; GS: 147/151]. Thus, the thought of the infinite that was sketched out in the Jena *Logik* re-emerges at the very point where (and as the form in which) consciousness is able to become self-consciousness in the text of Hegel's thought, through its reading and recognition, which is also a recognition of infinity in the form of life. But, despite this sameness, there is still alienation and desire and the restlessness of negation, because the form of infinity cannot ever be fully satisfied in life or in consciousness: 'This life is disquiet, the disquiet of the Self that has lost itself and finds itself again in its alterity; however it never coincides with itself, for it is always other in order to be itself; it always poses itself in a determination, and always negates itself in order to be itself, because this determination, in being as such, is already its first negation' [GS: 145/149–50].

Consciousness, for Hyppolite, is always unhappy consciousness, separated from itself and conscious of this separation, aware that it is changeable and finite, and yet also unchanging and infinite. It is important to realize that this structure is both that of the sentence and of thought, and it is as such that the speculative sentence can give rise to speculation. For in the earlier construal of the speculative sentence the subject was thrust backwards and forwards as it failed to find its ground in the object. Equally, scepticism oscillates between the contradictory positions of doubting itself and doubting the world, which is then transformed into unhappy consciousness as it is discovered that these two modes are part of the same thought and occur at the same time: 'This new form is thereby one that is *for itself* the doubled consciousness of itself as self-liberating, unchangeable, and self-similar, and as absolutely self-confusing and inverting, and is the consciousness of this its own contradiction' [PG: 121/126]. The sentence then becomes one in which it is both riven by uncertainty, as its predicative relation fails to substantiate itself, and yet it is also that in which this changeability is experienced as its form, which is thereby infinite in its self-relation. But the two aspects cannot be settled: the speculative subsists within the predicative and vice versa; at each point the sentence can pass from one perspective to the other, and its intrinsic ambivalence comes from this inability to ascertain which of the two perspectives is at any moment current. Hence there are no speculative sentences as such, but there are sentences that can become speculative if they are thought through in their negativity.[16] Rather than this negation leading to its own cancelling out, the movement of *aufheben* is such that its negativity is preserved as well as transformed, which is to say that what remains of the negative is never lost but is borne within the movement of *aufheben*, not through its assimilation but as that which persistently unsettles it, as in the negation *of* consciousness, 'which survives its own becoming-sublated [*Aufgehobenwerden*]' [PG: 112/115]. It is within this defile or penumbra that Blanchot's later writing finds its imperative, where the unrest of its particular contradictions is transformed into an infinite and absolute relation, a neutral thought. If language is already thoroughgoing scepticism, about what it is and what it does, what it means and what it intends, then it is only too obvious, he writes, that unhappiness is the writer's most profound talent:

> since he is only a writer by way of a consciousness torn into irreconcilable moments that are called: inspiration – which negates all labour [*travail*];

labour – which negates the nothingness of genius; the ephemeral work [*œuvre*] – in which he completes himself [*s'accomplit*] in negating himself; the work as everything – in which he withdraws from himself [*se retire*] and from others everything that he seems to give to himself and to them.

PF: 308/318

But as he would go on to write twenty years later:

> Just as the Book takes the name of Hegel, the work [*œuvre*], in its more essential (more uncertain) anonymity, takes the name of Mallarmé, with the difference that Mallarmé not only knows the anonymity of the Work as his trait and the indication of his place, not only withdraws himself in this way of being anonymous, but does not call himself the author of the Work, proposing himself at the very most, hyperbolically, as the power – the never unique, never unifiable power – of reading the non-present Work, of being the power of responding, by his absence, to the always still absent work (the absent work not being *the absence of the work*, being even separated from it by a radical break).

EI: 628–9/428–9

In this transition in Blanchot's thinking, the experience of negativity – which was central to the work of writing in his early thought – is found to reveal a more uneasy and elusive absence, a radical and formal disruption of the status of the work as such, through which the writer finds themselves (dis)oriented.

The thought that emerges in this transition is thus more alienated and exposed than it was even in the state of unhappy consciousness, as it is interrupted not just by the work but by the absence of the work, by which the very capacity of reading is reconfigured. For Blanchot this problem relates to the anonymity of the work, since Hegel's work is never wholly nameless as the system, however it is construed, still names him and thereby establishes a mutually determining relation of thought (or recognition), whereas between Mallarmé and the work there is no relation at all, or, as Blanchot says, there is at the most a relation of absence, which is what he now calls reading. Furthermore, this lack of relation is incorporated into the work as its power of completing itself without an author, 'not because it could be produced without anyone producing it, but because its anonymity affirms it as being always and already outside whatever might name it'. The work is thus outside the whole that still claims the book, and insofar as it does not complete itself it is linked to the disaster. However, there is nothing secure about this situation, for 'the disaster is yet another affirmation of the absolute' [EI: 629/429]. This is a rather complex and obscure reconfiguration of the relation of reading and its consequences, which will become clearer in the next chapters, but for the moment the following can be said: On the one hand, Blanchot is making an association between the lack of signature in the anonymous work and the fact that even in this lack there is a resignation that designates the absolute, which is to say that the disaster of the work can never entirely resist becoming the book. So, on the other hand, what is needed is an understanding of resigning that marks the passage between the book and the work, and perhaps does so in a way similar to the sense of renouncing found in Bataille's notion of sliding words. In this way, the work exists for as long as it avoids becoming the book, and does so through the absent relation of reading, which becomes absent as it is found that the only possibility of designating the voice of the work is as one that has been *souffler*, as it were, and it is this transformation in reading that will become apparent in Blanchot's later works.

There is a useful parallel in the *Phänomenologie* that will help cast light on this issue, that of the final form of unhappy consciousness, the ascetic, who renounces their subjectivity and gives themselves up to the movements of the object, just as the object is realized in self-consciousness. This is a movement of exchange and unity, as that which was the subject relinquishes its position in favour of the object, which thereby becomes subjective in the same move, so that each comes to realize themselves through the other. But this dynamic unity is still not grasped by consciousness, for even though the subject has made itself the empty vehicle for the object to express itself, it does not feel itself part of this movement of mutual realization and so it remains unhappy and unsatisfied, although the possibility of becoming so realized is what enables the transition from this form to that of reason. The difference between this thought and what Blanchot has discussed is that even though the writer resigns themselves from the work, such that it can be a work, there is no subsequent unity between these two aspects. As he made clear, there is no relation between them, and thus no reciprocal confluence, instead, the two aspects remain apart, which is the degree to which the work desists from the book. In the move by which the writer removes themselves there is a concomitant and further removal by the work, but even if this leads to a form of subjectification, as the work finds its own thought, this remains foreign to the writer in practice and in principle. There is no recognition between them, only alienation. While the subjectivity of the writer may have assumed that this other aspect was part of itself, instead, it only yields deviation, not union, which is what is found (and lost) in the absent relation of reading. This argument is taken up in more detail by Blanchot when he discusses the inter-relation of universality and individuality in literary activity in the first part of 'La littérature et le droit à la mort', and this is also the reason why the deviation of the work is examined in the second part of the article in terms of its inescapable ambiguity (which will be examined in the next chapter). As Blanchot realizes, Hegel's discussion of activity repeats that of the unhappy consciousness but reverses its positions, since here it is the individual who feels themselves to be unchanging while it is the work that is changeable, but the same tension and resolution take place, as the individual ultimately finds realization in their work when it is found to realize the universal in principle and in practice, that is, through its place within communal activity. By contrast, whatever universal (if any) may arise through Blanchot's writings, it is evident that it would relate to the intrinsic negativity of language, its resistance and evasion of thought, and its persistent contestation of sense.

This deviation from the authority of the book is only one way in which the work can avoid totality, but Blanchot makes it clear that what is required is a move by which the work discovers that which remains outside this relation and in doing so removes itself from any authority. But it should be recalled that this move is also implicit in Hegel's speculative thinking of absolute negativity, which must be thought through to the full extent of its contradictions. However, the problem with such an endeavour is that it is, as Hegel found, one of seeking to think totality in and through its contradictions, which does not inevitably lead to totalization but rather places thought on its limits in developing a logic that can be both of the whole and yet not, insofar as it holds to its contradictions. Such a logic appears barely sustainable at a formal level as it seems to be no more (but no less) than the movement of thinking, thinking itself. Thus, the question that Hegel raises concerns the relation that thought undergoes as it attempts to think through itself, which is what takes place in reading, as Blanchot saw, and what takes place, in its place, when this relation fails.

It is almost as if part of what Blanchot is attempting to think by way of literature is tacitly directed towards the key transitions within Hegel's thought – that of the transition from the understanding to reason, from predicative to speculative judgement, from the bad infinite to the true infinite – all of which arise through a realization of what is already taking place implicitly in these modes, but that has not been expressed in actuality. Within literature, Blanchot seems to find that the possibility of this realization is both deferred and yet also realized otherwise, as if it were instead to become the (endless, material) mode of realization of literature, without this then being expressed in thought other than through the alienation that arises in it by way of the encounter with literature. And this would mean that the transition of thinking that Hegel is seeking would perhaps only occur through this restless destabilization, through a movement in which thought loses itself without scope for anything other than a nominal recuperation.

4

Blanchot: nothing doubled

I The experience of negativity in language

At the beginning of *L'Entretien infini* Blanchot asks if there is not something between being and nothing that has been missed by Hegel's logic. However, this would seem to imply a misreading as being and nothing do not exist as distinct opposites but only as becoming nothing and becoming being. There is no interval between them, as Blanchot suggests, which would hold a nothingness more profound than the nothing that relates to being [EI: 7–8/7]. The latter is the point that Heidegger raises in his critique of Hegel, and he does so by claiming that, insofar as Hegel has failed to grasp the difference between being and beings, he has failed to grasp that from which this difference comes forth, which is the abyssal unground of nothingness.[1] So, by contrast, to think nothingness without transcendence, as Hegel does, and with a view to understanding what is underway in the constant unrest of negativity that subtends the back and forth transitions of being and nothing, is not to step outside this relation into some (quasi-)transcendental ground, or unground, but to attempt to think the liminal outside of this transition, its hollow, in Blanchot's words, which is always hollowing itself out. Hence Blanchot's reading is not entirely invalid in Hegelian terms, for what it does is make it possible to think a nothingness outside and irreducible to being, the shadow of its negativity, that which is not put to work in the absolute, and desists from any relation whatsoever, even from its own lack of determination.

A thought such as this nevertheless risks nonsense in becoming a hyperbolic apophatic avoidance of sense or form. Except that Blanchot goes on to specify how this nothing can be found when language is distorted, so that 'a relation of infinity would always be involved as the movement of signification itself [. . .] in such a way that the continuity of the movement of writing would let interruption as meaning, and rupture as form, intervene fundamentally'. Thus, this movement does not ignore the unfolding of *aufheben* but instead leaves space for its infinite rupture and evasion, insofar as it 'begins with the decision (or the distraction) of an initial void' [EI: 9/8; cf. AO: 21/8]. Language would then occur at the borders of its own deterioration so that it cannot be known if it bears form and meaning or not, not in terms of a reciprocal or harmonious balance between them but as their ever-present fragility. As a result, it is impossible to determine whether this void is open to a decision or to a distraction, which indicates that this writing only arises out of and as its stuttering egress. A distraction is to some degree its own decision but an evasive and contingent one, occurring by way of its resistance to organization. As such, the unfolding of being and nothing would not take place according to any teleology of presence but would occur by accident, as it were, by way of its own negativity, insofar as this is the overturning of (positive) action and determination. There is a slip or lapse, a clinamen that cannot be decided – as Blanchot made clear with the emphatically uncertain signs that mark the openings of *Aminadab* and *L'Attente l'oubli* – and space opens up, but a space that is marked by an undecidable initiation, an absence of determination, so that it is not simply the case that we do not know the status of what there is, as it is unable to determine itself, but we also do not know whether it actually occurred or not.

It is important to recall that these remarks come from the essay that introduces his most substantial theoretical work, *L'Entretien infini*. In the first part of this book Blanchot seeks to articulate the possibility of a thought beyond and between Levinas and Hegel by examining the nature of the relation marked out in the plurality of language (the distance, repetitions, and interruptions of its appearance as both speech and writing). As a result, the title of this book comprises the tension of this double articulation, which is explicated in its opening pages when he states that the 'speech relation in which the unknown articulates itself is a relation of infinity' [EI: 6/6]. This claim does not primarily refer to an ethical relation to the other but to the fact that speech, which 'is in advance always already written', is interrupted by the unknown in such a way that this unknown becomes its (infinite) measure. Hence it is not so much what the relation is attempting that is at issue but rather the manner in which it is ruptured by an indirect, non-symmetrical, and irreversible deviation in this attempt. As a result, 'an entirely different relation announces itself that calls into question being as continuity, or the unity or gathering of being': that is, it does not form a whole and does not take place at the same time, as it is a function of the unknown, and so it becomes an infinite and incommensurable relation [EI: 11/10]. Taking up this challenge, which is necessary if thought is to respond to the demands of the unknown, cannot mean that either continuity or discontinuity can suffice as an answer; something more radical and more subtle is needed, which it is then the project of *L'Entretien infini* to unfold. What is at issue is the notion of relation as such, whether in thought, language, or otherwise, and what happens when this is subverted by an infinite deviation. The unknown is demanding not because it is innately mysterious but because it is immeasurably accidental and unpredictable: these are the specific yet intangible ruptures that pervade the formal occurrences of thought and language as the deformations that are persistently ignored or suppressed in favour of sense, but that are the very form and (im)possibility of sense.

That the unknown takes place in the form of the infinite means that it cannot entirely be brought to being and, moreover, insofar as it is made to appear, it is only further removed from this unknown relation, since its infinite unrest is suppressed in favour of presence. On the one hand, as Hegel pointed out, infinity realizes itself in self-consciousness, but on the other hand, this realization can only take place to the extent that self-consciousness refuses being [PG: 109/111; GS: 160–1/166–7]. For, as was noted in the Jena *Logik*, 'the determinate has as such no other essence than this absolute unrest: not to be what it is'.[2] Consciousness can never be anything but unhappy as its desire can never be satisfied: the infinite, as that which is endless, cannot ever be circumscribed or gathered up in anything other than a notional unity, the mere idea of infinity. And as such it marks the finitude of existence with an exposure that cannot even be called a relation insofar as it has no end; even within the finite as its endless becoming and unfolding it knows no point of culmination. The point of the infinite is precisely that its outer limit is limitless, and it is by way of this lack that it leads to the deterioration of thought. When Blanchot writes about the other night, and a dying that exceeds death, it is to these effects on thought, language, and existence that he is referring; an infinite corrosion of sense that is not a bad infinite but the infinite as that which bears itself out through its own negation and the negation of this negation.

Blanchot's insight was to view the work in such terms: to apply to the work the contradictions that are found in the path to self-consciousness and to pursue its consequences, which can only distort what is meant by both work and consciousness. As Hegel explains, while the infinity of desire is brought to some kind of form in work, its endless dissatisfaction takes shape in such a way that 'the negative relation to the object becomes the *form* of the same, and something that *remains*' [PG: 115/118]. Thus, the work becomes a form *of* negativity, so that consciousness in realizing itself in this relation only does so to the degree that it is drawn into its negativity. It is necessary, then, to examine what consciousness has to endure as it thinks through its works in their negativity, for in this encounter there is not only alienation but also the risk of absolute ambivalence, as Hyppolite points out: 'If he were to stop at this anxiety before death the slave would doubtless be only a sick animal, really internalising sickness, but in transcending it after having recognized it he opens new perspectives, he makes of the life of the spirit a *creative* life that continually surpasses its destiny'.[3] The 'life' of the spirit, as Blanchot would emphasize, is unavoidably marked by this ambivalence and negativity, part of which is elaborated by Hyppolite in the following lines:

> [Hegel] thus becomes capable of understanding how the self-consciousness of organic life raises itself above life and, in reflecting it, can oppose itself to it. This reflection, which is at the same time negativity, this creative emergence of consciousness [*prise de conscience*] that "raises the omnipotence of Nothingness to Being", generates a new dimension of being. The self-consciousness of life becomes other than life in manifesting truth, in making itself capable of being *the truth*. The difficulty consists in understanding how the self-consciousness of life can, precisely in this reflection, negate the life of which it is only the reflection, or how it can generate a new form of being, while not confining itself to being the contemplation of what already exists. To repeat within itself the cosmic process of life that makes it possible, and in this repetition to create a history distinct from this life – because spirit is higher than nature since it is the reflection of it – such is the enigma of an emergence of consciousness that is authentically a creation. But this enigma is the existence of man, or rather of men, for in repeating the cosmic movement of life Hegel brings to light the conditions of self-consciousness and within it, the mutual relation of self-consciousnesses between themselves as the process of *recognition*.[4]

If Blanchot is at this time thinking through his response to Sartre's ongoing discussions of literature in the same journal, then in Hyppolite's reading of Hegel there emerges an aspect of his own understanding of the remove of literature, and its inherent negativity, which inevitably inflects its status and relation to thought.

Of particular significance is that which Hyppolite specifies under the name of reflection, and the questions it raises: what kind of relation is this when it is constituted by negativity; what is the nature and status of the space that is opened up in this reflection; how does it relate to that of which it is a reflection; and what do these questions entail for the attempt to relate to this object of reflection through thought and language? The difficulty comes from the fact that creativity is linked to negativity, but this relation is intrinsically unclear for is it a negative creation or a creative negation; a negativity that creates or a creation of negativity? This enigma is human existence, as Hyppolite writes, but insofar as it is realized through acts and projects it is also an enigma that is of these works, which only doubles and extends their uncertainty and ambivalence, as Blanchot will explicate. For it is now a question of what they are as works, if that can be ascertained at all: not just in terms of the difference between what they intend and what they do but whether or not they are works as such, and whether the new mode of being that Hyppolite refers to is in fact still of being as its key categories have been called into question.[5]

And, as this question has been raised, it becomes necessary to ask what the place or role of nothing might be in these works if they comprise a deviation from being. Paradoxically, the varieties of nothing are manifold and Blanchot's thought is evidently drawn to this fact, but it is noteworthy that he finds a way of talking about it that is not abstract or limited to simple negation, and to some degree thereby takes up the analysis of Hegel. For in order to avoid the abstractness of discussing nothingness as such, Hegel moves to examine negativity in its determinacy, as had been introduced by Kant.[6] Heidegger, by contrast, continues to discuss nothingness as that which is more primordial than negativity, but in doing so does not manage to explicate its abstraction other than in terms of not-being, which later becomes assimilated to the thought of being as event. Blanchot instead takes up the combined task of analysing the negativity of language and the experience of nothingness, and their interrelation. In this way, the abstract quality of nothingness becomes understood in terms of its experience of negativity, as a restless ambivalence that is not merely the inverse or absence of being, while the movement of negativity in language becomes an experience of that which is not only tied to its unfolding determination but is also its enervating hollow, a doubled movement that together constitutes the labour of the negative. It is thus that the abstract and concrete, particular and universal, aspects of the negative are exposed in the work of literature, so that thought can come to experience it as such. As a result, it is worth considering whether this experience becomes available *because* Blanchot is working through literature, which does not permit of a clear separation of concept and object, and uncovers an experience of nothingness that is lived as a concrete emptiness while yet being specific, insofar as it is 'the nothingness of that *from which it results*' [PG: 57/51; cf. WL2: 70/83].

The challenge is one of thinking through a statement like 'nothing remains' or 'nothing is more real than death' to the extent of its speculative ambivalence, which is both abstract and specific. For on the one hand, we cannot think about nothing without in some way construing its existence, but on the other hand, in so doing, by drawing nothing into some form of proposition, the determinate negation that allows for such positing is drawn from the nothingness that is latent in this relation, and is thereby determined (and distorted) by it. Hence this is not to allow language and thought to vanish into some hyperbolic apophatic rapture but to enter into the movement of becoming in both its determination and indeterminacy, which is what its speculative thinking unfolds. As Hegel indicates at the beginning of *Wissenschaft der Logik*:

> Insofar as intuiting or thinking can be mentioned here, it counts as a distinction [*Unterschied*] whether something or *nothing* is intuited or thought. To intuit or think nothing therefore has a meaning [*Bedeutung*]; both are distinguished, thus nothing *is* (exists) in our intuiting or thinking; or rather it is empty intuition and thought itself.
>
> WL2: 69/82

In reading this opening carefully, it can be seen how the determination of indeterminacy arises and carries its concrete abstraction into thought. So when, at the very end of this text, Hegel states that negativity 'constitutes the *turning point* of the movement of the concept [...] the *simple point of the negative relation to self*, the innermost source of all activity, all living and spiritual self-movement', we need to recognize that as negativity does not have a determinate locus or extent, so its turning point is without centre or horizon [WL1: 246/835]. Absolute negativity would thus be that in which negativity exists both of and as the absolute, and so this point can be clarified, for, as Blanchot wrote, the turning point exists only if we are not certain about it [EI: 394/264].

To examine these issues it is necessary to look more closely at how Blanchot's understanding of the work translates the fear of death encountered by the bondsman in the life and death struggle into the context of the writer's relation to their work, an absolute fear that is, as it were, sublated in the work, that is, not merely cancelled but preserved as its motive force or moment. As mentioned above, in the work, desire is suspended (or checked, *gehemmt*, as was the passage of thought in the speculative sentence) such that its negative (unfulfilled) relation to the object becomes the form of the object, and it is thus that it remains (desire). Hence, in making the work, the bondsman's own negativity becomes an object for him and 'this objective *negative* is exactly the alien essence [*fremde Wesen*] before which he had trembled' [PG: 115/118]. There then occurs a transformation, a turning around in the relation to the work, which bears its ambivalence into the thought that it manifests:

> In the lord, being-for-itself [*Für-sich-sein*] is *an other* for the bondsman, or it is only *for him*; in fear, being-for-itself is *in him itself*; in creative works [*Bilden*] being-for-itself becomes for him *his own*, and he becomes conscious that he is himself in and for himself. Hence the form, in *being made external* [hinausgesetzt], does not become something other than him; for it is just his pure being-for-itself, which thereby becomes the truth for him. Thus, through this rediscovery of himself by himself, he realises his *own sense* [eigner Sinn] exactly in the work wherein there seemed to be only *alien sense* [fremder Sinn].
>
> PG: 115/118–19

This is the movement of alienation in work, and it must be understood that this rediscovery is also a further estrangement, since the bondsman or writer do not come back to themselves but rather find a new existence by way of (the) work, which is to say that this existence is sustained and articulated by the negativity of the work as it (un-)realizes itself. The fear of death, before which the bondsman had trembled absolutely, is thereby extended across the work as the function of its thought, and it is this absolute fear that is then experienced by the writer or reader in their encounter with the literary work.

Hegel had written that thinking of nothing would result in an empty thought, which means that the nature of this nothingness can only be brought out in a more concrete form in a work in which the writer encounters objective negativity, that is, before which he is not only brought to the point of finding everything solid shaken to its roots but also finding (and losing) his own sense in this negativity. Such would be the scope of the speculative thinking of literature, but exactly what the form and status of such a thought would be remains unclear. Since, as was shown in *Wissenschaft der Logik* itself, which had begun with its own empty thought, the form and status of the realization of this thought appears to be that of infinite return, so that to write according to it would be 'to trace a circle in the interior of which would come to be inscribed the outside of every circle ..', in Blanchot's words [EI: 112/79 (ellipsis in original)].[7] Developing this understanding requires a sustained study of how thinking is transformed through the peculiar speculative quality of literary language, and how far its existence and sense is maintained through this transformation. While the conclusion to 'La littérature et le droit à la mort' emphasizes and extrapolates the ways in which the ambivalence of this transformation affects language, it is important to grasp the force of this ambivalence in terms of its experience, which is not without its effects on thinking, and it is perhaps upon thought that these effects come to bear most severely.

As Hegel concludes this section of the *Phänomenologie* before going on to discuss the forms of stoicism, scepticism, and unhappy consciousness, he reiterates the significance of the encounter with objective negativity for the possibility of recognition, which is studied in more detail in the later analysis of work as 'the thing itself':

> If consciousness fashions the thing without that initial absolute fear, it is only the vanity of its own sense; for its form or negativity is not negativity *in itself*, and so its formative activity cannot give it a consciousness of itself as of the essence. If it has not withstood absolute fear but only a few anxieties, negative being remains for it something external, its substance has not been infected by it through and through. If the contents of his natural consciousness have not all been shaken, he still belongs *in himself* to determinate being; his own sense is *obstinacy* [*der eigne Sinn ist* Eigensinn], a freedom that remains stuck within servitude.
>
> PG: 115–16/119

Such a thought is echoed in Blanchot's remark that reading must overcome the resistance of the reader to remain themselves through the act of reading [EL: 207/198]. But this transition does not lead to an alignment with or subsumption into the work, quite the opposite, as Blanchot makes particularly clear in his readings of Hölderlin: the rejection of immediacy does not lead to a thought of transition as mediation; instead, mediacy is rejected just as firmly as immediacy. While Hölderlin had written in his fragmentary commentaries on Pindar that the immediate is impossible, Blanchot does not take this to mean that we should now refer to mediation in our relation with the unknown, but rather that *impossibility* is the form of our relation with the immediate (thus he departs from Hölderlin's position).[8] This is to say that 'if the immediate is the presence of that which is infinitely absent, exceeding and excluding any present, the only relation with the immediate would be a relation reserving an infinite absence, an interval that nevertheless would not mediate (that should never serve as intermediary)' [EI: 54/38]. This infinite contestation is part of the displacement that Blanchot finds Hölderlin (and Nietzsche) nevertheless affirming, a displacement that, like that of *aufheben*, arises from the movement and moment in which the work is no longer *and* not yet, such that 'the poem's space is entirely represented by this *and*, which indicates the double absence' [EL: 260/247; EI: 244/163]. It can be understood why this double refusal would need to be developed by way of forms such as literature or experience, as this is to seek a form in which change occurs less through mediation than through a sudden transition or repetition, a form in which contestation and contradiction are existed, as Hyppolite stressed. However, this double refusal remains a supposition or hypothesis for Blanchot (in a way that will be spelled out in the next chapter) as nothing guarantees its possibility, let alone its actuality, since its form is that of impossibility, even as its experiences paradoxically remain concrete and specific.

It has been suggested that Blanchot's thought on this point can be articulated by way of the notion of 'the other night', the night that is not engaged in an alternation with the day, but nor is it the mystical night of intellectual intuition that Hegel criticized; instead, it is the night that is indistinguishable from the day insofar as light has become as obscure as the dark.⁹ The other night is a wholly different form of obscurity that is not in relation to clarity but is rather the lack of illuminated presence, yet without the sheer absence of determination that marked the night in which all cows are black [PG: 17/9]. This is the sense of a contingent nothingness, or concrete emptiness, which is to be found in the experience of literature as a space and form that both is and is not. In place of the attempt that Derrida pursued, to rethink the economy of *aufheben* without relief, Blanchot addresses himself to the question of mediation, which is reconfigured by way of the negativity of language as an issue of doubling, or repetition. The transition from one form to another that takes place in Hegelian dialectics is displaced in Blanchot's thought of the two slopes of literature, whose refractory and irreducible duplicity does not support a simple transformation of sense but inverts and complicates it with the ambivalence of negativity. Ambivalence is not dissemination as it is the experience of contradiction, of the nullity that is both sense and non-sense, the night and the other night. It is also not a thought of dualism as this doubling is not a fundamental division but a movement of uncertainty that, insofar as it is borne by experience as its contestation, is not related to a thought of presence or essence. As has been mentioned, relation as such is distorted by this ambivalence just as much as is mediation. Moreover, with this change to the sense of mediation, the nature and possibility of dialectics becomes reconfigured and re-emerges by way of deviation, rupture, and duplication. This is not to dismiss dialectical thought but to find that which replicates its forms with greater eccentricity or hesitation. Language does this to the degree that it has no system or goal in itself but proceeds according to its contingent historico-material exposures, which can only be addressed through a systematic logic of transformations by reducing them. What takes place in language, just as in death, cannot be assimilated by thought but is not lost to it either, instead, as Blanchot writes in relation to the space of memory, but that can also apply to literature, its space 'is at once the mediating site and the space without mediation' [EI: 463/316]. It is apparent that by staying within the vocabulary of experience and negativity Blanchot is able to develop a reading that manages to be critical of Hegel's thought without falling into the trap of attempting to oppose it and, as a result, finds a space that opens up by way of the replication of his thinking, which thereby carries its critique further:

> The correct [*juste*] criticism of the System does not consist (as is most often indulged) in finding fault with it or in interpreting it insufficiently (which occurs even in Heidegger) but rather in rendering it invincible, invulnerable to criticism [*incritiquable*] or, as they say, *incontournable*. Then, as nothing escapes it because of its omnipresent unity and its gathering up of everything, there no longer remains a place for fragmentary writing except by extricating itself as the impossible necessary: as that which is written in the time outside time, in a suspense that, without restraint, breaks the seal of unity, precisely by not breaking it but by leaving it aside without being able to know it.
>
> EDB: 100/61

The impossible is again the (almost apophatic) response, as if the idea that *nothing escapes* means that nothing does in fact 'escape' the system, and it is from this nothing that fragmentary writing finds its imperative. Such is Blanchot's reading in his later works, at which point even the association of thought and experience is in question, but in his earlier writings this is not the case, and so it is more helpful to examine these before trying to understand how the very form of experience is disrupted as thought is transformed in the fragmentary.

After studying the section in the *Phänomenologie* dealing with the *geistige Tierreich* and *die Sache selbst* in the first part of the essay that would become known as 'La littérature et le droit à la mort', Blanchot moves on in the second part to discuss the nature of language more directly. He refers briefly to Kojève in this discussion, and also to some lines from Hegel's first *Philosophie des Geistes* writings that deal with the peculiar power of naming, which would be taken up in more detail in the *Enzyklopädie* discussion of memory. From this starting place Blanchot launches into the explication of the two slopes of literature, which would be his first sustained attempt to provide something like a general analysis of the effects of negativity and ambivalence in language, and in doing so he draws out the strange suspense that occurs in literature when it encounters these slopes, which it is unable to balance or reconcile. The doubling of language becomes inescapable, and the effects of this, as he goes on to examine, are profound, as they expose the distance that language takes from ontology and what this experience means for the place and role of negativity in life and thought. Blanchot begins by rehearsing the Hegelian point about negativity in language, which states that, as Kojève puts it, '*conceptual*-understanding (*Begreifen*) is equivalent to a *murder*'.[10] Just as the concept makes the object unnecessary, so the absence of the object is the necessary condition for the concept. In discovering the name for an object, the latter is summarily despatched as it is now replaced by its name. Death thereby exists within words as their condition of possibility; if words could not substitute themselves for objects, they would not be possible. Names may thus enable mastery but equally, in speaking, I separate myself from myself: 'When I speak, I deny the existence of what I am saying, but I also deny the existence of the one saying it: if my speech reveals being in its non-existence, it also affirms that this revelation is made on the basis of the non-existence of the one making it, of his power to distance himself from himself, of being other than his being' [PF: 313–14/324]. Thus, a double manoeuvre takes place in which the object is made absent just as its absence is made present, alongside a similar movement in the speaker themselves. Hence two distinct absences occur in a non-identical, non-reciprocal exposure and estrangement.

This negativity becomes the very basis of language, to the degree that 'nothing finds its being in speech, and the being of speech is nothing' [PF: 314/324]. However, as Blanchot explains, this does not mean that there is scope for language to accomplish itself by allowing these absences to coincide with each other, as these two vectors diverge from each other, and it is to the analysis of these two vectors that the rest of his essay turns. The problem with understanding this analysis comes from its quasi-dialectical form, for each of these vectors is split in itself, which lends it the sense of a dialectical argument in which there is transformation by way of negation. But Blanchot extends the negativity of each of these vectors to show how it only deviates from itself. For example, nothing finds its being in speech, which means both that nothing finds its *being* and that it finds *its* being, that is, it finds being, and also its own being, in the sense that it finds meaning in words and that it finds the absence that is its own being. Equally, the same takes place on the other side, as it were, in that the being of speech is *nothing* and also that the being of speech *is* nothing, that is, whatever the nature of speech may be it finds its form in nothing, and it is nothing. The chiasmus-like form thus sketched out is not centripetal but centrifugal, and in reading Blanchot's essay it is sometimes difficult to parse these movements as he will move from one to the next without clearly specifying them. This is not accidental but part of the way that literature operates, as it does not pursue this negativity analytically but rather inhabits it and so passes back and forth by way of its deviations. In doing so, the dialectical reversals are not separated sequentially but interrupt each other as differentiations of negativity, and this is the case because literature does not deal with negativity in part or in isolation, but in and as its entirety. Literature does not simply seek the absence of the object but rather 'to attain this absence absolutely in and for itself, to grasp in its entirety the infinite movement of the understanding' [PF: 315/325]. Literature becomes this infinite movement in its negativity, which has implications for the status of the understanding, in its Hegelian sense, as Blanchot's essay will begin to show.

Hence pursuit of this movement only leads to more difficulties, for if language seeks to express the absence into which the object has disappeared in being named it cannot, for in speaking it brings that absence into being and distorts it: 'How could the infinite absence of the understanding consent to being confused with the limited and restricted presence of a single word?' In response to this difficulty, the literary writer tries to attend to words more closely, to uncover the nothingness and disquiet that they bear in obscuring the absence and non-existence of the object, but in attempting to refine language in order to better approach this nothingness words in general start to become uncertain. Names and their meanings become unfixed by their negativity and begin to slide, and thus language as a whole begins 'to accede to the uneasy demands of a single thing deprived of being and, after having wavered between each word, seeks to lay hold of them all again in order to negate them all at once, so that they will designate the void as they sink down into it' [PF: 315/326]. That is, once the insufficiency of a single word has been found, there is nothing to stop this corrosion of sense affecting all others. So, where language had sought to embrace the negativity of its grounds, it only becomes hollowed out and ungrounded.

However, language is not just a negation of reality, but is itself a reality. The failure to achieve satisfaction through the proliferation of its negations becomes the means by which language finds objectivity, as its words make things '*really* present outside themselves'. The distortions of language become things themselves, but this only brings further deviations, for literature thereby reveals that it no longer needs the writer, as it is now 'playing its own game without man', it is no longer 'inscribed in the world as the absolute perspective of the world in its totality. It is not beyond the world, but it is not the world either'. It is thus that it is 'outside', as it is before or after the appearance of the world, outside presence and the illuminating gaze of consciousness. Literary language, in seeking to undo itself and reach the moment before its own existence, becomes absent from presence without fully disappearing; it is drawn into its own negations such that it undermines its own appearance and definition. It becomes '*my* consciousness *without me*', the ever-marginal abandon of both existence and non-existence, and the receding horizon of sense outside its determination:

> It is not the night; it is the haunting of it; not the night but the consciousness of the night that keeps watch without ceasing in order to surprise it and because of this dissipates itself without respite. It is not the day; it is the side of the day that has been rejected in order to become light. And it is not death either, because in it is manifested existence without being, existence that remains below existence, like an inexorable affirmation without beginning or end, death as the impossibility of dying.
>
> PF: 317/328

In these formulations, Blanchot is seeking to draw out that which evades the positing of thought by this use of negation, which breaks down the sphere of reflection so that what is not this, is not simply its negation or opposite, especially when it is referring to the key metaphors of light and life. Except that these are not simply metaphors, for with the transformation of language through negativity the parameters of experience are also transformed, and the very dimensions and extent of life. Initially, it can be seen how far this set of inversions comes by way of the explorations that have occurred in Blanchot's fictional writings, as well as his readings of Lautréamont and Kafka. But it should also alert us to the difficulty of recruiting Blanchot's language to a philosophical discourse, without merely reverting to a poetic-literary figuration of negativity in its place.

For what is at issue is a language that bears its own thought by way of this negativity, and does not follow the logical rules of contradiction, but is rather trying to respond to its material distortions to uncover that which does not fall into the formal patterns of this or that, or position and negation. Hence this is not a poetic evocation of existence without being but an attempt to draw thinking into its own alienation by way of the eccentric convolutions of language. To this extent it seems to follow Hegel, for whom language is the form in which the externalization of consciousness coincides with the spiritualization of externality, so that it becomes the 'completed element in which inwardness is just as external as externality is inward' [PG: 388/439]. But there is no coincidence or completion of language for Blanchot, for what he is focusing on are the contours of this transformation, the hollows and outlines that fall outside its mutual reinforcement. Equally, this point seems to take up the Heideggerian critique that dialectics fails to consider its abyssal grounds, which withdraw and conceal themselves and become conditions of impossibility as much as of possibility. But Blanchot is in fact focused on the more marginal and contingent role of literary articulation, which never takes place without enduring and extending its own displacement, without thereby essaying any (quasi-)transcendental conditions. For example, language that addresses itself to its materiality does not thereby uncover its earthly constituents:

> Literature has certainly triumphed over the meaning of words, but what it has found in words taken outside of their meaning is meaning that has become thing: thus, it is meaning detached from its conditions, separated from its moments, wandering like an empty power [*pouvoir*], which one can do nothing with, power without power, the simple inability [*impuissance*] to cease to be, but which, because of that, appears to be the proper determination of indeterminate and meaningless [*privée de sens*] existence.
>
> PF: 319–20/331

Thus, Blanchot is not re-essentializing Hegel's thought by way of the Heideggerian critique, but is exploring the actual problems of literary existence, its effects on actuality, as it extends (beyond) itself to become the thought or image of its non-existence, of inapparence and absence, the shadow doubling (of) existence. As Hegel explained, diurnality means that there is neither light nor dark (which in their purity would be identical voids) but only darkened light and illuminated darkness, as each determines the other [WL2: 80/93]. For Blanchot, the question of the other night is precisely that of the failure or limits of this determination; that which cannot be negated as it negates its own determination through its weakness. Or, said otherwise, it is to find the other night as that which doubles it, the night of the night, as it were, which would be neither pure nor determined. Insofar as literary language provides this doubling, it not only reflects on what is but also on itself and in doing so moves undecidably between the two, and so fails to be fully transitive or intransitive, thereby opening up a lacuna that could be called the night of language, as he later writes [EI: 524/357].

The analysis of the two slopes of literature then goes on, for as much as language seeks to name things and thereby abolishes their existence, it cannot in doing so prevent itself from indicating this disappearance. It thus forms its own restless infinity in which each disappearance is remarked since, as Blanchot clearly states, 'what is abolished is maintained', but this is not the transition from non-existence to meaning that Kojève had earlier discussed. For in literature this sublation occurs alongside another that is of a different order: when the word refuses to name an object in seeking to appear itself, the destruction of meaning is replaced by mere signification in general, 'the meaning of the meaninglessness embedded in the word as expression of the obscurity of existence'. This is the nightside of language as it seeks the thing without its revelation, before its appearance, by way of its own concrete negativity, and in doing so it is not the essence of the thing that is abolished and sustained in its name but the inverse: the nonexistence and insignificance of its absence, which is made manifest as the sheer possibility of signification. So, on both sides literature has receded from meaning, neither revealing the object nor its sense, but in its place finding that which lines appearance; its ever contingent penumbra of nothingness, which is also the darkness of necessity, since 'what is prior to the day, of prediurnal existence, is the dark side of the day, and that dark side is not the undisclosed mystery of its beginning, it is its inevitable presence', its inescapable fatality [PF: 318/329]. The existential pathos that echoes through these lines does not substantiate nothingness and the night but is rather there to indicate how the failures of language are experienced, that is, they are not merely failures of signification but of existence itself as that which bears or does not bear meaning, and of the world that arises when there is only nonsense and obscurity, of the night of the world, as Hegel calls it, 'this empty nothing that contains everything in its simplicity – a wealth of infinitely many representations, images, none of which occur to [the human] directly, or are not present'.[11] For Hegel, this night is the human in its interiority but, as Blanchot is showing in this essay, this night is made real in literature, not as the night of pure self, as Hegel terms it, but as the impersonal light of consciousness deprived of self, which is what becomes concrete in the language of literature. Thus, the nature of the haunting that this language introduces can be understood as that of an absent presence that refuses to disappear, and that seems to double the night as its obscure and selfless thought.

Confronted by the strangeness of both objects and their sense, literature appears faced with a choice. For Hegel, the unity of spirit is such that whether we start with concepts or things we are drawn by way of their contradictions into realizing their reciprocal determination. For Blanchot, the two slopes of literature, which might crudely be called idealist and materialist, also lead into each other but only in a movement of ever further estrangement and instability, as will be seen. It is worth emphasizing that Blanchot retains the immanent critique that Hegel develops, by examining the differing experiences of literature through their contradictions and then extrapolating them, but in doing so these contradictions only become more subtle and disconcerting. For example, on the idealist side, literature that seeks meanings instead of words is involved in the endless negation of words to reach this meaning, a negation that becomes global insofar as it seeks not the negation of individual words but the whole movement of negativity, both in itself and as a totality. The search for meaning thereby comes to constitute an imaginary whole: that which would appear if this endless search for negation could realize itself. On the other side, literature that seeks to be a thing associates itself with the formless materiality of language, which remains indeterminate and uncertain. But this transformation of language occurs through the appearance of meaninglessness, which is both the coming about of meaninglessness and the meaning that this appearance takes on. It can be seen that Hegel himself straddles these two slopes in the tension between his thinking of the system and of language, but Blanchot is not interested in showing how they lead into each other in the transformation of materiality into meaning, and vice versa, but in drawing our attention to the strange power that underlies this endless ambivalence. Firstly, it is important to note that the two slopes do not reflect or lead into each other: although the first slope may seek to focus on meaning and end up finding an array of empty images, this is not the same as what happens on the other side, where the search for materiality led to the emergence of the sheer sense of senselessness. It can be seen that these two outcomes are not the same, nor are they exact inversions; instead they only indicate how the slopes diverge from themselves as much as each other. Thus, the dialectic of language completing itself that Hegel had proposed is undone in ways that are not obvious but are more disturbing because they are undefined. Literature cannot choose sides when faced with this problem, but nor is it enough just to recognize this aporia. Instead, it is necessary to seek to grasp what this undecidability implies for a literature that would not follow this oscillation blindly, a literature that would seek to draw out its fractured movements by not allowing the drive towards either systematicity or materiality to become dominant. What is at issue is not only the realistic or non-realistic status of literature but the relation between language and the world, as it is construed by way of their negativity, and the thought of this relation.

Blanchot's understanding of literature is as the work, the power, and the thought of the negative, by which it relates to the world, history, and humanity. And insofar as it is a work of negativity, rather than the spirit, it bears no possibility of systematic completion, for what it uncovers is the problematic of the 'meaning for the meaning of words that, in wholly determining them, also surrounds this determination with an ambiguous indeterminacy' [PF: 330/343]. The ambiguity at stake here is that of the uncertainty over whether language is primarily a thing or its meaning, an ambiguity that cannot be settled as there is no position from which such an adjudication could take place. Thus, the indeterminacy of determination exists in a region outside the whole, not as history or fantasy or concept, but as its undying ferment that arises through the power of the negative. In effect, Blanchot has doubled Hegel's thinking to suggest that we not only consider negativity from the point of view of spirit but also vice versa, and, consequently, we consider the human from the point of view of language as well as the opposite. There is an intimation here of what would take place in the (post-)structuralist turn, but that Blanchot is developing in a broader perspective insofar as he is keen to approach the experience of literature as such, as far as this is possible, that is, without the anthropological concern with goals or works, and to rethink the human from this revised perspective. If literature is this thought of the negative, then its experience is such that it will unsettle any humanistic spheres of meaning, for, as he goes on to conclude:

> nothing can prevent this power [*puissance*] – at the moment in which it works towards the understanding of things and, in language, the specification of words – from continuing to affirm itself as an always other possibility and perpetuating an irreducible *double meaning*, an alternative whose terms are covered in an ambiguity that makes them identical in making them opposed.
>
> PF: 330/343–4

The last point does not revert to the Hegelian identity of identity and non-identity but shows how the notion of identity is rendered irreducibly ambiguous, since it is an identity whose status is itself uncertain and ungrounded, as it is only an aspect of the ongoing power of negativity to unravel (into) its own estrangement. This negativity and the ambiguity that it gives rise to are indicators of the final important factor in Blanchot's essay: the impossible fact of death that lies at the heart of the problem of literary language, which indicates that this problem is not merely artistic, but nor is it simply existential. Death takes on this role insofar as it brings about the unending difficulty of a negation that cannot be delimited, which takes shape in and as literary language.

As he has shown, death is the mark of finitude without which language and thought would not be possible, but why should the experience of writing become aligned with that of death? This question can be made clearer by examining how Blanchot reformulates key lines from the *Phänomenologie* in the second half of 'La littérature et le droit à la mort'. Firstly, in the discussion of the master-slave dialectic, Hegel speaks of the way that the consciousness of the slave implicitly bears the truth of pure negativity within itself, for it has experienced the fear of death as its essence [PG: 114/117]. Blanchot rewrites this point by saying that if true language is to begin, then the life that bears it must have experienced nothingness and been shaken by the fear of death [PF: 314/324]. Language thus takes up the position of the slave encountering the possibility of death, and while this indicates how it begins with the nothingness of death, the fact of negation, without which there could be neither sense nor senselessness, it also shows the radically disturbing and inescapable consequences of this encounter.

Secondly, Hegel speaks in the Preface of the unique importance of the understanding, which actualizes the tremendous power of the negative, and goes on to say that the life of the spirit does not shrink from this power but bears it and maintains itself in it [PG: 27/19]. Blanchot directly cites this phrase, but for him it is language that is 'the life that bears death and maintains itself in it', a point he repeats several times (he also states that speech is this life, and that the ideal of literature is the moment in which life bears death, etc.) [PF: 311/321-2, 316/327, 324/336, 330/343]. Again, this does not so much alter Hegel's sense but rather particularizes it within the field of Blanchot's concerns, for to say that language is that life that endures the power of the negative, which can also be called death, as Hegel notes, is to say that it is carrying out the work of the understanding, which for Hegel may be powerful but nevertheless remains the perspective of negativity. Thus, this would be to say that literature does not accomplish itself as reason, or perhaps only does so implicitly, without actively realizing its sublation, since it is precisely that which maintains itself in death and negativity.

These points are important for the way that the status of death is then drawn out in Blanchot's essay, and for what he has called 'the right to death'. Although there are passages in the first part of the essay that illuminate what is meant by this phrase (as when he discusses the French Revolution), in the second part, death is not a right but the very basis of language, that in and through which it exists, which is made explicit in literature. As he writes: 'If we want to restore literature to the movement that makes it possible to grasp all its ambiguities, it is here: literature, like ordinary speech, *begins* with the *end*, which alone allows us to understand. To speak, we must see death, see it behind us'. To some extent this is the same argument about the grounding of language in finitude that he has already elaborated, but Blanchot goes on to say that it is because of this grounding that death is also 'man's greatest hope', for it is through it that there remains for us 'the future of a completed world'. Conversely, this significance is what brings out the horrifying fact of existence (as it excludes death) and of death itself, which necessarily makes death impossible once it occurs [PF: 324/336–7]. These aspects indicate what is underway in the absolute fear that language unveils, and that the life of the understanding makes real as persistent negativity, but it is the uncertain combination of these aspects with the determining finitude of death that leads to its most profoundly destabilizing ambivalence, which is exposed in literature as its inherent contradiction:

> It is negation, because it pushes the inhuman, indeterminate side of things back into nothingness; it defines them, makes them finite, and it is in this sense that it is really the work [*œuvre*] of death in the world. But, at the same time, after having denied things in their existence, it preserves them in their being: it causes things to have a meaning and the negation that is death at work [*au travail*] is also the advent of meaning, the activity of the understanding.
> PF: 326/338

Death is never not death, it is never merely the finitude of definition, or, rather, the latter is never distinct from real death, death that is real as it has a being and is in the world. This is why Blanchot discusses it in terms of actual figures – rephrasing Mallarmé's description of the idealization involved in poetry in terms of the death of a woman; and, emphasizing a literature that moves away from resurrected meaning towards that which refuses being, like a Lazarus who remains in the tomb – in order to demonstrate the place and role of death. Consider the effect of Blanchot's revision of Mallarmé's lines from *Crise de vers*:

> I say a flower! But in the absence where I mention it, through the oblivion to which I relegate the image it gives me, in the depths of this heavy word, itself looming up like an unknown thing, I passionately summon the darkness of this flower, this perfume that passes through me and that I do not breathe, this dust that impregnates me but that I do not see, this colour that is a trace and not light.
> PF: 316/327

Instead of the transposition from object to word, or idea, that Mallarmé envisages, in which the absent object becomes an idea of absence, there is a transition of thing into word as a movement of word into thing, where negation leaves both word and thing incompletely emptied and uncomfortably coexistent.[12] There is an end because there is death, but also, there is no end because there is death, and the two cannot be separated, undermining any simple transposition to ideas or any certainty about presence. This is a death that cannot die, a nothingness that cannot be annihilated, which is the basis and the form in which ambiguity occurs in language, thereby bringing about the transformation in Hegel's thought that has been running throughout this essay, in which negation is not merely finitude and determination but the life of death in all the complex reconfigurations of life and death that this double genitive will imply. As Blanchot concludes the essay, literature makes real the ambivalence of the expression 'death ends in being' (*la mort aboutit à l'être*), which marks both the hope and the fate of existence as that in which death *ends*, and yet also that in which *death* ends. And so, in a final reversal, literature is that which makes death possible, in the sense that it can now be thought and realized, but in doing so we can only understand it 'by infecting what we understand with the nothingness of death', which is exactly how and how far death can be thought, which thus becomes the form of the understanding [PF: 331/344]. The relation of Blanchot's thought to that of Hegel would thus seem to be closer, but also more tensed and distorted, than that which Derrida claimed, which demonstrates his response to the dialectic as that which must be criticized from within by pursuing its strengths and successes to the point where they invert themselves.

It is in no way inconsistent that Blanchot would then, years later, come to question the very possibility of an alternative to the dialectic. For even if we start from its inexhaustible strength, and consider that language in its formlessness may activate a negativity that exceeds it, then the implications of this reversal from life to language might not disavow the dialectic by removing its point of closure, but 'only serve to prolong it in other forms, in such a way that one would never be sure that the dialectical imperative does not aspire to its own renunciation in order to renew itself from what renders it obsolete [*met hors de cause*], ineffective' [EDB: 119/73]. At this point any scope for a refusal of the dialectic is thereby put in suspense, as Blanchot's subsequent remarks in this fragment indicate, which is not to rule out such refusal but to reconsider how its negativity relates to thinking. While it is not possible simply to refute or escape dialectical thought, it is also necessary to be wary of any reification of the dialectic as insurmountable, just as was found with *aufheben*. Thus, it is worth considering how the *labour* of the negative is displaced by an equivalent movement *sans emploi* and how its idle, workless operation might expose the suspense in which this refusal occurs to a neutral thinking – without relation.

This point is at the heart of the thought of Bataille, which Blanchot reflects on in a piece written after Bataille's death in 1962. Here, the limit-experience that concerns Bataille so heavily is shown to be without limits, in that it puts everything in question by putting the human itself in question. Consequently, the limit-experience is paradoxically unlimited, and in its elaboration demonstrates that the human concerns everything, as it is already everything within itself. Thus, the issue of the end of history raised by Kojève is recalled, but more profoundly and extensively, for the limit-experience, in drawing out the experience of everything, makes of this experience that which is not completed and finished but realizes the immanence of the end in itself. It is as such that it is a limit-experience, since it is an experience of and on the very edge as that which is in itself endless. Despite its extremity, this experience can still look like the work of negativity, which endlessly prepares the end by converting itself into action without satisfaction, and with which dissatisfaction the human completes and satisfies itself through and as the work of history. But here, as Blanchot writes, Bataille's intervention occurs:

> No, humanity does not exhaust its negativity in action; no, it does not transform into power [*pouvoir*] all the nothingness that it is; perhaps it can reach the absolute by making itself equal to the whole and by becoming conscious of the whole, but then more extreme than this absolute is the passion of negative thought, for faced with this response, negative thought is still capable of introducing the question that suspends it and, faced with the accomplishment of the whole, of maintaining the other exigency that again raises the infinite in the form of contestation.
>
> EI: 304/205

This passion is not a casual pathos but a reminder of the force and experience of thinking, and the manner in which its negativity occurs, since it is that in and by which negativity occurs while remaining in place. Passion is thus a relation without relation, as Blanchot had earlier called it, which emerges in/as the hollow of negativity, and in which there is an experience of impossibility [EI: 66/46]. Passion may be related to pathos, passivity, and patience, but it is also the very movement of the negative as that which is (not) a step (*pas*) or passage.

There is in negativity that which is not used up in the conversion to action: a surplus of nothingness, a plus/minus that marks the fact of our double relation, the relation *of* non-relation, in which events are experienced as comprehensible and useful and also as useless and unattainable. This is the dimension of impossibility that surrounds and undercuts possibility by virtue of the endlessness of its contestation, which frees all possibilities of their meaning and their actualization [EI: 307–8/207]. If the limit-experience is that in which this radical negativity is affirmed, then it does not substantiate or recuperate it in doing so, for it does not affirm anything but its own affirmation. It is the empty moment of the sovereignty of its own affirmation, which expiates itself:

> Thus, the limit-experience is experience itself: thought thinking that which will not let itself be thought! thought thinking more than it can think by an affirmation that affirms more than can be affirmed! This more is the experience: affirming only by the excess of the affirmation and, in this surplus, affirming without anything being affirmed, finally affirming nothing. Affirmation in which everything escapes and that, itself escaping, escapes unity.
>
> EI: 310/209

Again we come to a point of apophatic excess, but in this case it is as a sheer surplus that is a mark of the infinity of the limit-experience, which is always more and, as more, always other (as the Hegelian understanding of the true infinite in part showed, in that it is related to the transition from mere quantitative endlessness to a qualitatively new form of infinity), and that thought can only echo in its affirmation as this surplus, the thought without thought of the experience of the infinite. (In the above quotation, Blanchot's rather unusual use of exclamation marks would seem to mark this excessive experience as a rupture of thought that is also its own empty affirmation.)

The dialectic of experience is thereby rendered hyperbolic, extending beyond any form or system and becoming deformed by this excess, whose stakes are continually being raised such that this endless contestation becomes an affirmation of the infinity of experience. This is Bataille's version of dialectical transformation and so, despite his sympathy towards it, it cannot be assumed that Blanchot follows this path exactly, since this is primarily an experience, as has been shown, that cannot maintain itself in any form and so cannot even be claimed as an experience. While it is thus that it is most fully a limit-experience, to some degree this leaves it outside the particular forms of literary experience that Blanchot pursues. As a result, Blanchot's reading of Bataille is helpful in designating the distance that separates him from the latter, and also the way that experience passes beyond any empirical or phenomenological sphere into a notion of absolute transgression, a surpassing of what cannot be surpassed, by which it inflects the very form of thinking [EI: 308/453]. But insofar as Blanchot is pursuing this experience by way of literature, it is necessary to understand how it affects language – which is to turn to the loss of relation and mediation in language, and its experience – and contests its unity, and thereby contests the syntactic form by which it establishes relations. Part of this undoing has already been found in the changes that occur through the speculative sentence, but Blanchot is seeking to uncover that which remains outside this form, whose echoes can be detected by a concerted negation and fragmentation of the sentence.

II A neutral relation

The primary approach to the question of relation that occurs in Blanchot's writings is that which is addressed in the transition from the first to the third person, which he finds to be intrinsic to the space of literature. That is, this transition in which the writer passes from speaking in the first person to speaking in the third person is that which effects, and is effected by, the transition into the space of literature. This point is repeated across many of his writings, both fictional and critical, and forms the basis of the discussion that opens *Le Pas au-delà*, which begins by returning to Blanchot's first novel, *Thomas l'Obscur*, whose opening sentence was: 'Thomas sat down and looked at the sea'. This phrase seems unremarkable, but what is underway in the transition when one ceases to speak as I and instead speaks in the third person, what is the nature and status of this narrative voice? For one is not only not speaking in one's own voice but also not speaking directly in the voice of another either, the third person is not the perspective of a person at all and hence not a voice, and yet it speaks. And so, in this transition into literature, there is an estrangement of and into language in another form, into a voice that is a wholly different kind of voice. As Blanchot writes, the third person 'does not simply designate another me any more than aesthetic disinterestedness', hence 'it remains to be discovered what is at stake when writing responds to the demands of this uncharacterizable "it". We hear in the narrative form, and always as excess, something indeterminate speaking that the evolution of this form elaborates [*contourne*] and isolates until it gradually becomes manifest, although in a deceptive way' [EI: 558/380–1]. This is, in effect, the voice of estrangement in language, but Blanchot goes further, since it also raises the question of the nature of the relation drawn out in this neutral voice, as it is intrinsically formless; being neither one nor many, and having neither place nor direction. Thus, in entering the space of literature, the form of the 'I' is displaced, and the relation thereby exposed is itself distended by this displacement. The transition cannot be said to occur at a particular moment as it appears to be both sudden and absent, as if it were always to come and already apparent, yet without any substantiating measure. Hence it cannot be located, and it is thus that we can begin to understand the peculiar openings that mark many of Blanchot's narratives, especially *Au moment voulu, Celui qui ne m'accompagnait pas, Le Dernier Homme*, and *L'Attente l'oubli*, where the first sentences dramatize this aporetic approach. It is not so much the other who is being approached in these phrases but rather the broaching of the space of literature, and the intrinsically uncertain nature of this transition. Although this transition opens and leads into literature it is a transition that, in its elusiveness, cannot be read. Thus, the narrative begins with this moment of illegibility, this neutral rupture of the third person or *il* (it), which enfolds into life that which is not simply its opposite, that which somehow unlimits it. It is not just a case of what happens to the 'I' when it moves into literary space but of the effects of the latter on the former, of the way that life itself is forced into its own reformulation by that which was thought to exist outside it: 'The sentence I pronounce tends to draw into the very inside of life the limit that was only supposed to mark it from the outside'. In the narrative voice life does not cease to be finite 'but it takes from language the perhaps unlimited meaning that it claims to limit: the meaning of the limit, by affirming it, contradicts the limitation of meaning, or at least displaces it' [EI: 556/379].

The thought of the *neutre* that Blanchot pursues in his later works arises out of his attempt to think the undying force of negativity (a force that comes from its endless weakness and uncertainty) beyond the negative, and it also seeks to reaffirm the importance of this thought beyond Levinas's condemnation of Heidegger's thought as a thinking of neutrality.[13] But it is equally apparent that the examination of the *neutre* by way of the *il* is a recasting of the notion of the *il y a* that Levinas had explored, as well as of the primarily ethical manner in which he understood relation. The latter point is the most contentious, as the mode of relation is understood by Levinas on the basis of the responsibility for the other while presupposing its nature and status. Thus, Blanchot's re-examination of these issues comes from a need to understand relation more closely, without assuming its ethical basis, and in the opening of the literary work the third person reconfigures relation so that it becomes infinite or discontinuous, 'always in displacement, and in displacement in regards to itself'. This reconfiguration affects the self as much as relation, insofar as the indefinite form of 'it' comes to inflect the form of 'itself' by the doubling of its unlimitation: 'does "it" indicate "it"-self better in the double use that this sentence has just made of it, as a repetition that is not one'? This repetition suggests that 'the second "it", if it restores the first, gives it back to rectify [*redresser*] the verb in an unstable position', which implies that the self occurs by a repetition that is itself empty or useless; nothing is added but the same again [PAD: 12–13/5].

This relation *of* the 'it' in its neutrality is thereby absolute and on the borders of that which it exposes, whether it is of fiction or critique. Consequently, the openings of Blanchot's more theoretical writings become as fraught as those of his fictional works, as can found in *Le Pas au-delà* in particular. Throughout this text Blanchot is seeking to unsettle its designation by drawing out the lack of fixity in its voice, which makes us focus on the peculiar status of each of its fragments and prevents us from gathering it up into a unitary whole. For as a work it is made up of a series of fragments that are each marked by a black diamond, some of which are in italics, while some are presented in a narrative voice. Furthermore, the text opens with a fragment that is not marked by a black diamond, a fragment that is distinct from and thereby on the borders of the rest of the text: 'Let us enter into this relation'. This would seem to be some kind of invocation, but if it is, then it is quite complex, as it is a figuration of the verb *entre* in the first person plural, such that the text is already mobilizing a transformation of the subject position and its displacement in and by language. *Entre* is also a preposition, meaning 'between' (or, through, among, within), which is evidently part of the thought of relation and so this phrase actualizes a form of pleonasm, a repetition of its own disfiguring: *Entrons dans ce rapport*. The movement of going into is coupled to its transformation of the subject, so that in going in the subject not only enters into but becomes transformed by this relation, as between. Thus, the edge of the text folds (its own border) into itself and in doing so opens (itself) into relation, in which its neutral voice, which has already sounded in the uncertain source and location of this phrase, can be heard. The step into literature that language makes possible and vice versa is (not) the step beyond; there is only the solitude of its sky, the same sky.

This problem is one of distance and approach and thereby pertains to philosophy as much as it does to literature since it refers to the question of the opening. What Blanchot has brought out is the way that this problem finds its response in its recapitulation, in that the distance to be addressed in the opening is the manner by which it can be broached. It is thus that his writings persistently figure a distance that can neither be bridged nor reduced, but instead hovers in place as its own suspension of relation, a relation without relation. Such an opening does not mediate its inassimilable distance but presents it in the placelessness of its neutral voice, which to some degree is echoed in the work of philosophy through the necessary deferrals of its prefacing, as Hegel showed. The distance to be crossed (which cannot be crossed) to enter the work, re-enters the work by way of its ever-receding horizon of strangeness. Blanchot refers to Kafka's *Das Schloß* here, but the effect can be found just as strongly in Hegel's *Phänomenologie*, which forms its own persistent interrogation of (the approach to) alienation and estrangement. The recurrent transitions in Hegel's thought draw our attention to these problems, and especially the necessity that they should not only be traversed but comprehended, as if one were to realize the bridge in crossing it, which inevitably only further defers and displaces its crossing:

> This distance is not only lived as such by the central character who is always at a distance from himself, as he is at a distance from the events that he lives or from the beings that he encounters (which would still only be the manifestation of a singular self); this distance distances him from himself, removing him from the centre, because it constantly decentres the work in an immeasurable and indiscernible way, at the same time that it introduces into the most rigorous narration the alteration of another speech or of the other as speech (as writing).
> EI: 562/383–4

The *pas au-delà* of literature thus becomes isomorphic with the *entretien infini* as a relation without relation, and without mediation or sublation; an infinitely suspended hesitation that accompanies every step.

As Blanchot goes on to say, this distance remains aporetic, as it cannot be ignored once it has been noticed and yet it remains unavailable and remote, unconcerned with the disorientation that it has brought about. The step into language and reflection, by which there is writing, not only estranges thought but also remains absolutely foreign to it. Insofar as the step is never completed, its distance is never encompassed and so it persists in its destabilizing effects. The experience of the third person in language can never be eradicated, and so its lack of location begins to affect all thinking through language, all dialectics. In lines that also refer to Hegel's phenomenological narration of the shapes of consciousness, Blanchot outlines this disruption: 'Narration ceases to be that which lets us see through an intermediary and from the viewpoint of a chosen actor-spectator. The reign of circumspect consciousness – of narrative circumspection (of the "I" that sees everything around it and holds it in its gaze) – is subtly shaken, without of course coming to an end' [EI: 563/384]. In narrative, the subject experiences its emptying out; not just its disorientation but its loss of identity and selfhood. While language in general carries out this alienation, literary language draws out its lack of satisfaction. Hence philosophy, in passing by way of language in its writing, also succumbs to this displacement, which can only be partially and provisionally curtailed by thinking, for in writing it becomes the speech of no one, not of the I that is We and the We that is I (in Hegel's terms), but of the nondescript third person, without substance or location.

This is because the transition, which has always already occurred even if it is yet to be completed, is also neutral in not being central, as Blanchot puts it, which is to say that it remains an illegible pre-position. As such, it neither reveals nor conceals anything, it is not part of the thematics of light and life, but is merely a clinamen without measure, and is thus without predication as it goes beyond any position or negation of being and relation. In Hegel's books, as Derrida discusses in 'Hors livre', the preface suffers from this combined difficulty in that it is necessary and unnecessary, possible and impossible, as it is contradictory to the text that follows it. For if the text is satisfactory in its exposition then the preface is unneeded, but as the preface exists it indicates that the text itself is only preliminary. So, if the preface is part of the work, then it is not a preface, but if it is not part of the work, then it is extraneous or superfluous. The speculative operation of the preface is to sublate these differences, so that the preface dissolves its own exteriority in introducing the subsequent text by anticipating its own realization and redundancy [e.g. WL2: 65/78]. Hence the text realizes itself by way of an exteriority that is folded into the text, but in this move Blanchot discerns that what subtends its possibility is also that which displaces it through an exteriority that unfolds as the text. This is to invert the relation of sublation, so that it is the text that dissolves in the wake of its own liminal estrangement. The *pas au-delà* is thus perhaps 'the enfolding, self-unfolding [*le repliement, se déployant*] of a relation of strangeness that is neither suffered nor assumed' [PAD: 167/122]. Rather than the speculative proposition of the text as a whole becoming one in which its anticipation and anteriority, inside and outside, tautology and heterology, are all brought together in the self-realization and self-dissolution of the preface as it presents itself (in Derrida's words), Blanchot has found the underside of this manoeuvre that is never entirely realized but instead propagates its instability and formlessness [D: 37/31]. It is not so much a question of what remains outside this movement and evades or resists sublation, which would imply a superficial reading of Hegel, but of the extension and deviation of the opening that, in its failure to be surpassed, constitutes the ever-present lining and liminality of all that follows.

We can thus begin to understand what is underway in the opening movements of Blanchot's writings, especially his fictions, before they fragment and start to take place as forms of self-negation and self-cancellation, which nevertheless do not dissolve themselves. This mode had always been part of Blanchot's writings, as can be seen in the following lines, and so to some degree the changes that become apparent in his later works are simply a distillation of an approach that had long been explored. I will not attempt any kind of comprehensive or synthetic reading of these openings but rather isolate some of their distinctive features, which can facilitate our awareness of how Blanchot responds to the manoeuvres of the negative in writing.

Blanchot's opening lines

Thomas sat down and looked at the sea. *Thomas s'assit et regarda la mer.*

Thomas l'Obscur, 1941

It was broad daylight. Thomas, who had been alone until then, was pleased to see a robust-looking man quietly occupied in sweeping his doorway. *Il faisait grand jour. Thomas qui jusque-là avait été seul vit avec plaisir un homme d'aspect robuste, tranquillement occupé à balayer devant sa porte.*

Aminadab, 1942

I wasn't alone, I was anybody. How can you forget that phrase? *Je n'étais pas seul, j'étais un homme quelconque. Cette formule, comment l'oublier?*

Le Très-Haut, 1948

These things happened to me in 1938. I feel the greatest difficulty in speaking of them. *Ces événements me sont arrivés en 1938. J'éprouve à en parler la plus grande gêne.*

L'Arrêt de mort, 1948

I am neither learned nor ignorant. I have known joys. That is saying too little: I live, and this life gives me the greatest pleasure. *Je ne suis ni savant ni ignorant.*

J'ai connu des joies. C'est trop peu dire: je vis, et cette vie me fait le plaisir le plus grand.

La Folie du jour, 1949

In the absence of the friend who lived with her, the door was opened by Judith. My surprise was extreme, inextricable, certainly much greater than if I had met her by chance. *En l'absence de l'amie qui vivait avec elle, la porte fut ouverte par Judith. Ma surprise fut extrême, inextricable, beaucoup plus grande, assurément, que si je l'avais rencontrée par hasard.*

Au moment voulu, 1951

I sought, this time, to approach him. I mean that I tried to make him understand that, if I was there, I still couldn't go any further, and that in turn I had exhausted my resources. *Je cherchai, cette fois, à l'aborder. Je veux dire que j'essayai de lui faire entendre que, si j'étais là, je ne pouvais cependant aller plus loin, et qu'à mon tour j'avais épuisé mes ressources.*

Celui qui ne m'accompagnait pas, 1953

As soon as I was able to use that word, I said what I must have always thought of him: that he was the last man. In truth, almost nothing distinguished him from the others. *Dès qu'il me fut donné d'user de ce mot, j'exprimai ce que j'avais dû toujours penser de lui: qu'il était le dernier homme. A la vérité, presque rien ne le distinguait des autres.*

Le Dernier Homme, 1957

Here, and on this sentence that was perhaps also meant for him, he was obliged to stop. It was almost while listening to her speak that he had composed these notes. *Ici, et sur cette phrase qui lui était peut-être aussi destinée, il fut contraint de s'arrêter. C'est presque en l'écoutant parler qu'il avait rédigé ces notes.*

L'Attente l'oubli, 1962

± ± The feeling he has, each time he enters, and when he takes notice of the robust and courteous, already aged man who tells him to enter, rising and opening the door for him, is that the conversation began long ago. ± ± *Le sentiment qu'il a, chaque fois qu'il entre et lorsqu'il prend connaissance de l'homme déjà âgé, robuste et courtois, qui lui dit d'entrer, se levant et lui ouvrant la porte, c'est que l'entretien est commencé depuis longtemps.*

L'entretien infini, 1966

♦ (A primal scene?) You who live later, close to a heart that beats no more, suppose, suppose this: the child – is he seven years old, or eight perhaps? – standing by the window, drawing the curtain and, through the pane, looking.
♦ (Une scène primitive?) *Vous qui vivez plus tard, proches d'un coeur qui ne bat*

> *plus, supposez, supposez-le: l'enfant – a-t-il sept ans, huit ans peut-être? – debout, écartant le rideau et, à travers la vitre, regardant.*
>
> Une scène primitive, 1976

> I remember a young man – a man still young – prevented from dying by death itself – and perhaps the error of injustice. *Je me souviens d'un jeune homme – un homme encore jeune – empêché de mourir par la mort même – et peut-être l'erreur de l'injustice.*
>
> L'Instant de ma mort, 1994

I have left aside the early pieces collected in *Le Ressassement éternel*, and also the narrative passages from *Le Pas au-delà*, which for the most part occupy slightly different narrative spaces. And, insofar as Blanchot himself refers to the beginning of *Thomas l'Obscur* as the starting point, it makes sense to pursue these opening lines across the major narrative works that follow it, including the fragmentary conversation that opens *L'Entretien infini*. It is important to stress that there is not any kind of simple development across these texts, although of course there is change. Instead, we find a number of different variants on the approach that emphasize its different dimensions – sometimes the threshold, sometimes the encounter, and sometimes the transition – alongside the problems that writing brings to these dimensions in its refractions of them. I have in some cases rather arbitrarily cut off the citations after what seemed to be their initial manoeuvre, but it is part of the nature of Blanchot's openings that this cut could be deferred almost indefinitely. As has been pointed out, to some extent all of Blanchot's fictional writings comprise a negotiation of the demands of its approach, so the opening passage often has no fixed limit where it passes into the text proper, as it were. In reading the Introduction to Hegel's *Phänomenologie*, Heidegger claimed that its reading demonstrated both that there could be no introduction to phenomenology (as it had necessarily always already taken place) and also that phenomenology entailed its own actualization of introduction.[14] Along these lines, much could be said about Blanchot's literary openings, except that there is in each opening no phenomenological return to presence in which we might find ourselves to be genuinely, originally situated, for in the self-demonstration of each opening there is a further deviation that can never complete itself.

What becomes evident in these extracts is a kind of passivity, a convolution of prose that gives rise, even within the first person, to a passive voice, which is perhaps the form in which its subjection to literature is made apparent. The effect of this making-passive is to suspend the movement of the writing, to hold it to the moment of its occurrence as transition. For in proceeding it finds itself caught up in qualifications, sub-clauses, indirections, doubts; the step does not seem able to fulfil itself and in doing so finds another mode of entering or opening (its) space, and this move is both a moment and a transcription, a writing of its own temporal passage or lack of it, as absolute. But this is not the obvious and self-referential passage that is sometimes found in more explicitly experimental forms – Blanchot is still writing fiction, narratives, however convoluted – because the experience of literature must remain an experience: that which is endured as well as that which is reflected upon, and so neither side can override the other for this would be to remove the literary from its specific historical occasion. Thus, despite these generalizations, what is more apparent in these extracts is their singularity, their concrete uniqueness; they do not aspire to a universal theoretical position but to particular differentiations of literary experience, which are each time irreducible and in passing. From this arises the aporetic delicacy of these openings, a delicacy that has as much to do with the actuality of the traversals as it does with the difficulties of expressing them, which is what leads to its syntax of inability, a phrasing that is intrinsically preliminary not just because what is at stake resists articulation but because, in being expressed, it appears as hesitation. In doing so, the opening fails to proceed and falls into contingent deviation and, as such, broaches its threshold.

The syntax of 'without' expresses something of this eccentric branching, in which a term only deviates from itself in its failure to ground its own progress, as its negativity leads to the phrase falling away from itself at each turn: the declination is multiple and inescapable. The nothingness in each word, as Blanchot writes, 'digs tirelessly, striving to find a way out, nullifying what encloses it: infinite disquiet, formless and nameless vigilance' [PF: 315/326]. But this general idea is more than can be claimed in relation to each of these openings, what is necessary is to take their movements singly and seek to grasp their vicissitudes, as I have done elsewhere in some of these instances, and will do in regards to *L'Attente l'oubli* in the next chapter.[15] What is found here is the insufficiency of a general reading, which indirectly reveals what is specific to each of these openings. Literature, in this aporetic delicacy, is not offering itself up to the unity of the concept but remaining stubbornly attached to its deviations. Hence this language is not only eccentric but singularly (un)grounded, which is to say that the thought that undergoes its experience will also become singular, which is not merely to estrange it but to remove it from the universality of thinking that is thought. The thought that emerges is thus literature's own, in all the self-contradicting, self-relinquishing senses that this will bring about. On the one hand, this formation gives rise to the association with oracular speech, and on the other, to the fragmentation of the speech of the streets, of crowds and pamphlets and graffiti. For in both cases there is a form of language that is anonymous and yet bears its own thought, however ambivalent and groundless. Such language can no more be defused than it can be comprehended, and as such it remains challenging and unsituated: it cannot be ascribed a location or source and so it is, in a sense, exterior, like the speech of madness. The effect of this writing is

> to establish the centre of gravity of speech elsewhere, where speaking would not affirm being and would no longer have need of negation in order to suspend the work of being, which is ordinarily accomplished in every form of expression. The narrative voice is, in this respect, the most critical that can, unheard, suggest [*inentendue, donner à entendre*]. That is why we have the tendency, in listening to it, to confuse it with the oblique voice of misfortune or the oblique voice of madness.
>
> EI: 567/387

Dispelling these associations is an additional demand on and of literature, for through them it becomes too easy to diminish the challenge of literature, just as is possible in relation to the thematics of the ghostly. What is experienced in the narrative is not any of these approximate forms but rather neutral, that which suspends both form and formlessness, which is why Blanchot pursues this thought in order to grasp that which deviates from even the negative.

The thought of this neutral writing is what is most difficult to grasp, even as a notion. As the interplay between *inentendue* and *donner à entendre* demonstrates there is an uncertainty about the relation between hearing and understanding in which what is not heard (or meant) still gives us to understand (or hear). The intonation bears an irresolvable ambivalence such that it can imply (but not be heard) or be unintended (but still understood). There are effects apparently without cause, either because they are accidental or because they are inaudible; language acts, as it were, without agency, whence its uncanny power, but also its weakness. Indeed, its power arises from its weakness. As a word, *entendre* brings together the double aspect that has been in question throughout this book – that of the word as thing and also as that which means – as the problem of *entendre* is whether it is a case of hearing or understanding, listening or interpreting. It is precisely this illegible traversal that is marked in the neutral thought, which is consequently barely a thought as it fails to reach any kind of clarity or definition. But it can also be seen that this notion provides a different kind of critique of Hegel than that which emerges through the modes of *différance* and dissemination, for example. And, as Derrida has largely avoided this thought of the *neutre* as being too close to that of negativity, it is perhaps the case that he has also avoided the possibility of this more insistent critique.

The *neutre*, as that which occurs between position and negation (as though it were akin to the null space between two similar magnetic poles), as much as it occurs between being and sense, is an entirely different kind of thought, and, as has just been noted, barely a thought at all. It is perhaps more like an insinuation that takes place alongside thought as its echo, as the quasi-form of the ambivalence of sense as such, or the contingent deviation that occurs through language, as thinking seeks to take place and resonates with its uncertain loss of sense. Some of the most detailed comments on the *neutre* occur in the middle of *Le Pas au-delà*, where Blanchot takes pains to distinguish it, primarily, from the thought of Hegel. To begin with he explains how it derives 'from a negation of two terms: *neutre*, neither one nor the other. Neither nor the other, nothing more precise'. Thus, the back and forth movement between one and the other is 'altered', as he writes, by the other, such that the form of the speculative proposition is itself estranged. The peculiar form of affirmation that the *neutre* bears is such that being neither one nor the other 'signifies also one of the two and in some way always that which is never only one': being *neither nor* the other. The *neutre* pluralises the binary, as he writes, 'to the point of indeterminacy' by following through on the implications of this othering [PAD: 104/74]. (If, in speaking of or from the *neutre*, 'the one who says it is always other', then this means that there is neither one nor the other [EI: 582/396].) As such, the form of the *neutre* allows for a juxtaposition of affirmation and its indefinite negation, which does not permit of a dialectical reversal but re-circulates the bad infinite of this othering into its own form of non-work, or worklessness. It thus echoes but also distorts the labour of the negative and the movement of the *Aufhebung*, and if, in doing so, it suspends and retains anything, as *aufheben* would imply, then it is only by retaining its suspension, its distance, rather than its work [PAD: 105–6/75]. The *neutre* is close to becoming an impossible thought as some kind of negative diacritic of being and nothing, that which both marks and unmarks it through its repetition, suspending any attribution or predication.

An intimation of this manoeuvre can be found in the way that a word becomes meaningless if it is repeated often enough (and enters, as Hegel showed, the mechanical exteriority of the name by which it can be remembered and used in thought). However, what exactly becomes of the word here is not obvious, and when this operation is taken up by Blanchot it is even less so, for in his fictional writings such an effect can occur without explicit repetition, but by a process of fragmentary isolation in which the word becomes something other than a word. When a word becomes less than a word, it does not necessarily become a thing; instead, it seems to become something else entirely. Derrida examines this process in relation to Blanchot's use of the word 'come' (*viens*), as a term that is no longer an imperative and does not even seem to be associated with the verb 'to come' (*venir*). The instances in which this word occurs seem to suggest some other kind of relation and, furthermore, seem to do so in such a way that the term falls outside any order of language. As Derrida explains:

> *Viens* does not give an order, it proceeds here from no authority, no law, no hierarchy. I do indeed say *here*. And in order to recall that only on the condition of a context, of a very determined operation of writing – here the-récit-of-Blanchot – a "word", ceasing to be entirely a word, disobeys the grammatical or linguistic, or semantic prescription, which would assign it to be – here – imperative, present, in this person, etc. Here is a writing, the riskiest there is, subtracting something from the order of language that it, in turn, yields [*plie*] to with a very gentle and inflexible rigour. But what is to be subtracted in this way? "Thought"? A thought "outside language"? There would be enough here to scandalise a certain modernity.
>
> PA: 26/15

Derrida's account condenses several issues that need to be distinguished: first of which is the relation between this freeing of a word from the order of language, which still occurs within and with respect to a determined and rigorous context. Blanchot is not writing gibberish; his narrative works remain recognizable and comprehensible, but within their intricate negotiations of form and sense there are occurrences that appear to come loose from or to expose holes within this order and context. Thus, the second thread that emerges concerns the status of such a 'word', for a word 'outside' language is no longer a word at all, and its quasi-relation to its context is such that it is also not simply a thing. Instead, within this complex enfolding and unfolding, the word becomes something else that is meaningless but not senseless, as it were, or, perhaps, senseless but not meaningless. That is, despite its absence from the order of language, however this is construed, there remains something to the word that does not render it entirely without resonance. It may have become opaque and ambivalent (a materiality that is not materialist, in de Man's terms), but it retains a specificity that means that it is not inane.¹⁶

It is as such that Derrida can speak about the resonance of *viens* in a way that withdraws any sense of semantics from it, while still leaving it singular. Hence the third issue is that such a word becomes a 'thought', whatever is now meant by this term, insofar as it is not abstract or conceptual but appears, in Hegel's terms, more like an alien and individual self-consciousness, an autonomous form *of* language [PG: 381/430]. As a result, this formation puts in question the word's 'relation' to language, of which it is both a part and apart and is thus 'outside'. This careful destabilization and displacement of the word 'does not confer on it', as Derrida notes, 'a sort of non-linguistic wildness that lets the event *viens* come free [*en liberté*]', for it remains 'singularly insistent' in language, a phrase that itself confirms its paradoxical non-lieu. It is necessary to be cautious about associating this apparent liberation from the order of language with any kind of event, towards which Blanchot was sceptical – whether through repetition, chance, or death, the form and status of the event is persistently interrogated in *Le Pas au-delà*, which is why it comes to be figured in its passivity as the disaster. However, Derrida goes on to parse the 'sense' of *viens* as that of the quasi-transcendental call of the call 'come', which seems to place too much of a burden on it, for if this word falls outside language while remaining singularly insistent within it, then the degree to which it can still retain any semantic sense of the verb 'come' (and thereby operate at a quasi-transcendental level as the condition of such a call) remains in doubt. For, insofar as *viens* does not communicate – not saying, showing, describing, defining, or stating anything – as Derrida writes, then it becomes difficult to grasp how it can still refer to a call, however nuanced, especially as it is then formulated as that which provides the basis for all types of call, order, prayer, demand, or desire [PA: 26–7/16]. Instead, its specificity needs to be understood in a way that does not infer any semantic content, or (quasi-)transcendental status, which is what takes place through its formation as *neutre*. This reading is reinforced in the way that *viens* recurs across Blanchot's texts from *L'Arrêt de mort* to *L'Attente l'oubli* to *Le Pas au-delà*, each time singularly punctuating its context but each time recurring, rendering it in some way resonant with an affirmation, but also exposing the peculiarity of the imperative form of the verb as such, an imperative without source or aim, subject or object, and yet continuing to bear some urgency or force.

This distinction from Derrida's thought is subtle, but it is of the nature of the *neutre* that its status is exactly that of a subtle uncertainty between form and content, substance and meaning, which demands that even in regards to Derrida's careful deliberations it is necessary to continue to think through the evasiveness of this notion. It is only in doing so that we can come to an understanding of literary language and especially, as Derrida insisted, its specific but uneven localization in the text, and the apparent thought that this exposes. This point is extended further when a phrase or sentence is considered, where the emphatic refusal of definition that the *neutre* introduces begins to affect the manner in which the sentence, any sentence, attempts any predication. Thus, the uncertainty of the *neutre* contests the rule of identity and contradiction that underlies the forms of predication, so that its appearance within a proposition is such that it contests its own form and insists as such, in its passage. This means that we cannot privilege any one word, not even one like *viens*, without abstracting it from the multiple refractions it would undergo by way of other textual instances. Significant in this regard are the odd asides that sometimes appear in Blanchot's writings, like the remarks on poison and black magic in *L'Espace littéraire*, the comments on fleeing in *L'Entretien infini*, and the fragment on cancer in *L'Écriture du désastre*. No analysis of Blanchot's key terms (so-called) and their 'syntax' can begin without taking into account the peculiar eccentricities that also punctuate his thinking, for these are evidence of a kind of *hapax* of thought that takes place with the *neutre*: notions that have no certain status or relation, and whose identity is thus always in question. That which occurs in only one place disrupts the systematic movement of the concept and the unity of philosophy and, in its relation to thought, comes to operate like the sliding words that Bataille discussed. This point is important because it indicates that the syntax of a *rapport sans rapport* that occurs across Blanchot's writings is not limited to its appearances at the level of the sentence or phrase but is also active in the thematic organization of the fragmentary texts as well. Discussing x without x is not merely an apophatic manoeuvre as it also entails a topological transformation; 'without' is always a category of relation and thereby figures an outside of some form. In this way the English term is more sensitive to the ambivalence at issue, since it is precisely a question of how relation is reconfigured 'without'. The *rapport sans rapport* is like an inversion of the *pas au-delà*, as if it had been turned inside out, and as such the two aspects operate together in Blanchot's reconsideration of the movement of dialectics as one of transformation, mediation, and reversal. As Derrida writes, the multiple negativity of the *pas* is such that it is not even itself, hence, as a step that is not and a not-step, 'it is labyrinthine and immediately, singularly multiple, *digressive* of itself'. The border of the *pas* is thus not outside it but within, so that it breaks free of itself through its 'immediately transgressive nature' [PA: 38/27]. This duplicity of the *pas* removes it from any negation of negation (dialectical or otherwise), for insofar as it is not identical to itself it becomes other, which is also to say that it is not only within itself but without, and as such the *pas* begins to mutate into the *sans*: the *pas* within the *pas* becomes the *pas sans pas* [PA: 46/34].

The category of relation being the minimal category of philosophical thought, Blanchot's narratives, by their interrogation of this theme, are at the heart of traditional philosophical discourse. But, as this category is reconsidered to the point of rendering it unfamiliar, these narratives expose an exteriority within philosophy. Relation involves both proximity and predication, for it is not simply a question of the relation between x and y but also the nature of this relation as that which involves a form of belonging or propriety; the necessity and possibility of this relation. There is an intrinsically ontological dimension to relation, but it also necessarily involves an understanding of what is not related. Hence Blanchot's rethinking of this category addresses it on multiple levels, for if relation is rethought from the perspective of without, then it is the negativity of predication that is foregrounded.[17] However, this rethinking becomes immeasurably more difficult when subject and object are ostensibly the same. If we say, 'death without pain', for example, then the relation is readily understandable, even if death remains poorly grasped insofar as it is only defined in one dimension and this only negatively. But if we go on to say, 'death without death', then the phrase becomes dizzying in its complexity, for not only is the identity of the subject (death) rendered indeterminate (as it is without death) but the very form of its relation is unsettled (as there is no way to determine the order of the relation between subject and object: is it death *without death*, or *death* without death, or some other anomalous form?). Furthermore, in this undecided and unresolved self-cancellation, the relation of subject to itself, its identity, is replaced with negation, so that the phrase no longer bears a subject and object but two non-identical non-subjects (or non-objects), and thus the phrase is no longer part of an ontological predication. Whatever death may have meant, this phrase removes by preventing it from having any identity with itself, as it is impossible to determine its nature or status when it is made to undefine itself. So, what had been a sentence with some ontological definition has become a phrase in which the only point of navigation is its negative relation, *without*, without delimitation. And yet the torsions of this phrase remain specific in their vertigo, however indeterminately or negatively, so that the narrative 'logic', as it were, that Blanchot pursues in this way is not vacuous but carries its own 'experience'.

Critically, the phrase remains perfectly legible, there is nothing challenging about its syntax, and so at first glance nothing has changed, everything is in its (syntactically arranged) place. But, as Derrida points out, returning to his discussion at the end of 'Le puits et la pyramide', it does not work: it no longer functions as a sentence, it neither says nor means anything, and yet it is not nothing. Something remains that is neither a remnant nor a thing but that ensures that each term remains singular and irreplaceable [PA: 91/77]. Hence whatever the nature of the phrase that emerges, it still 'works' in some (workless) manner, which is to say that its 'operation' persists, and yet it does so without any possibility of generalizing or formalizing this operation, since what is at work neutralizes its own thinking *as* an experience. Derrida thus comes to grasp the neutrality of this operation as that which exceeds negativity, thereby revising his critique of the *neutre* that had arisen in his earlier essay on Bataille [PA: 70/57; ED: 402-3/273-4]. For in the distortions of the phrase of without, the negativity of the latter is displaced into a *neutre* state in which it is neither negation nor non-negation. Derrida goes on to say that this *neutre* is affected by an absolute heterogeneity, as the word is exposed to a wholly other in losing its status as subject, which resonates with the status (and affirmation) of the call that he had earlier addressed [PA: 91/78]. However, this thought again needs to be treated carefully, as both subject and object are unsettled in the phrase, and in doing so they are rendered uncertain to the degree that they are neither themselves nor another. There may be alterity here, as Blanchot had noted in relation to the alteration of the phrase, but this is suspended through the *neutre* as that which is *neither nor the other*. Nothing permits us to move from a privilege of the subject to that of the other. There may be threads of heterogeneity running through the *pas* and *sans* by way of their negativity, but as they also undermine the distinction between noun and verb, syntax and semantics, signifier and signified, word and thing (without blurring or assimilating them), as Derrida remarks, then it is not possible for there to be an other in place of the subject, or towards which the subject tends, for the latter is always already traversed by a suspension of both identity and difference.

Strictly speaking, there is an aspect of impossibility to reading Blanchot, for at every step the narrative undermines itself abyssally even as it proceeds with what appears to be a smooth and unremarkable prose. What Blanchot has found is a way to draw out the problematic that is intrinsic to literature, in which the reader's attention becomes punctured by the text, interrupted critically, as they are struck by the impossibility of deciding what is at stake (and in play). This is not so much a form of speculative prose, for thinking is radically estranged in and by literature. As an image in *Aminadab* had suggested, the plane of the literary work is suspended between being a picture that one gazes at and a window that one looks through, an aporetic dilemma that fundamentally displaces any possibility of it being a mirror in which the gaze returns to itself.[18] The reader can no longer regard this relation but is instead held by it as it transgresses and deviates from itself. There is not an other that the text seeks to approach, but there is an infinite othering into which reading falls, which affects any understanding that might surface through the literary: any dialectical negation that it might attempt to develop would have to pass by way of its loss through doubling and dissimulation, its ever-eccentric estrangement from self or other.

5

Blanchot: wholly impossible

I Out of circulation

As has been mentioned, the circularity of Hegel's thought – in the sense of it being all-inclusive, and also of returning to itself so that its end reappears as its beginning, and vice versa – is a persistent target of criticism. There is a suggestion of a rotation in and of his thinking, which enables it to bear out the same and the different, as well as to be a completion in which everything is encompassed.[1] As the last section of the *Phänomenologie* makes clear this circularity is a necessary result of Hegel's method, in terms of the coming together of the subjective and objective aspects of this method in both its concept and its actuality. But whence comes this idea and image of circularity? Does it always imply closure, and does the movement of returning to itself necessarily involve unity and identity? A rotation may return to the same place, but does this also mean that it returns to itself? The perfection of the circle is a geometric assumption. While we can look to circular objects – a wheel, a ring, a dish, a ball, and so on – and see that this closure is intrinsic to their identity as such objects, this closure does not take place in the same way across the apparent forms of temporal or even logical circularity. Assessing Hegel's thought in terms of its circularity is not straightforward, since the curvature through which something returns to itself (and thereby gives rise to its own end) is not simply a transparent expression of perfect closure, unless the latter is its presupposition. At the end of the *Phänomenologie* we are called as readers to realize the recapitulation of everything that has preceded the end and to perceive this as a return to its beginning. However, this return does not lead to that which was first encountered, as we and the text have changed in the reading of it, so this is not a return, and, moreover, this ending also leads into *Wissenschaft der Logik* by way of the recapitulation that has just occurred. Thus, the turning of its circle always occurs over time and is logically without external ground and so, in its ambit, it both turns and unfolds itself. Its turning thereby happens across more than one dimension and as a result it cannot return to 'itself', even as it is only turning out of, around, and on itself. In each rotation there is no immaculate self-identification, but a return through and over time in its difference and deferral from itself. Circularity is therefore surprisingly complex and refers to the behaviour and identity, and status and operation of what is at issue, so that the one doubles and distorts the other. To understand it, we would need to use all the words that bear elements of torsion, revolution, inversion, deflection, and complication, which leaves the picture of Hegel's thought, if the analogy still holds, very far from any simple circularity.

Nevertheless, the issue of the 'self' involved in any movement around itself remains, and even if this is rethought on the basis of its lack of grounds and its complex dynamics, a form of centripetal focus seems to persist, however transient or mobile. It is as such that Blanchot's insistent requirement to think the eccentricity of curvature becomes critical, for here the possibility of any 'self' identity is removed. Instead, we are led into a thought of the absolute as non-relation, and all the various metamorphoses of the circle that Blanchot (after Georges Poulet) considers – such as the reconfigurations of the forms of symmetry, curvature, and exteriority that take place throughout *L'Entretien infini* as his understanding of the ramifications of literary space changes – indicate their previously unexamined topological possibilities of flight and extravagance, and not just as dissemination but as an infinite negative curvature that is irregular and inconstant [EI: 513–14/350]. While the effects of these changes are developed on a small-scale through the thought of fragmentation, their extrapolation to the broader effects on not just literary space but also the space of language leads to a reconsideration of the nature of negativity in space. As one unusual but particularly relevant example shows:

> Man flees. First he flees something, then he flees all things through the unmeasured force of flight that transforms everything [*tout*] into flight, then, when it has seized everything – making of all things what must be fled as much as what one cannot succeed in fleeing – by a repulsion that attracts, it makes everything steal away [*se dérober*] in the panic reality of flight. In panic flight, it is not that everything declares itself to be what should be fled or what is impossible to flee: it is the very category of everything – the one borne by the question of the whole [*ensemble*] – that is deposed and made to break down. We are here at the juncture where the experience of the *whole* is shaken and gives way, in this shaking, to panic profundity.
>
> When we flee, we do not flee each thing taken one by one and one after another from the perspective of a regular and indefinite enumeration. Each

thing, equally suspect, has collapsed in its identity of a thing, and the whole of things has collapsed in the sliding that steals them away as a whole, flight then makes each thing rise up as if it were all things, and the whole of things – not as the secure order in which one might take shelter, nor even as the hostile order against which one must struggle, but as the movement that steals and steals away. Thus, flight not only reveals reality as this everything (totality without gap and without issue) that one must flee: flight is the very everything that steals away and to which it draws us while repelling us. Panic flight is this movement of stealing away that realises itself as profundity, that is to say, as a whole that steals away and from which there is no longer any place to steal away to. Hence flight finally accomplishes itself as the impossibility of flight.

EI: 28–9/21

These lines come from an article on the nature of questioning first published in 1961, and refer to some degree to the mode of the question in Greek tragedy (and particularly to the figures of Oedipus and Phaedra), but, as can be seen, Blanchot is drawing out the Hegelian dimensions of what may be entailed by questioning while also persistently drawing them away from their familiar points of reference in a manner that anticipates Derrida. It is thus, *in nuce*, that literature puts thinking in question, and puts its whole out of balance by turning it aside without measure. And it is with this extraneous possibility in mind that we should rethink the movement and the moment in and by which philosophy takes flight, in Hegel's words. For the question that Blanchot raises, and that he calls the most profound question, the question of the profound, is the one that is raised and left aside by dialectics, that of the whole itself, as that which puts it in question just as it is made to falter.

When the 'whole' is mentioned in discussions of Hegel's thought, it is often conceived as a form of inclusive totality, a unitary gathering in which everything finds its essential place. But as a conceptual universal this is not how it should be understood; rather, the whole exists in the same way as the referent of terms like 'nature' or 'society'. When nature is discussed in general terms, we do not simply mean the various forms of plants and animals, microbes and fungi, and so on, but something more that is constituted by these realms and yet is not reducible to them. That there is a sense and value to the use of the word 'nature' is not disputed, even if it is not clear what its limits or grounds might be, and the same is true for the word 'society'. It is as such that we can understand what is meant by the whole of which Hegel speaks, without it becoming exclusive or deterministic. Indeed, it is intrinsic to these terms (and that which makes them exist) that they refer beyond themselves to some putative sense that is as real as it is unreachable, since they are abstractions, and the same can also be said for the word 'literature'. In order to understand what is at stake in this point, it is helpful to consider Adorno's argument that spirit in Hegel's thought can be understood as social labour. This argument is developed in his 1956 essay 'Aspekte' and responds to the general problem of how we are to approach Hegel's thought when its categories are so intangible, and none more so than that of spirit itself. Understanding that spirit is neither mystical nor essentialist in bearing means grasping how it is, like the categories of nature or society, concretely developed even as it leads beyond this concrete form. The insight that spirit can be thought more easily if it is read as social labour was first put forward by Marx, but for Adorno it takes on manifold implications. For current purposes, not only does this insight enable us to see more closely how the universal and the individual, and the abstract and the concrete, come together in the movements of labour, but it also shows that we must take account of the way that literature alters the dimensions and possibilities of labour while still operating within its (socio-historical) terms. Labour may be the sphere in which universality becomes apparent in the form of individual action but in literature the combination of the concrete and the abstract only leads to an eccentric universality, since it does not adhere to any formal or material constraint and thereby puts in question the very nature of such universality. After all, while an eccentric universality is perhaps a contradiction, it is nevertheless what literature makes apparent against the illusion of its normative conceptions.

In the labour of the concept and the labour of the negative the same sense of labour is ongoing – that of the process of realizing itself in and through its own activity – but literature brings a strangely evasive tendency to this realization such that, if it occurs, it does so only to the degree that it also loses itself, without return. This is the literary estrangement that unsettles philosophical discourse, for the labour of the concept leads it into material deviations and contingencies, just as the labour of the negative finds (and loses) itself in its inability to draw this negativity to any completion, and so only proceeds by undoing itself. This same process of self-undoing is, for Adorno, what is key to Hegel's notion of the absoluteness of spirit, which, because it can only be worked through in terms of its ongoing social concreteness and overreaching, cannot sustain any sense of itself as whole except as that which is intrinsically contradictory and antagonistic. Such is the way that Adorno approaches the problem of the whole, which is not inexistent or illusory but is real in the sense of the disharmony that it bears. Any sense of the whole as truthful is merely an illusion that suppresses and conceals the actual labour that bears it out through its diremption and excess:

> the whole realises itself only in and through the parts, only through their cracks, alienation, and reflection [...] His whole is above all only as the quintessence [*Inbegriff*] of the partial moments that point beyond themselves and are produced from one another; not as beyond them. This is what his category of totality aims at. It is incompatible with any harmonious tendency, no matter how much the late Hegel may subjectively have had such tendencies. The noticing of the unconnected and the principle of continuity are both equally overtaken in his critical thought; connection is not a matter of steady transition but of overturning, the process happens not through the approximation of moments but through their rupture.
>
> DS: 253–4/4–5

The actual experience of the whole, as one in which thought passes into and out of objectivity through an ongoing dialectic, gives rise to both a surplus and an inadequacy in the relation of thought to objectivity, a penumbra of sorts, in which is found its sense of truth. And in this experience, there is a critique of those forms of totality that exist as attempts to establish a perfect coherence between thought and objectivity, from the coercions and manipulations of fascist ideology to those of the digital totalitarianism of modern corporations.[2]

So, when Adorno says that the whole is the untrue, this statement can be read in two directions: firstly, as what is said to be the whole is untrue, in the sense of it being a deception; and secondly, and conversely, that the whole is as what is untrue, in the sense of it being out of true, not perfectly aligned. This point can be further refined, since truth, in Adorno's reading, lies precisely in its movement beyond itself, whether in terms of the concept or the object, by which each actualizes itself through time [DS: 283/38].[3] This means that truth is never perfect or complete, nor is it fully available to (finite) thought, instead, there is only its infinite passage. If we turn to notions like nature or society, then it is apparent that, insofar as these abstract nouns are also concepts, they have a certain history and grounding alongside the speculative sense that grants them the capacity to operate as concepts, to go beyond themselves and to name that which has not yet been thought. Thus, it is in this combined sense that they exist as wholes, even if they cannot be grasped as such. The whole is of course its own concept as well, and so as conceptual it is incomplete in the sense just outlined, without this failing rendering it inoperative. Indeed, concepts are constitutively incomplete, which implies that even as they are thought they are not yet thought through, for they are thoughts thinking beyond themselves. Any sense in which the thought of the whole (or any of these abstract nouns) is said to be grasped, and in so doing is definitively determined, is thereby false and misleading. What needs to be understood in the usage of these terms is the way that they lead thought astray by exposing it to their ongoing imperfections.

The occurrence of circularity, systematicity, and totalization in Hegel's thought is undeniable (especially in the last part of *Wissenschaft der Logik*) but their existence is not simple. Within his thinking there lies a constant dialectical tension between the effort to think and the effect of thinking, in which the whole is never given or predetermined:

> The system is not to be abstractly preconceived; it is not to be an all-encompassing schema but to be the effective centre of force [*wirksame Kraftzentrum*] latent in the individual moments. These should, through their motion and direction, come together from out of themselves in a whole that is not outside of its particular determinations.
>
> DS: 298/56–7

To hold thinking to the point where this tension is greatest is not to find the balancing point between the effort and effect of thinking, as this is neither stable nor harmonious, but to keep it exposed to its own undoing, which is perhaps why it is most apparent in Hegel's written works, especially the *Phänomenologie*, where the effect of thinking becoming carried away by its own thought is compelling and concrete as this is not an idle eccentricity but the actual experience of thought in its conceptual estrangement. And it is as a result of its inability to find any satisfaction or adequation in this labour that spirit finds itself akin to truth [DS: 285–6/41]. For, as Adorno states, truth is 'the dynamic totality of all the propositions that can be generated from one another by their contradictions' [DS: 260/12].

Truth is thus the sense of the whole, which in its dynamism remains grounded in the infinite contradictions from which it is drawn, while yet taking place in the generalized subjunctive form of the concepts that they bear, such that time itself becomes a moment of truth, the supposition of its function. Adorno is clearly reading Hegel by way of Benjamin's understanding of the relation between history and truth (although in doing so he is perhaps doing no more than drawing out Hegel's own affinity with Goethe), but he is also drawing this relation into the analysis of thinking by making it constitutive of the nature of concepts as such. With this in mind, it is important to recall that this conceptual flight is profoundly materialist, which allows us to perceive the form in which its totality (of sentences) might appear (and it is not insignificant that the system as described by Adorno has the form of an emergent phenomenon like that of a flock or swarm). If the temporal moment of truth arises out of the ongoing contradictions of its concepts, then this means that it only occurs through the permanent confrontation of its objective and subjective moments, between its material grounds and its possible exposure. This is, in turn, to perceive the movement by which the natural and the historical are brought into a reciprocal displacement, by which the material becomes historical in the form of fate, and the historical becomes material in the form of decay, as I have suggested elsewhere.[4] And, in Adorno's terms, this leads to the combined necessity of thinking history at its most historical extreme, where it appears as natural (impassive), alongside a thinking of nature at its most natural extreme, where it appears as historical (transient), for in doing so the concreteness of each is given its conceptual form. Adorno's own aim thereby becomes apparent in the wake of Hegel, since in this dialectical rethinking of history, metaphysics is itself secularized, and 'the life of the absolute becomes equated with the totality of the transience of all finite things'. And so, the task of philosophy is to be found 'in the shards that arise from decay and that are the bearers of objective meanings'.[5]

The totality of propositions that arise from their own contradictions is therefore a whole that can only be read by way of this transience and decay, which is its precise conceptual form, albeit one that in its infinity yields to opacity. That the whole is the untrue thereby holds a further resonance, as it is only in the negation of the true that the whole is to be found, which reveals its sense of exteriority. In Hegel's words, 'thinking is essentially the negation of what lies immediately before it', and it is as such that it remains insatiable, caught in the constant misalignment between the effort and the effect of its own negation [ENZ: §12, 53/36; cf. PG: 69/65]. This means that there can be no formal theory of knowledge, as Adorno notes, which leads Hegel to the further point that the content of philosophy is to be understood as actuality itself [DS: 306/66; ENZ: §6, 44/29]. Given the natural-historical dimensions of actuality just sketched out, this means that thought is condemned to wander through the world without homeland or natural language. This condemnation is not the mark of a theocratic judgement but of a fall without beginning or end, a declination that takes on the form of an endless decay and an implacable fate. Such is the secularization that Adorno speaks of, which thereby exposes the Hegelian dialectic to the irresolvability of its absolute contradictions. Thus, the flight of philosophy, in its actuality, is such that thought is lost into the world in its ever-ongoing negations. It is perhaps as such that we can come to recognize the significance of the move by which Blanchot's explicit return to politics in the late 1950s coincided with his pursuit of a literature of fragmentation, of the actualization of the literary by way of its breakdown.

II Transitions and transcriptions

For a writer who could remark in a Hegelian vein in 1949 that literature, in following the demands of the symbol, can only 'assert itself as universal negation, and not as an abstract universal but as a concrete emptiness, a realized universal emptiness', this sense of a whole will, ten years later, come to be submitted to a new pressure in Blanchot's writings, that of the fragmentary [PF: 86/81]. This happens because the relation of the symbolic to the imaginary, and to the work of literature as universal negation, leads to a more serious problem:

> The imaginary is a not strange region situated beyond the world, it is the world itself, but the world as a whole, as everything. This is why it is not in the world, as it is the world, grasped and realised in its whole by the global negation of all the particular realities found in it, by their disqualification, their absence, by the realisation of that absence itself, with which literary creation begins, for in going back over each thing and each being it cherishes the illusion of creating them, because now it is seeing them and naming them from the starting point of *everything*, from the starting point of the *absence* of everything, that is, from nothing.
>
> PF: 307/316

The whole, even insofar as it is not whole, is still deceptive simply because it desires to be the whole, and thus to be itself, to some degree, in place of the world, without the world. It is thus that the literary will come to change in its relation to the world as Blanchot's thought starts to question the possibility of its form, of form as its possibility, and how its reality might proceed otherwise.

The fragmentary text does not simply oppose the systematic one, as it can still aspire to a whole even in its fragmentary form, nor does fragmentation on its own imply any less sense of asserting its own presence in place of the world. What is at issue in the fragmentary imperative is its relation to the world, and how the sense of the whole is to be found in an entirely different and eccentric form, in what might be called the fugitive (or perhaps furtive) place of its formations. Even before we come to the pressures inherent on the writing of sentences, there is that of the space that is opened in the text to come, which is not reducible to the blankness of the empty page. In this opened and indeterminately empty space there is both absence and impossibility, as it can never be filled or circumscribed despite the fact that it is not, and not there, and yet in its moments there are seemingly fragments to come, indiscernible distinctions within its emptiness that arise from its remove, its separation from the world, which is not, for it itself is not. Hence there are opaque material transients that traverse the emptiness of the space, which are its (non-)relations to the world. The space is not there as an existent void, the slate or canvas we have been told about, but as the patches of fugitive absence that comprise its non-unified expanse and that arise from its detachments from the world. Thus, fragmentation is already latent in the space before it gives rise to phrases and movements. In this way Blanchot can find in Mallarmé's *Un Coup de dés* something like a notation of this space, as if its variations were given form in the lines of the poem, and so were in some way to become legible as

> movements of "retreats", of "prolongations", of "flights", movements that accelerate and slow down, divide and superimpose by a burgeoning animation all the more difficult to the mind since it does not unfold, does not develop and, refusing the alleviation of succession, forces us to support all at once, in a massive though spaced effect, all the forms of the disquiet of this movement [...] this proliferation in the heart of absence, this infinitely restarted coming-and-going that is the emptiness of indeterminate space.[6]

This is not to grant the void some mystical force, but to recognize that even in its emptiness it is never quite absent from the possibility of figuration, which is the form of the abstraction of thought itself, the explication of indeterminacy that allowed Hegel to write out its logic, an indeterminacy that may be the emptiest and poorest imaginable but in the abstraction of the empty page still takes shape.

The demand of responding to this indeterminacy places an extraordinary pressure on the writing of the work, which is persistently focused on its outside at the expense of its 'self', even though this self becomes its outside as it proceeds. This is why there is a sense of evasiveness to the work, and of work as such, since it is constantly seeking to flee its own force of attraction and to respond to this flight. This is to some extent no more than the effort and effect of the negative that was mentioned above, but now given material, textual form in its ongoing evasion of form. Blanchot's *L'Attente l'oubli* draws out this expanse and shows how these indeterminacies are given form in a way that is only partly legible, but as a result, more materially demanding, as they draw our attention outwards from the text. Given the period in which Blanchot is writing, and the manner in which the text unfolds, it makes sense to see certain ethical and political dimensions to this extravagance, but it also presents a rigorous philosophical analysis and actualization of a form of spacing out, an exemplary opening. From this point of view it becomes possible to see how the text exists as if it were the reverse or underside of what would ordinarily be seen as the work, so that what is found is less the material cartography that Foucault saw in Roussel's texts than a patchwork of traces. These could be seen as the fragments that precede the work as a whole, or succeed its breakdown, but they are also on their way to not being fragments at all insofar as they take up their own kind of linguistic form, which is neither complete nor incomplete, for instance:

❖ She did not wait, he did not wait. Between them, however, the waiting.
AO: 47/22

It is a striking feature of this text that it contains many seemingly definitive assertions, statements that appear straightforwardly transparent, but that unravel themselves by their contradictory or equivocal senses. This is a feature of much of Blanchot's writing, but in *L'Attente l'oubli* these fragments often appear in a much more isolated and simple manner, lending them the appearance of an assertion only for this to dissolve, leaving something more elusive. And because it cannot be grasped easily it becomes disquieting, not leading to thought and meaning but remaining at a level somewhere between material opacity and semantic transparency. There is something vaguely irritating about this equivocation, which is a marker of its refusal to be fully grasped, but this irritation is an indicator of the way that reading has become materially engaged, as it is the form in which thought becomes bogged down in this refusal of sense and thereby exposed to another mode of reading, as if snagged in or on its formation.

It follows that much of the text should be occupied by transits, with the difficulty of arriving or leaving, speaking or remembering, for each of these is a movement that is perhaps unfulfillable; what would be their limit, their natural term, when would we know that they are done, and what form would this knowledge take? Such are the demands that Blanchot seeks to respond to in writing this text and that are thus the basis for its form, so it is worth looking more closely at what is taking place. It is possible to start almost anywhere, which is of course the result of a text that refuses any order or development, as it exists all at once, without presence.

❖ The mystery is nothing, even as a mysterious nothing. It cannot be the object of attention. The mystery is the centre of attention when attention, being equal and at perfect equality with itself, is the absence of any centre.

In attention, the centre of attention disappears, the central point around which are distributed perspective, sight, and the order of that which is to be seen inwardly and outwardly.

Attention is idle [*désœuvrée*] and uninhabited. Empty, it is the clarity of emptiness.

Mystery: its essence is to be always on this side of attention. And the essence of attention is the ability to preserve, in and through itself, that which is always on this side of attention and the source of all waiting: mystery.

Attention, the welcoming of that which escapes attention, an opening onto the unexpected, waiting that is the unexpected of all waiting [*l'inattendu de toute attente*].

AO: 44–5/21

This is one fragment, and it seems to be no more than a series of meditations on the interweaving of two terms, but although this is partly the case, it is also reflexively concerned with these meditations. As such, it is not just that Blanchot is seeking to understand these two terms but also to follow what they put into play, to find their sense not only as meaning but as a demand on the form of thinking. This is to find in these words a sense that is ongoing rather than complete and that consequently insists and persists in its demand on thought. So, even as we see nothing but a series of statements, on reading them they are found not to be statements as much as marks of experience, adumbrations of what is still (and so has not finished) taking place.

Rather than seeking to understand change through a form of dialectics or phenomenology, Blanchot finds in the movements of sentences a kind of material transcription that allows thinking to emerge in and as the wake of its experience, as that which results from it without ever completing itself. For what also occurs in this text is the rupture of meditation by narration or dialogue, and vice versa, so that the focal point of what is underway is dissipated, not to render it simply vague but rather to allow for a differential force of supposition.

❖ She began a short time later: "I would like to speak to you." From then on she had not stopped conversing with him, but nothing had struck him so much as the first words.

> She proved, with respect to herself, to be so astonishingly indiscreet that her only aim – this he had no doubt – was to confine him to a discretion that was almost incompatible with life.
>
> "You listen to this story [*histoire*] as if it concerned something moving, remarkable, interesting." He does listen in this way.
>
> A story that requires only a little attention. But also the waiting that gives attention.
>
> AO: 45–6/21–2

This fragment follows directly after the previous one, but there is no articulation to this movement of following, the text simply moves from one point to another without designating how they might be related. However, we cannot but seek to find some kind of articulation, and it is thus that thought becomes unsettled by the text, since formulations at one point may or may not be supported by others at other points. We are led into a kind of mosaic that is without centre or hierarchy, so that it is not possible to know how the pieces are to be read together (as it is neither a narrative nor an essay, nor is it a narrative with meditative asides, or an essay with narrative moments, since neither side forms its ground or aim), and as a result the very sense of the ensemble that is drawn out is neither whole nor total.

These sentences not only transcribe how the text takes place as it is taking place but also indicate how it is to be approached, without suggesting that the two movements of taking place and approaching are either identical or reciprocal, since as she remarked, and he had noted, all she had said was that she would like to speak to him; their approach remains in the realm of the possible, the hypothetical. And yet the sentences hover at the border of this non-relation, which is not a coming together of the text and the world, or of reading and the text, but a kind of movement around its avoidance of such a meeting point. It is by way of this doubled non-approach that the formation of the text occurs, which is also how the negativity of its indeterminacy is thought through. Rather than finding a dialectical emergence of becoming, there is a non-appearance and non-arrival of that which remains underlying the emergence of form as that which is still undetermined, which is why the text does not progress in a syllogistic fashion but simply iterates its positions again and again. There is in this movement a resistance to development that is quite foreign to reading; an insistent demand not to proceed by any kind of sequential order but to render this progress uncertain at every stage. (This point is made particularly explicit by the use of a plus/minus sign for some of the texts in *L'Entretien infini*.) The movement of order, from one to two to three, and so on, seems obvious and unavoidable, but there is little intrinsic necessity to thinking that *this* and *this* should be seen as two rather than as one and one. The movement from one to two requires an assembly or gathering in which this new form is named as two; it requires recognition of a whole (and a decision to recognize it) that imposes itself on its individual forms.[7] But if the indeterminacy of its emptiness does not fully emerge, then it cannot be subsumed into such a determinate group: there are only its dissipating particularities.

The indexical mark placed next to most of the fragments in *L'Attente l'oubli* not only distinguishes them from any order or sequence but also marks the moment of reading with a reflexive point of illegibility, in that it exemplifies the movement by which the reader returns to each fragment rather than passing on to the next. The fractured diamond icon is thus a marker of the indexicality of the fragment that each time says, this, here, for in its moments of incomplete transition it can only mark its inability to be read as part of a process. Each fragment is a point of exteriority as it cannot be incorporated into the movements of the text as a whole, so that what is found in the reading of *L'Attente l'oubli* is an explosion of its form. While the book opens with a short narrative sequence, this stops after the fifth paragraph, and there is then only page after page of fragmentary notations, which do not lead or follow into each other. Reading thus stops at the end of the fifth paragraph as any kind of summative reading through of the text, for each of the fragments in the pages that follow is a new interruption, a new point of exteriority, not part of the narrative in the sense of being included within its course but apart, each time, again. As such, the text finds a way of being without limits, and for each of the fragments to be a form of space, a flickering moment of hesitation, neither in the world nor beyond, but apparent in its passing.

What is found is an opening that is incessant even as it does not progress and that, as the narrator remarks (in part reflecting our own situation as readers in relation to the text), seems to confine him to a lack of linguistic movement (a discretion or illegibility) that is almost incompatible with life. There is a point, as Blanchot later wrote in response to Kafka, where the forces of life seem to fail, but in stating this in writing or speaking this limit is rendered uncertain (as was cited earlier): 'Language modifies the situation. The sentence I pronounce tends to draw into the very inside of life the limit that was only supposed to mark it from the outside'. We can then understand how such a form of language can be *almost* incompatible with life, as the limit 'does not disappear, but it takes from language the perhaps unlimited meaning that it claims to limit: the meaning of the limit, by affirming it, contradicts the limitation of meaning, or at least displaces it' [EI: 556/379]. This would seem to follow the transition from the finite to the true infinite in Hegel's thought, but, as Blanchot points out, there is a problem (just as there was with the life of the spirit): how are we to experience this form of language? If the limit is also transformed, then how are we to know it or speak of it, and how does this lack manifest itself without rendering its experience impossible? Waiting becomes a tentative answer to this question, for as an experience that is both empty and limitless it is almost not an experience at all, and, as a result, different forms of history and language become apparent through it, forms in which things do not take place as such but where there is an unfocused non-relation. Not in a centripetal circling around each other, but through a mutual hesitation that is marked by the chiasmus of the following sentences: 'Mystery: its essence is to be always on this side of attention. And the essence of attention is the ability to preserve, in and through itself, that which is always on this side of attention and the source of all waiting: mystery'. There is no movement from mystery to attention and then back, as in some hermeneutic gathering or assimilation, but a suspense that affects both their form and relation. After all, the essence of the mystery remains mysterious, and the nature of attention is still to be awaited, and although the experience of each is brought out through reading it is only as incomplete, not fully determined.

Thus, in this reading, the terms of its experience are lost or displaced, rendered indeterminate, and as such it becomes exposed, not confined to the text but released as its horizon dissolves, and the space that is thereby found is not blank but marked by these indeterminate fractures. This is not a generic indeterminacy but that which arises from a specific situation, that of an attempt to open a relation between a man and a woman, and the distortions that language and its situation bring to this attempt. This is not primarily a sexual situation but one in which the very possibility of relation is at stake and, furthermore, the possibility of relation to another as that which is indeterminately remote such that their very appearance is not given. Hence there is no assumption of recognition or reciprocity, no circularity of relation, only that which happens when attention is cut loose from any movement of simple return. There is no life and death struggle in which one party seeks to dominate the other but an encounter in which each comes, accidentally, to interrupt the other, without return, just as each are interrupted within themselves by the evasions of language. In an article from the same period Blanchot explicitly modifies Levinas's thoughts on the relation to the other, which might seem to be in question in *L'Attente l'oubli*, to state that there is no symmetry or asymmetry between the self and the other, but rather 'a double dissymmetry, a double discontinuity, as if the emptiness between the one and the other were not homogenous but polarised, as if it constituted a non-isomorphic field bearing a double distortion, at once infinitely negative and infinitely positive'. Blanchot terms this exploded non-relation, which is as far from Hegel as it is from Levinas, *neutre*, adding that we should not think that this term implies a neutralization or nullification of 'this double-signed infinity, but bears it in the way of an enigma' [EI: 100–1/70–1].

As a result, these deviations are not only specific in their historical and material deviations but also indicate another form of relation, and another mode of language:

> "Explosion", a book: this means that the book is not the laborious gathering of a totality finally obtained, but has for being the noisy, silent, bursting, without which it would not take place [*se produirait*] (would not affirm itself), since it itself belongs to burst being – violently overflowing, thrust out of being – it shows itself as its own violence of expulsion, the blazing refusal of the plausible: the outside in its becoming burst [*devenir d'éclat*].
>
> EDB: 190–1/124

Blanchot is referring to a phrase drawn from Mallarmé ('there is no explosion except a book') but, as can be seen, the formal ruptures of such a mode of language bear on the structure of being itself.[8] These ruptures are never simply literary concerns, for in radically restructuring the possibility of relation as such, the modal qualities of being are themselves reformulated. What might be considered to be the ground of relation is shown, by way of the uncertainty of its infinitely positive and negative curvature, to be such that it does not necessarily support reciprocity and return, instead, relation has to be considered otherwise. Being, as what is, is restructured on the basis of this explosion, which continually expels it from itself, leaving it without rule or measure, and as such it is difficult to see in what way it remains possible to refer to this inconsistency as being.

Instead, Blanchot is essaying the strong claim that we should think what is underway in being by way of the explosion that is the book, by way of the eccentric expulsions that the text brings to bear on the relation of language, and on relation as such, which raises the question of what this means for the reading of such a relation, especially in terms of the reconfiguration of what might be understood as the parameters of such excess when it has no horizon, no order, and no centre.

While Blanchot had observed in 1943 that it 'seems absurd and pitiful that anguish, which opens and closes the sky, needs the activity of a man sitting at his table and tracing letters on a piece of paper in order to manifest itself', this revelation of the disquiet at the heart of existence is found to occur in *L'Attente l'oubli* through the attempts of a man and woman to meet and to speak to each other [FP: 12/4]. Language strips the innocence from these scenarios; they can never be insignificant when the very possibility of relation is at stake, when the situation in which language may appear is such as to make that appearance infinitely questionable. For this doubt, once raised, cannot be curtailed but finds itself proliferating ceaselessly, and it is then incumbent on the writer or reader to attempt (impossibly) to take the measure of it and the world that it unfolds, a world of particularities without clear or certain forms that begins to take shape as the world before or outside the world, its inverse or underside, the world without.

III The rupture of actualization

Speculative thinking, in relation to the work of literature or art, thus comes across a considerable challenge, as Adorno explains: 'Anyone who does not, as it were, retrace [*nachzeichnet*] the work under its discipline sees a painting or a poem with the same empty eyes' [AT: 183/120]. This idea relates to Adorno's understanding of interpretation, particularly as it operates in regards to music, in which the interpretation of the work involves its re-creation. That is, reading is never generic or impartial but is contingently affected by its situation, such that its interpretation each time actualizes the work anew and thereby brings about changes in that situation. The response to the artwork indicates that speculation is a highly specific form of actualization in which thought comes into the world in the formations of the work just as the latter are themselves brought out in the concretion of thinking. Reading in this way is no longer entirely of the subject or the object, but is its own form, its own material thought, particularly in those cases where the text puts its own presence in question and seems to realize itself otherwise, in a different order or modality. This issue of actualization is of critical importance for Adorno in terms of how he responds to the thought of Hegel and Lukács, for in relation to the former he grants a greater variability to the modes of actualization, and in relation to the latter he urges a greater scepticism and complexity in understanding its possibility in practice, which then become the keys to how thought takes place in the world.

At the beginning of his career, Adorno set out the (materialist) task of philosophy by stating that its concern lies not with the meaning of the world, by which the world is merely justified, nor with its explanation, which only refers to another supposedly more real world, but with its interpretation through images that illuminate and transform its problems. In this act of interpretation, the riddle of the problem, by which it appears, is dissolved and a movement into praxis thereby enabled, as the 'interpretation of given reality and its sublation are connected to each other. Not, of course, that reality is sublated in the concept; but that out of the construction of a figure of reality the demand for its real change always promptly follows'. Adorno is naturally aware of Marx's condemnation of the philosophical interpretation of the world, and the imperative for praxis but, as he points out, this thesis is itself made from the position of philosophy as an interpretation, and it is this perspective that gives it its transformative force.[9] However, this optimistic and rather obscure programme is modified thirty-five years later when he opens *Negative Dialektik* by announcing that philosophy lives on only because the moment of its actualization has slipped (*versäumt*) past it [ND: 15/3]. This implies that although philosophy has survived, its manner of living has changed, since if it can still be actualized it can only do so in a disjointed way, as out of step with reality. As he remarks in relation to the form of the essay, whose actuality is that of anachronism, reality 'continuously forces upon [philosophy] the risk of experimentation [*Versuchs*]', so that its actualization always remains an attempt, an essay.[10] This complicated set of concerns carries over into the interpretation of the work of art, which in its re-enactment or re-creation stutters its own formation alongside that of the work, thereby dissolving the enigma of the work by reposing it otherwise, and it is as such that philosophy both finds and loses itself. This image can also help us to grasp the problem of speculative thinking itself, which can appear to operate in a somewhat magical fashion.

The idea that acts of thinking can bring about real changes in the world needs to be treated carefully to avoid the senses of domination and instrumentality that arise in magical acts. Nevertheless, a work that is mysterious in and for itself creates a sense of obscure effectuation, of possibilities that have not been realized but may become so through unusual or indirect channels. This idea has a particular resonance in relation to forms of writing that are not easily readable and yet appear to bear hidden lines of influence. What this suggests is something of the variability of actualization, of the unrealized possibilities that remain latent in a work and that retain the potential to be realized in unexpected ways.

The basis of sympathetic magic, for example, rests in the mimetic belief that because x resembles (or is contiguous with) y, then actions on x will bring about effects on y.

> The world of magic still retained differences whose traces have vanished in linguistic forms. The manifold affinities between beings become supplanted by a single relation between the sense-giving subject and the meaningless object, between rational signification and its accidental bearer. At the magical stage dream and image were not regarded as mere signs of things but as linked to them through resemblance or name. The relation is not one of intention but kinship.[11]

Much as was the case with Cratylism, the lack of a rational basis for this belief is not enough to refute it, as the mimetic notions of resemblance or contiguity are such that in themselves they bear unconsidered possibilities, and it is this potential that allows for the formation of thought in writing to take advantage of the ways in which the text enables different modes of resemblance or contiguity; visually, aurally, symbolically, or otherwise, as was found with Roussel's writings. The modes of actualization are thus multiple and indirect and bring about associations that rest in non-obvious and non-rational associations, and in doing so manifest that which lies outside ordinary possibilities. Such is what is at work in the movement of symbolic action and the rhetorical force of thinking; those modes of relation that are neither direct nor transparent but persist and make up the ways of thinking's occurrence in the world.

The aim of magic, as Blanchot writes, is thus twofold, for it is 'to arouse things as reflections and to thicken consciousness into a thing'. But there is also a prior operation in which an equivocal realm is brought out within which this double transformation can take place, and the enabling of this realm is itself equivocal as it is an act (on the world) that still aspires to be entirely passive (in relation to the world). To this extent, it is an act that aspires to operate from that place or moment that precedes acting, to act without and before action [EL: 275/262]. There is a further equivocation to this double transformation as its two movements do not coincide or mirror each other, rather they remain out of step, which means that even as thought is able to grasp the sense of that which has no relation, by virtue of making itself like it, it can only so to the degree that it becomes as strange as it. Hence the thing emerges in reflection as thought finds (and loses) itself in the morass of things, so that this discovery risks leading to inertia, and it can be seen that this problem is also involved in the act of responding to artworks by way of their retracing. So, in Blanchot's words, thought finds that everything is possible but also that nothing is possible and, conversely, in seeking to approach the thing, thought only finds and loses itself.¹² Responding to the mystery of the artwork thus reposes the conundrum of magical acts, in which any approach recapitulates their distance and estrangement, which suggests that philosophy, even within the broader framework of socially and historically informed praxis, can only proceed by this mutual but uneven repulsion.

While the instrumental and dominating senses of magic may determine its appearance, as it is conducted for a specific purpose in a specific situation, this also means that, as Horkheimer and Adorno note, 'in magic there is a specific representability [*Vertretbarkeit*]', unlike the universality of language in general. It is as such that the specificity of the thing can be recapitulated in its own language, but, as with the retracing of artworks, this sense requires performance in order to be understood, indeed, understanding is consequent to actualization:

> Musical interpretation is the act of execution [*Vollzug*] that holds fast to linguisticality [*Sprachähnlichkeit*] as synthesis, and at the same time erases every individual language-similarity [*Sprachähnliche*]. Hence the idea of interpretation belongs to music itself and is not incidental to it. But to play music properly is, above all, to speak its language properly. This demands that it be imitated, not decoded. It is only in mimetic practice – which may, of course, be sublimated into unspoken imagination in the manner of silent reading – that music discloses itself, never to a consideration that interprets it independently of its execution. If one wished to compare an act in the languages of meaning [*meinenden*] with that of music, it would rather be in the transcription of a text than in its comprehension as signification.¹³

This understanding of musical interpretation relies on a dialectical form of relating subject and object and is crucial to the way that Adorno approaches artworks. That is, it is through a modulation of speculative thinking that the artwork is approached, to the extent that the former cannot be grasped outside of its actual modifications in the latter. It is from this concrete perspective that the issues of praxis and actualization as such are to be examined and, intrinsic to this movement is its moment of illegibility and disjunction. As a result, the critical aspect of this movement concerns the intelligibility of the work, since there is the suggestion that its esoteric qualities will make it hermetic and thus not only opaque but also open to the risk of the worst: re-enactment without thought. In this regard, Adorno's notion of co-execution (*Mitvollzug*), which is the basis for his understanding of interpretation as re-enactment, becomes revised, for if the artwork is not necessarily intelligible, in that it does not offer itself primarily to any form of conceptual understanding, then not only is the conventional form of significatory interpretation disrupted but the manner in which the work might be retraced also comes under pressure. This risk does not reduce the significance of the unintelligible but renders its encounter more critical, as there is now the burden of its responsibility without conceptual reassurances. Thus, there arises the need to respond to the work by suspending (its) actualization.

Blanchot's writings are not as formally or explicitly challenging as those of Joyce or Stein, but they seem to share a similar form of resistance, although in Blanchot's case this leads to an interrogation of what occurs to thinking when it encounters that which cannot simply be read, and its concomitant rupture of actuality. For what is evident is that any retracing cannot bring about a clarification of the meaning of the work, if that work does not primarily appear in a clearly meaningful form. A text like *L'Attente l'oubli* does not abandon meaning but equally it does not present a coherently meaningful form that could be reconstituted through its reading. Instead, the belief that a text exists in a necessary and immediate relation to the reader is replaced by something more oblique and contingent. Accordingly, the understanding of such a text for Adorno needs to be reconsidered 'as a kind of following-after [*Nachfahren*]; as the co-execution of the tensions sedimented in the artwork, of the processes that have congealed into its objectivity'.[14] Such a reading does not disinter the intended meanings of a text but retraces and reproduces its formation, even with works that appear illegible. In these moments of illegibility are found those points where the retracing of the work brings out its initial contingencies and occasional ruptures; those points where language neither conveys nor expresses meaning but touches on what is, and remains heterogeneous to it through the accidents of its existence. It is thus that the space of literature opens onto exteriority even as it is rigorously consistent and faithful to its own construction. The apparent interiority or subjectivity of the work, which gives it the impression of hermetic enclosure and of being a whole, is inverted or exploded, leading not to a re-established relation to the world by way of its contingencies but, rather, to a re-marking of the distance from the world as a result of the loss of that to which these contingencies putatively refer, their fractured context. Hence, in the text that does not offer itself immediately to reading, the compulsion to retrace its appearance leads away from any purported meaning and towards another form of actualization: of what has not taken place.

It is important to recognize that the dream of direct effectuation that magic shares with the ideology of pure praxis is both remarked and undercut in the work of art, which restages the moment of its appearance and the manner in which its transformation takes place:

> The artwork has in common with magic the postulation of its own self-contained sphere removed from the context of profane existence. Within it special laws prevail. Just as the sorcerer begins the ceremony by marking out from all its surroundings the place in which the sacred forces are to come into play, so each work of art is closed off from reality by its own circumference. The very renunciation of effects by which art is distinguished from magical sympathy only binds it more deeply to the heritage of magic. It places the pure image in opposition to corporeal existence, whose elements it sublates within itself. It is the meaning of the work of art, of aesthetic semblance, to be what was a new and terrible event in the magic of primitives: the appearance of the whole in the particular. The work of art constantly brings about the duplication by which the thing appeared as spiritual.[15]

Thus, it is of considerable significance that the role of fragmentation in Blanchot's writings will challenge this notion of a work's circumference and the consequent appearance of a whole in its particularity. For what occurs by way of the fragmentation of the work is merely its own specific evasions: not the complete replacement of reality by a sudden and absolute transformation but its pervasive and contingent erosion.

In a text that refuses to make this transition to the universal, that holds itself to its own appearance, a strange reversal takes place, for in this case thought does not move from the text to the signification that it ordinarily bears but, in being brought up against the text, is forced to change in order to reconsider its relation. Thought becomes as strange and as singular as that which it contemplates, and thereby gleans the sense of its eccentricity far more than would have been possible by any other means. And in doing so it makes the transition beyond itself in a manner that is neither instrumental nor dominating as it is led to an understanding of the strange as strange. This transformation of speculative thinking in literature has significant consequences, for in such singular texts we find that these 'fictions that we understand are not written for us. Thus is formed the idea of a mystery completely deprived of enigma, of a fantastic newness without finality, more capable than any other of displacing man, of giving him a profound image of disarray and unease that would seize him if he could endure the thought of a world in which he would not be' [FP: 259/226]. This is the world without, which thinking reveals through its own rupture, and by which it is left as that which is no longer thought. What makes Blanchot's writings in this area remarkable is that he has found a way of rendering this passage in thought, so that even if the rupture remains illegible, its contours can still be negatively essayed, which allows for a consideration of this movement (even in its evasions) through the hesitations of reading, its *pas au-delà*.

IV Parataxis of relation

The steps beyond that the text makes are still thought insofar as they are abstract, which has the effect of making *L'Attente l'oubli* appear to be a kind of literary version of Hegel's *Wissenschaft der Logik* in its persistent focus on the movements of thought thinking through its own negativity, but with an inverse effect. The moment of beginning in *L'Attente l'oubli*, despite its poverty, opens into an eccentric series of fragments that keep returning without progress or summation, neither cancelling nor sublating each other but leading only to further deviations and hesitations. And yet it remains thoroughly rigorous and precise, to the extent that the examples that punctuate the text (whether these are considered to be the narrative or meditative elements) provide it with a persistent foil to its reflections that means that its progress cannot be decided. As has been mentioned, it is neither a narrative with meditative asides, nor an essay with narrative moments, but that which maintains itself through a suspension of the decision between them, between *histoire* and thought, description and analysis, fiction and truth, or praxis and theory, and thereby places itself at the very border of the world. A non-relation that is paradoxically, as is suggested by its title (and the very possibility of the encounter that it relates), held in relation and that becomes its key concern: how to think relation without the whole?[16]

It is as if we had been asked to imagine the following scenario: A man and a woman come together in a hotel room and attempt to come to terms with their meeting, they discuss it and he seeks to write their discussion down, but the event seems to slip away, as if it had not actually happened. And if it had not happened, did they meet at all? There is a sense in which this is a kind of primal scene for the modern, urban world: two strangers in an anonymous space, both confined and released to each other but without any establishing ground, and so lacking any purpose or reason to their encounter.[17] As such, the narrative of this encounter, if we can still use these words, struggles to get beyond its starting point, for at each point at which it might move on it finds that there are no grounds for doing so and thus it returns, not to itself or even to its opening, but simply returns. If that which had seemingly occurred finds that both its event and its narration are uncertain, then it is also the case that its apparent beginning is in question, since it can only be an opening if there is that which it opens into, and if the latter is doubtful, then there is only adumbration without focus. Hegel had begun with the iteration of being and nothing in their indeterminacy, out of which arose the stream of action-based nouns that will characterize his thinking (negation, mediation, determination, alienation, transformation, speculation, sublation), but Blanchot cannot get past the point of beginning, as is emphatically remarked in the first sentence: 'Here, and on this sentence that was perhaps also meant [*destinée*] for him, he was obliged to stop' [AO: 7/1]. The deixis of writing does not lead to a generalization in which its singular location yields to universal meaning, but interrupts such a movement, for as an encounter that cannot guarantee any movement beyond itself, writing cannot proceed. But this sentence is, perhaps, reflexive, which is to say that its sphere of resonance is uncertain, as we can never know to what degree its words may refer to themselves as well as to something else, and so they turn back and come to a halt. This movement of ruptured generalization persists throughout the text, upsetting the nominalization of its acts and their purported 'destination', as he had noted. As the narrator goes on to explain, he is engaged in writing notes for that which would appear to have already happened, but these notes, like the encounter and the discussions around it, have not finished, their action is not over:

> It was almost while listening to her speak [*presque en l'écoutant parler*] that he had composed these notes. He still heard her voice as he wrote. He showed them to her. She did not want to read. She read only a few passages, which she did because he gently asked her to. "Who is speaking?" she said. "Who then is speaking?" She sensed an error that she could not put her finger on [*ne parvenait pas à situer*].

Such would seem to be the situation of a muse and amanuensis; she speaks, and he writes down what she says. But the voice carries on just as the writing does, neither of which find a form of closure, and it is perhaps for this reason that the notes seem inadequate, although, more fundamentally, there is also the inability of the voice to recognize itself, to find its identity. Writing only displaces their distance further, thus it is not only the problem of the encounter that is at stake but also its recording, just as it was not merely a question of the movement of being and nothing in their mutual negation and determination but also of the thinking through of this movement.

Just as the first sentence is ruptured by its failure to move beyond its deixis, so too is the woman's speech brought to a halt by the attempt to position herself at a certain point: '"Who then is speaking?" [*"Qui parle donc?"*] She sensed an error that she could not put her finger on'. The possibility of narration as an ongoing process is broken not merely because that which it sought to narrate cannot be said to have occurred with any certainty, but also because the act of narration itself doubles this uncertainty with further obstacles and hesitations. But this doubling is perhaps the only way of approaching, however haltingly, that which may have taken place, for in its stuttered progress it somehow gives form to what underlies, and also undermines, this encounter, its sense of having almost happened: 'She had the impression that, although he had assured her that he would believe her entirely, he did not believe her enough, with the force that would have rendered the truth present' [AO: 7/1]. If his belief is insufficient, then whatever is taking place is not of the order of truth, but if it is not possible for belief to make truth present at all, then this would mean that what is taking place is also outside the order of belief. The truth, if there is any, remains evasive, beyond belief, so that if it occurs it does so otherwise, in a different modality, for whatever may take place in their encounter is not grounded in their relation or their perspectives. What is going on is separate from any constitutive ontotheology of presence, and there is thus no proof of its existence, no way of substantiating what is happening.

It is important to recognize the relation between this first section of *L'Attente l'oubli* and that which comes after it, since this section brings out the issues and questions that lead into the fragmentary text that follows. That is, it is not only a methodological and thematic preamble but also a laying out of the problems that will lead to the fragmentation of the rest of the text. The breakdown is the result of the contingency of its opening, and in the way that this text also refers to Blanchot's other *récits* there is a sense that it is also partly the result of a long series of experimentations, which did not inevitably lead to this situation but persistently put themselves in question so that some kind of formal reflexive aporia becomes unavoidable. This aporia is apparent in the abruptly self-defeating first sentence, from which he will attempt to proceed, and that is borne by the verb *destiner*. Hence the fate of these halting experiments has an outcome that is personally imperative, even if the explicit form of its necessity remains in question. There is nothing inevitable about the progress or development of Blanchot's writings, nor is there any attempt to bring them to a point of summation in *L'Attente l'oubli*, but there is an increased negotiation with the burden of their imperative. Blanchot had already published material in 1958 and 1959 that would reappear in the book in 1962, suggesting that the final work was no more than a concerted attempt to give more attention to the work in progress, but in reorganizing these earlier fragments he is also making a stronger case for their consequence from the specific conditions of their aporetic beginning. To this extent the series of deictics in the first sentence almost appears to be a direct response to Hegel, not only to the discussion of such terms in the *Phänomenologie* but also to the introductory section of *Wissenschaft der Logik* where he had insisted on the necessity of beginning absolutely, with pure immediacy, without any presuppositions or mediations [WL2: 56/70]. As Hegel had pointed out, philosophy cannot begin with either something mediated or something immediate for in doing so it runs into a problem, as the one cannot be separated from the other. So, by beginning with pure or abstract immediacy he hopes to bypass this problem as he is not beginning with any 'thing' at all. In *L'Attente l'oubli* a very different route is underway, in which a specific incidental occurrence unravels itself, not into abstraction or generalization but only into more fragmentary occasions, which appear to be neither fully mediated nor immediate.

What takes their place is disjunction, a point that Blanchot makes clear in the cover copy for this book where, after apologizing for the fact that he cannot provide a simple account of the narrative, he offers the following remarks instead:

> What might strike and frustrate the reader is its discontinuous movement: often from one paragraph to another, sometimes from one phrase to another, there is an interruption, a halt [*arrêt*]. Let us suppose that an author habituated to the happy (or unhappy) continuity of narration has imposed on themselves the necessity of writing, sometimes almost simultaneously, brief, closed, separated phrases that refuse to go on [*se poursuivre*] and remain as if laid out in emptiness, rigid, obtrusive, and immobile. Initially, this simultaneity of phrases at a distance from one another can only be received as a disquieting trait since it signifies a certain rupture of inner connections. Nevertheless, in the end [*à la longue*], and after some attempts to brutally unify that which is scattered through an exterior constraint, it appears that this dispersion also has its coherence and that it even responds to an obstinate, indeed unique demand, tending towards the affirmation of a new relation, that which is perhaps in play in the juxtaposed words that give this narrative its title. I must add that the supposition I have just made is only a supposition.[18]

There seems to be a certain level of self-effacing humour in these words, which is perhaps drawn from an awareness of the peculiarity of the text that they are introducing but that only has the effect of reinforcing its novelty and specific demands. For what is intriguing about this supposition is that it is written from the point of view of an author and yet it is also that which imposes itself on the reader, as if the writer found themselves in the same position of coming across the text in its writing as the prospective reader. Conversely, the reader finds themselves in the position of the writer in coming across a recalcitrant array of word shards that refuse to be assimilated into any larger form. Finally, as it were, both reader and writer find that what arises from the text is a new relation that arises not out of an inner connection or an external constraint, but is paradoxically unique, and that – still in the mode of supposition – a sense of this unique relation can be gained through the titular verbs, in their undecidably transitive and intransitive forms.

And, indeed, the text that follows (without going on) is also to be understood as an extended supposition, which means that its movements remain discontinuous, neither mediated nor immediate, nor absolute or relative, and yet passing by way of deviating contours, waiting . . . forgetting . . . What is thereby brought out in such a text is permanently undecidable in its fragments and their ruptures, its halts and their phrases, such that the sense of its movement, and the 'whole' that (in whatever form) it constitutes, is left uncertain, suspended, so that we cannot even say that it has happened since it remains a supposition. Yet it is precisely this uncertainty that appears to take on the role of the imperative to which the text is attempting to respond, and that reveals itself as a new mode of relation; an uncertainty about the very possibility of movement from one phrase to another. It is thus that this is a text about relation, in perhaps its simplest, most basic form, and what takes place when it does not take place, when it founders in its lack of grounds and determinacy, when there is only waiting . . . forgetting . . . and hence only their own reflexivity, however impoverished, to answer this demand.

Waiting and forgetting clearly have resonances with Heidegger's thinking, particularly in its destinal mode (that Blanchot *perhaps also* puts in question by casting doubt on its universality), but the Nietzschean account of forgetting equally has implications for Hegel's understanding of memory, for the space of memory that is exposed when the language-relation is found wanting. This aspect is marked by what Blanchot calls the demand to be faithful to the space of forgetting in its orientation to what it may or may not be awaiting, as that which may or may not come, and the kind of relation that this entails. Of course, the discontinuity and uncertainty of sense can always be reconstrued as a *movement* of discontinuity and a *sense* of uncertainty, thereby muting its disruptive effects by making them part of a greater system. But, as Adorno makes clear, this approach depends on the assumption that the system, as a system, is ultimately rational, an assumption that reveals that Hegel's thinking fails to be dialectical enough, as it fails to consider the demands of both identity and non-identity, and so fails to grasp the depth of negativity at issue. For it cannot be presumed that such a movement and sense prevails over their ruptures, that their negativity can be wholly assimilated, and that there is always a system within which these movements finally take place [DS: 374–5/146–7].[19] Blanchot's point in stressing these undecidable terms is thus that their emptiness cannot be assumed to be always available to meaning.

Aside from its implications for the thinking of the system, the usage of a term like forgetting in a world where the possibility of political action is directly related to the possibility of remembering and where the scope for autonomy is undermined to the degree that the role of memory is handed over to technology, can only be received, as Blanchot writes, as a disquieting trait. And yet this is also a world where the scope for autonomy is directly related to the capacity to be forgotten, since it is precisely in regards to the totalitarian desires for complete technological surveillance and data retention that the lacunas in such a system become strategic as well as tactical. Forgetting itself is not at issue but rather what, how, and when it might occur, and how this can subvert the instrumentalization and commodification of memory. As with the role of waiting itself, which is not merely quietist or passive, Blanchot is not seeking to generate a political programme but to isolate the manner in which these terms unravel themselves and thereby expose a form of experience that is not available for use, in that they disrupt the immediate, and thus unthinking, actualization of thought.

To return to the imperative that the narrator seeks to respond to, and that the woman had reinforced by claiming that 'he did not believe her enough, with the force that would have rendered the truth present'. Thus, the belief that was thought necessary as a constitutive relation is not adequate to what is ongoing in the evasive facticity of writing, which renders any sense of presence, as well as truth, ambivalent, yet without relinquishing the claim of its imperative, which results in the sense that 'everything before her eyes was spinning: she had lost the centre from which the events had radiated and that she had held onto so firmly until now'. It is thus in the very nature of the beginning that there remains some form of possibility, in the strongest sense, some form in which truth, in whatever form, may remain and so she is led to say, 'perhaps because the first words say everything, that the first paragraph seemed to her to be the most faithful and also the second somewhat, especially at the end' [AO: 7–8/1]. In saying this, we, as readers, are inevitably drawn back towards the beginning that has just been read, and that may or may not have been forgotten, as well as on towards the end of the second paragraph that has not yet been read but is seemingly waiting for us. It is as such that the dimensions of its truth are sketched out, but nevertheless persist in remaining unclear, as the relation between the text that we have read and that which is being discussed is never made perspicuous, for although the text that we are reading does not seem to coincide with that which the narrator is composing it is also not entirely removed from it. We are in a sense reading a palimpsest of the notes for this encounter, notes that are neither within its terms nor without as they fall into a different mode of relation, and so cannot confirm either its presence or its absence. Again, the writing can only support a supposition of that which may have occurred, and so occupies a different place and time that is not clearly related to it in any form of proximity or orbit (it should be recalled that the 'primal scene' in *L'Écriture du désastre* is also explicitly marked as a supposition). If there is a doubt over whether what occurred actually took place, in actuality, then any documentation that would seek to come after it and provide its account can only take up a position that is equally uncertain and remote; there can be no guarantee of correspondence or isomorphism between them. And so, in its attempt to write in relation to what (may have) happened, writing only makes the latter (and itself) more unstable.

If the point of existence, that which it uses to situate itself, is not a point, then it cannot reflect on itself, by whatever means, through the form of a circumference. The circle arises out of the rotation of the point upon itself and it is this that gives rise to the idea of a totality of meaning that surrounds and encompasses it, and by which it literally makes sense of itself. But if the point is not a point, either because it is not certain that it is at all, or because, if it is, then it is so in the form of something less determinate and unitary, then this doubled uncertainty can only lead to a more fragmentary and eccentric form, pervaded by a negativity that would prevent it from returning fully to itself, if at all. A sense of this new mode of relation is apparent in the next lines, where the narrator states that 'he did not need familiarity in order to get close to beings. Was it chance that had placed them so intimately in relation, by giving him accommodation in precisely this room?' [AO: 8/2] It could always have been otherwise; the event can never completely surface out of the range of other possibilities that might render it non-existent: there always remains the penumbra of impossibility that undercuts its occurrence. The spectre of contingency, the ineradicable fact that this might not have happened, not only affects the nature of its presence but also that which would seek to designate it. The deictics of this, here, now, you, and so on, which would define the situation, are replaced by the pervasive suspicion that it might not be the case, that the world might be otherwise. And so the place of the narrative, in both senses of its genitive, is rendered uncertain, and this leads to another way of thinking of not only its presence but also any relation thereto, as there is no possible means of guaranteeing that we can ever be together, which is not simply nihilistic but rather exposes another form of relation that occurs by way of its contingency, with all that this implies for its cognizability. For example, that which we call love or survival are traversed by an awareness that things might have been different, which is also the force of that which is addressed in revolutionary politics, that things could be different, and to be so anomalously constituted leaves them permanently undefined (the notion of fate offers a powerful negative indicator of this issue). The experience of this anomaly is what is apparent and ineffaceable in the (dis)contours of waiting and forgetting and, although the discipline of maintaining them so as to have a sense of this difference is necessarily immeasurable, understanding this task is what is underway in Blanchot's writing in this book.

It is thus not a question of waiting for the event to happen, as if in so doing it would authorize itself, but rather of waiting as a mode of experience of that which does not take place but remains in the realm of the merely possible, which is why this is a mode of *désœuvrement*, just as forgetting is a mode in which what is unrecalled nevertheless persists, but outside the workings of memory. The narrator in *L'Attente l'oubli* describes what appears to have happened: he had seen her from his hotel room and waved to her, and she had come to his room. This is, in fact, the sentence at the end of the second paragraph that may or may not be the one she had said was more faithful, and there is very little more in the way of facts that could be added to an account of what happened. Then, at some later point, they try to put into words what seems to have occurred, and he tries to write this account down. This opening would not appear to be difficult, but every aspect of the situation starts to become doubtful, and the first question that the narrator asks himself to try to counter this lack of clarity relates to its initial conditions: why had she spoken to him? To be faithful here is ambiguous, as it could mean to remain faithful to her, or to what happened, or to the sense or truth of what may have happened, and it is this uncertainty of relation that underlies the recollection of the encounter, its attempt to return to itself. There is no why to their encounter, no reason why she spoken to him, and yet this question cannot be relinquished since it persists as an aspect of the contingency of their situation, the impossibility of discerning any grounds for what may have happened, which affects any sense of whether it may have something to which one could remain faithful.

The narrator suggests that there might be an Orphic dimension to their relation, which only complicates it further, in that it supplements it with the dimensions of life and death, alongside that of male and female, before and after, as well as the lack of patience and remembering. Hence this allusion is not there to define the relation but to emphasize its incommensurable deviations, for how is it possible for there to be any kind of relation between Orpheus and Eurydice when they exist in different worlds, separated at all levels of meaning and tense?

> To be faithful, this is what was being asked of him: to hold this slightly cold hand that would lead him by singular turns to a spot where she would disappear and leave him alone. But it was difficult for him not to seek the one to whom this hand belonged. He had always been like this. He thought about the hand, about the one who had held it out to him, and not about the itinerary. There, without doubt, was his mistake.
>
> AO: 10/3

Avoiding the allegorical sense in which Eurydice represents a figure of philosophy or poetry, the mistake that the narrator feels he has made is that of mistaking the companion for the path, the person for the route, which is to focus on the *relata* rather its relation, despite its remoteness and obscurity. But how can this mistake not happen? Just like the query about why she had spoken to him, these questions cannot be effaced even if they are unanswerable, and it is exactly this impossibility that is being addressed. Instead of believing that these questions can be passed over because of their impossibility, and replaced with more tractable issues about the path and the destination, it is necessary to hold on, to remain faithful, to that which cannot admit of such determination. Even if all there is to hold on to is a mere fact, the passing contingency of a hand already growing cold, the opacity of this moment of sense renders more of what is at issue because it is its only factual occurrence. The lack of sense that may accrue to such facts does not prohibit them from being thought but indicates that there is that which persists in thinking despite its opacity, and that this constitutes what there is in each relation to which we need to remain faithful. And it is insofar as this opacity is a mistake, a blot or accident of thinking, that it will take place as an aporia; that which cannot be surpassed but only endured in its anomalous form.

The narrator goes on to say that he 'felt bound to her by this failure [...] as if he had touched her across the void'. Moreover, he had seen her, if only for an instant, and this meant that 'he had seen who she was'. But this breach, by which the two had briefly been juxtaposed, like two fragments across the intervening space, was no more than a confirmation of their finitude, as it suggested 'the end [*point final*] of everything' [AO: 11/3]. The contingency of their encounter is no more than the breach of fatality in which each is not exposed to the other as they are, but only as they were in the moment of their mutual interruption, so this does not betoken further relation or reciprocity but only reaffirms their incommensurability. It is thus the space between them that is at issue, that which comes to pass when the sentence has stopped and the voice has gone silent, that which remains in/as the space between like a negative integument, an absence that cannot be bridged. And it is on the point of discovering this breach that the preamble comes to an end and the fragmentary passages begin, making it clear that the interstice that the fragments expose is precisely the space after the end of the sentence towards which each is seeking to attend. *Le point final* is a full stop or period, the emphatic declaration of finality when the sentence is over, and by way of which any subsequent sentence can only arise by parataxis: There is an end point. And then a new sentence. But this 'and then' is no more than an attempted supposition of the breach; nothing can guarantee or substantiate the transition from one sentence to another, each one is a new opening that can only forget or miss the moment preceding it. There is no relay from one to the next that does not obscure this lack of transmission, and so to be faithful to it is to recognize this absence (which undermines any assumption of an essentialized movement beyond) and the space of what might be otherwise. This is not just a textual space but that of pre-enunciation or pre-articulation, of that which has not come forth and so has not taken place in any form.

So, aporetically (again), the narrator states that he will give up, or rather renounce, unannounce himself from the course of action, so that he does not simply go on with it but instead does so, in his words, in a private word (*parole d'intimité*), the singular and wordless phrase or gesture that seemingly bound them to each other by not addressing them directly. This ambiguity brings him to a point of realization about the contingency of their relation, which he then writes down: 'What she says, the secrets that you collect and transcribe so as to give them their due, you must bring them back gently, in spite of their attempt to seduce, to the silence that you first drew out of them' [AO: 11/3]. This is the secret of their secret, that which lies concealed in their unknowable relation, which is nothing more than its chance conditions, that is, its conditions as that of chance, in both its weight and its gratuity (as opposed to the simple emptiness of the enigma that Foucault finds). The silence here is not that of a quasi-mystical ontological essence to which we must attend but merely that of an inescapable occasion, each time transient and singular and necessarily unspeakable. The preamble thus orients us to its conditions and thereby introduces the form of logic that it will seek to adumbrate. It is not engaged in laying out the conditions for a general logic of literary forms, which it could then examine in the text that follows, but rather in indicating its own specific and concrete mode of realization, which is never completed and so leaves a text that is both fragmented and unwhole. This unfulfilled actualization derives from the fact of its chance, as that to which the text remains faithful and so cannot leave behind. It is for this reason that the text remains on the borders of its own formation, never fully legible and yet also never fully realized in its negativity.

In an interview with an Italian journalist in 1978 Foucault discussed the idea that certain of his books could be considered as 'experience-books', in his words.[20] By this phrase he suggests that these books do not exist to prescribe or demonstrate a certain truth but primarily operate as experiences in which his own thought changed in the writing of them, and, subsequently, as invitations for a similar operation to take place for the reader. While he links this idea to that of the limit-experience that appears in Bataille's writings, there is less of a sense of the loss of subjective experience per se, as there is for Bataille, and more of a sense in which the lesson that Foucault has discovered in the writing of these books (*Histoire de la folie* and *Surveiller et punir*, especially) is shared by the reader in their experience of the book. To this end, he suggests that these books exist to disturb our conventional way of thinking about certain terms and notions so that they can be approached with a new understanding of their intelligibility. There is some degree of equivocation in Foucault's descriptions, for while he dismisses the idea that he is trying to teach, and insists that these works are merely fictional gestures designed to provoke and enable a transformation of thought, he also insists on their firm historical and empirical grounding and that the new understanding he is seeking to generate should be capable of being linked to collective practice. As a result, despite mentioning Bataille and Blanchot in relation to this idea, the experience-book more closely resembles a traditional form of academic discourse. Even if it is occasionally aporetic, in that it disrupts ordinary modes of thinking, the lesson of these books is ultimately to impart a form of knowledge in the mode of a new experience, which is to say that they inhabit a rhetoric of illumination that is startling or dazzling but finally clarifying.

Nevertheless, this comparison is helpful not just because Foucault states that he is following Blanchot in taking up this sense of experience, but because he is operating in a direction and a tenor that is very different from that of Blanchot's writings, for which, as has been noted, philosophical discourse can only proceed if it recognizes the necessity of becoming a dis-course, of losing itself as much as it finds itself. As such, there is no scope for suggesting that there may be any lesson that could be drawn from a text like *L'Attente l'oubli*, despite its evident philosophical and political dimensions. Instead, the mode of experience that might be discerned in Blanchot's writings is closer to that which Hegel discussed, and precisely to the degree that it articulates itself in a constant interrogation of the possibility of any thought of the whole or the system, or of the mediation and determination of negativity. Hence whatever may be gleaned from Blanchot's writings exists only insofar as it activates a sense of the ineradicable negativity of thinking, of the persistent opacities and contingencies that permeate thought, which force a reconsideration of its unannounced situation and possibilities.

To consider the way in which thought might lose itself just as it finds itself is not to return to a Hegelian thought of the recuperation of alienation, but to uncover a very different kind of topology in which the centrifugal and centripetal do not coincide but sketch out a space without regularity or unity. It is the experience of this space and time that becomes apparent in *L'Attente l'oubli*, not as an experiential fact that can be imparted and shared but as an uncertain rupture, an interruption of hesitancy, a pause in thinking. The furthest extent of the solar system is marked by what is known as the heliopause, where the radiation emitted by the sun finally ceases to overpower the interstellar void. The pause in thinking is also a point where it encounters its own limit; however it is not at some distant external point but pervades it from within, and forces it to think its own absence and its ever-present burden of unrealized possibilities and contingent impossibilities, which undermine the certainty of what has or has not happened by leaving it permanently undecided, and in suspense. Consider the way in which the first three sentences of *L'Attente l'oubli* bring these issues out:

> *Ici, et sur cette phrase qui lui était peut-être aussi destinée, il fut contraint de s'arrêter.*
> *C'est presque en l'écoutant parler qu'il avait rédigé ces notes.*
> *Il entendait encore sa voix en écrivant.*

The difficulty of reading these sentences presents itself straightaway, as we have seen, and can be given more concreteness if we to try to isolate their moment:

what is the time of these phrases, when are they written in relation to what is going on, and to when are they referring in their designations? The situation of *il*, the one who narrates these sentences, seems to exist both after and alongside what has been (and/or is still) happening, and so in reading these lines this ambivalence of moment is made apparent and encountered.

He had composed these notes almost while listening to her speak, and, conversely, he still heard her voice as he wrote, *presque* and *encore* are brought into parallel such that what comes after is aligned with what is ongoing, the past lingers on into the present just as (and perhaps only insofar as) the present lingers back into the past. But this positioning is complicated by a narrative perspective that is both current and retrospective, and also somehow follows the first sentence in which he had been forced to stop, but it is not possible to say when this occurred since we do not know what sentence he is referring to when he says 'here' and 'this'. The suggestion of reflexivity is hard to displace but it must be recognized that whether it is real or not, the actual sentence upon which he comes to a halt is not given, not just because he does not stop or because it is perhaps not meant for him, but because, even if it is the same one that is before us, it is still not the one that he designates as 'here'. The sentences are thereby not only parataxically arranged with each other but also within themselves, as it were, so there is no possibility of any progressive dialectical syllogism from one sentence to the next. That which would purport to be the term or limit of a sentence no longer passes through it as its determination by holding it together but expels it from itself, leaving it at all points exterior to its own sense in that it refers elsewhere for its grounding. This is not merely a provisional disruption, as if the grounding could at some point be found and re-established, but an aporia that separates it from itself from the beginning. In being obliged to stop in reading this sentence, the reader encounters a form of illegibility that is constitutive and extraneous, and in constraining one to its end the reader is brought to read this ending as that which leaves the sentence outside itself.

But, as he had written, this aporetic ejection leads to the affirmation of a new kind of relation, of the facts that lie without the narrative – the hand, the voice, the paper, the room, and so on – and that constitute their own mode of parataxis, a non-relation in the form of supposition, which would seem to be what Blanchot is suggesting as the only possible basis for a thinking of community or politics outside the whole. A sense of community that writing cannot approach but can only indicate through its moments of contingent illegibility, which is to imply a necessary and permanent engagement with the end of writing, an end that can of course only take place within writing, and that *L'Attente l'oubli* materially demonstrates by its breakdown. The word that Blanchot comes to use in this context is the most discreet and unassertive, as he speaks merely of friendship, the most minimal and undetermined form of relation, a term that is barely philosophical at all, and yet within which he finds the possibility of a relation that is non-prescriptive in regards to both its form and its ends. As such, although this word comes to take on the burden of much of his thinking of politics, it never receives any detailed examination. Instead, and remaining faithful to its singular discretion, it is only apparent in his discussions of the actual friendships he experienced, with Bataille, Levinas, Mascolo, and Paulhan, for instance. This means that the contingency of its relation remains legible despite its fragility and yet resists being assimilated or transformed into any greater universal form. Thus, friendship is never understood as the basis of community, for example, in any sense that might construe it as being instrumental to a model of praxis. But, in one of his most compressed sentences, Blanchot does indicate the force of its significance, which shows how its near non-existence bears an extraordinary complexity and imperative: 'friendship is also the truth of disaster'.[21]

The density of this sentence demonstrates something of its demand as it requires us to examine the relation between its three terms: firstly, that disaster has a truth; secondly, that this truth can be understood as friendship; and thirdly, that truth is the form in which disaster and friendship somehow come into relation. Any sense of such truth is thereby between disaster and friendship and bears the form of both as rupture and relation, so that friendship is perhaps no more than a name for the form in which the disaster reflects on itself. It should be noted that this does not imply a Hegelian identity of identity and non-identity but something much more refractory, as he had indicated a few years earlier in a piece that, alongside the fragments collected in 'L'attente' in 1958, also marked the beginning of his work on *L'Attente l'oubli*, a piece that was simply entitled 'Le refus':

> Refusal is absolute, categorical. It does not argue, nor does it voice its reasons. This is why it is silent and solitary, even when it asserts itself, as it must, in broad daylight. Those who refuse and who are linked by the force of refusal know that they are not yet together [*ensemble*]. The time of joint affirmation is precisely that which has been taken away from them. What they are left with is the irreducible refusal, the friendship of this certain, unshakable, rigorous No that keeps them united and in solidarity.[22]

Blanchot's concern is to think through the relation of abstraction and negation in their concreteness, that is, as concrete abstraction and concrete negation, and it is in literature that this takes place, in literature and also in the Revolution. In this way Blanchot is seeking to hold literature to its revolutionary rigour, the moment in which negation and abstraction are experienced together in their concreteness. This is the freedom that literature exposes, a concrete freedom of thought, which Blanchot seeks to sustain in the moment before it is collapsed into genres and forms, and that thereby leaves literature in an abstract turmoil of negativity. Even if the force of this turmoil is muted in his later works, it remains no less severe, for it now takes the form of a radical suspension of modality.

Blanchot, no less than Hegel, is haunted by the caesura of the Revolution, which recurs in literature from Sade to Mallarmé, and from Hölderlin to Lautréamont, and is recapitulated in the persistent ruptures of his own time, which again and again reaffirms its anomalous force in the face of the institutions that would seek to reduce it. Thus, the Revolution is not just the fury of disappearance, in Hegel's words, but the very life of literature for Blanchot, the negativity that is its right [PG: 319/359; PF: 309/319]. With Mallarmé, for instance, literature undergoes an upheaval as universal as that which Robespierre unveiled, which is why this form of literature, in appearing in the world, bears its own kind of life, and why it indicates a point beyond which thought cannot go, precisely because it is already beyond thought. This is why Derrida can say of Blanchot's writing that it is the riskiest there is and why, in the pursuit of this risk, it becomes its 'own' thought and experience in their minimal (non-)relation and their perpetual instability and expropriation.

Coda

At the end of *Thomas l'Obscur* is found a passage that is among the strangest that Blanchot wrote. Tonally, the last chapter of the novel is already very odd in that it is concerned with the joys of spring as opposed to the toxic darkness that has pervaded the narrative thus far. But, equally, this last chapter presents an extraordinary apocalyptic vision that seems to be both utopian and dystopian, as if it were expressing a kind of negative idealism. It is thus worth looking at it more closely in order to essay the possibilities and impossibilities inscribed in this vision, which will in turn allow for a form of conclusion to this reading of the nature of relation.

> Thomas went out into the country and saw that spring was beginning. In the distance, ponds spread forth their murky waters, the sky was dazzling, life was young and free. When the sun climbed onto the horizon, the genera, the races, and even the species of the future, represented by individuals without species, peopled the solitude in a disorder full of splendour. Dragonflies without wing-cases, which should not have flown for ten million years, tried to take flight; blind toads crawled through the mud seeking to open their eyes that were only capable of vision for the future.[23]

Between a vista of waters thick with burgeoning life and the openness of the sky, the life that emerges in this new world is pervaded by paradox, to the point of seeming almost impossible. For it is a life that appears in some way to be constituted by its futurity, conditioned by that which is yet to come, and so grounded incompletely, dependent on an always future unfolding.

And, critically, in this future (which separates it from the similarly future-dependent vision of Koyré) the kingdoms of life disintegrate into solitude, the genera and species giving way to sheer individuality. This vision of life is thus oddly ideal; phrased in joyous and apocalyptic terms it appears to depict a world that is unfinished and unorganized, which is the form of its utopia, its ever-apparent impossibility. What we perceive are not the possible forms of a future existence but the impossibility of their formation, their permanent incompleteness, without degeneration or regeneration, indeed, without genre or generativity at all. The larval quality of this world (much like that of Lautréamont's writing) would seem to undermine its utopian aspects but, instead, it suggests that there is a mode of life outside progress or decay that is not tied to linear, teleological, or circular models of growth. This is not a form of life in which negativity is assimilated but one in which it remains adjoined to every form and mode of existence such that every step is cancelled and not cancelled. In addition, this negativity occurs in the relation of each form, to others and to itself, which thus affects the possibility of identity as well as community. There is no organizing *logos* to this mode of life, no system within which it finds its order and aims, there is only its dissembling. Such a life cannot be the ground for anything but, paradoxically, it is as a result of this that it most radically opens the future as such.

Within the narrative of *Thomas l'Obscur*, this chapter comes after the long musings following the death of Anne and so seems to mark a kind of rebirth (without birth) of life itself. However, as the last chapter in the novel, it also proceeds by way of an intimation of return, of a closing of the circle of life, which, as the peculiar descriptions suggest, will always remain incomplete and to come. The apocalyptic nature of the vision is not one that reveals any truth or summation of the narrative and its world, but shows that this vision itself cannot return to itself and therefore cannot marry light to light; the light of vision with the light of understanding, the light of revelation with the light of assumption. The very opening of the sky is tarnished by its inability to realize itself fully and thereby only reveals its negativity. Hence what is discovered in this revelation is the irresolvable ambivalence of its opening, which is precisely the nature of the vision that Thomas is given, and that concludes the narrative. This realization is perhaps what a negative idealism involves; an idealism of the negative alongside a negative ideal so that the ideal is persistently undermined just as the negative is made pervasive.

Intrinsic to this negativity is its effects on relation, as mentioned, which is emphatically marked as non-reciprocal: the forms that Thomas encounters do not return to each other but are rather constituted by their non-relations. Examples proliferate in this section, not just in terms of sight but also sound and smell, which only confirms the immense solitude of this world, and throughout it all Thomas advances. After passing through this darkly bucolic landscape of birds and flowers and insects that exist through their own negation, Thomas comes to a city in which the same occurs, even at the level of its construction and the very space itself. (It would be too much to say that this landscape is in some allegorical sense, Literature, for any sense of there being a code that could translate this work is undone by its own ongoing and formless translations of itself.) And, by way of this non-relation, the inhabitants of the city find themselves released from themselves: untied from the bonds of memory and the body yet still constituted by the absence of these bonds. Such a situation, as this chapter of the novel has emphasized, seems (wholly) impossible, but this is precisely insofar as impossibility excludes the whole, and vice versa, and thereby indicates that which persists otherwise, not so much outside as without the whole. Thus, the form (without form) of this exteriority is that of its negativity, the refusal and evasion of relation, which is addressed in the last lines of the book. After somehow assisting in the release of the city's inhabitants, in a manner that partly recapitulates Plato's cave allegory, Thomas watches as they plunge into the ocean:

> But when, from the deepest of shadows there arose a prolonged cry that was like the end of a dream, they all recognised the ocean and perceived a glance whose immensity and sweetness awoke in them unbearable desires. Becoming men again for an instant, they saw in the infinite an image they enjoyed and, giving in to a last temptation, they stripped themselves voluptuously in the water.

> Thomas also watched this flood of crude images, then, when it was his turn, threw himself into it, but sadly, desperately, as if the shame had begun for him [*comme si la honte eût commencé pour lui*].[24]

Although Thomas is said to be like a shepherd in these last pages – leading 'the tide of star-men towards the first night' as if, in a Mallarmean sense, the constellations (as configurations of absent relations) were to realize themselves in the void – his position is more minimal, more like a witness to this transformation. This plunge into the ocean should not be seen as either a simple return to the beginning of the novel, as I have noted, or as a lemming-like self-annihilation. Instead, it is the image of the infinite that is pivotal here and, as Thomas discovers, the response to its endless exposure is not a peaceful abnegation of the self, but one of shame.

It has often been noted that this last line recalls that of Kafka's *Der Process*, where Josef K. watches the faces of his executioners as he is killed: '"Like a dog!" he said, it was as if the shame would outlive him [*als sollte die Scham ihn überleben*]'. But in rewriting this line, Blanchot only draws out the peculiarity of the sense of shame. This is a highly complex emotion and a challenging point upon which to end any novel, for shame has to do with a sense of exposure, a self-conscious awareness of negativity, of loss or lack. If this emotion is withdrawn from its moral constraints and the standards against which it is normatively drawn, as Blanchot's account would suggest, then we are left with a much more elusive sense of what might be termed, very provisionally, ontological shame, an awareness of the exposure that is involved in the loss of an aspect of being, with the implication that this loss is related to the lack of ground or whole that has been demonstrated thus far.[25] Shame would then be the corollary of the futurity mentioned earlier, the reflexive awareness of the constant negativity that undermines any sense or order to life, which thereby renders it inassimilable to any system of thought.

In Kafka's sentence, Josef K. experiences his death with shame and to such a degree that it would seem to outlive him, as if it would survive in his place, rendering his death even more ignominious. For Thomas, the situation is different, since he plunges into the sea with a combined sense of urgency and resignation, sadness and desperation, as if there were finally no other chance for him, and it is in this sense that the shame arises, the shame of a commitment to that which offers no alternative and of the living on that it bears. It is in this survival that the shame begins, both in its fact and its form, and as such it becomes definite. A few years later Blanchot would make this point a little clearer, and in doing so he makes apparent that it is the very limit of the work that is at issue, the transition that occurs when the book ends, whether for the writer or the reader, which is its final point of illegibility:

> Literature appears linked to the strangeness of existence that being has rejected and that escapes every category. The writer feels himself prey to an impersonal power [*puissance*] that does not let him either live or die: the irresponsibility he cannot surmount becomes the translation of that death without death that awaits him at the borders of nothingness; literary immortality is the very movement by which is insinuated into the world, a world undermined by brute existence, the nausea of a survival that is not one, a death that does not put an end to anything.
>
> PF: 327/340

Thus, the contradiction and loss that is the mark of shame, and grants it the sense of survival of which Kafka speaks, is rendered more complicated in the survival of the literary work, which leads to it living on in a way that is no longer one's own, and no longer human or finite, since it bears its own after-life. In thereby disturbing the movements of life and death, literature also undermines their temporality, exposing a future in which the pervasion of negativity renders all forms (both in and of time) incomplete and uncertain, permanently ruptured by their unreadable contingencies. Consequently, shame becomes the experience of the negativity of contingency, and vice versa, of its anomalous burden and of the thought of this experience, which cannot itself be thought as it is the very disowning or exposure of thought. Hence when Blanchot later comes to comment on this line from *Der Process*, he writes that there is no end to the ordeal, 'since Kafka specifies that the shame survives, which is to say the infinite itself, the mockery of life as life's beyond' [EDB: 89/53]. Shame, as a mark of finitude, is infinite, and becomes its own form of life or thought, which is however neither living nor thinkable but is the sense of the bad infinite as it turns on and suspends itself and, as this contradiction insinuated into the world, shame is, as Marx wrote, already a revolution.[26]

Notes

Introduction: marks of experience

1 The discussion of the life and death struggle first appears in Hegel's writings in the 1803–4 manuscript on *Sittlichkeit* where he uses the words for both slave (*Sklav*) and bondsman (*Knecht*), see Hegel, *Jenaer Systementwürfe I*, ed. Klaus Düsing and Heinz Kimmerle (Hamburg: Felix Meiner, 1975), 307-15; *"System of Ethical Life" (1802/3) and "First Philosophy of Spirit" (1803/4)*, ed. and tr. H. S. Harris and T. M. Knox (Albany: SUNY Press, 1979), 235–42. It should be recalled that the life and death struggle is not the only scenario in which self-consciousness emerges, for Hegel also develops such an account in reference to love, see, *Vorlesungen über die Philosophie des Rechts* (GW 26.3), ed. Klaus Grotsch (Hamburg: Felix Meiner, 2015), §158, 854; *Elements of the Philosophy of Right*, ed. Allen W. Wood, tr. H. B. Nisbet (Cambridge: Cambridge University Press, 1991), 199. As I am examining Blanchot's relation to Hegel, it would take the discussion too far afield to consider this important counter-scenario, but it could be argued that it is because of Kojève's privileging of the life and death struggle (which was crucial for Blanchot's generation) that Derrida begins his own reading of Hegel in *Glas* with exactly this counter-scenario.

2 Blanchot, *The Instant of My Death*, tr. Elizabeth Rottenberg (Stanford: Stanford University Press, 2000), 6–9. This account recalls the opening paragraphs of Blanchot's 'La Folie du jour'. To grasp the significance of this narrative it is also necessary to contrast it with the versions provided closer to the time. Six days after the incident, Blanchot wrote to Paulhan and described it in more prosaic, almost absurd, terms, emphasizing the loss of his pens and manuscripts and the way he was treated after it was discovered that he was a writer, with one of the German officers angrily telling him 'that getting involved with writing was a highly serious crime', cited in Christophe Bident, 'Maurice Blanchot à *La NRF*: secrétaire, critique, écrivain', *Letras de Hoje* 48.2 (2013): 163–71 (170). See also the memoir by Pierre Prévost, *Rencontre Georges Bataille* (Paris: Jean-Michel Place, 1987), 116, which appears to carry the first confirmation of the event when Prévost recalls receiving letters from his friends towards the end of 1944: 'These letters told me that despite the euphoria of liberation, material life was not ameliorated but rather aggravated. However, Bataille was, he wrote, rejuvenated and very lively. Lignac, librarian at the Bibliothèque nationale, worked regularly at *Combat* with Pascal Pia, Albert Camus, Albert Ollivier, Romain Petitot. Blanchot had almost been shot by the Germans'.

3   Hegel, *Aesthetics: Lectures on Fine Art*, tr. T. M. Knox (Oxford: Clarendon Press, 1975), 387. As is well known, the text of the *Ästhetik* was largely written and compiled by Hegel's student Hotho, and Hegel's original manuscripts are missing. Consequently, it is necessary to be careful in claiming that any lines from Hotho's text accurately reflect Hegel's thought, since Hotho reorganizes, elaborates, and consolidates ideas that Hegel seems to have presented more tentatively. The student notes from these lecture courses having now been published, it is possible to compare the notes taken at the time with the version published by Hotho by 1835. In this regard, the comment about the language of slaves is representative, since the notes from the 1823 course are not nearly as definitive as the later formulation, see *Vorlesungen über die Philosophie der Kunst* (GW 28.1), ed. Niklas Hebing (Hamburg: Felix Meiner, 2015), 357; *Lectures on the Philosophy of Art: The Hotho Transcript of the 1823 Berlin Lectures*, ed. and tr. Robert F. Brown (Oxford: Oxford University Press, 2014), 303, where, in relation to the form of Aesop's fables, Hegel is reported to have said, 'this is not a free form, it is even attributed to a slave as its originator [*Urheber*]'.

4   As Derrida explains at the start of his course, *La vie la mort, séminaire (1975–6)*, ed. Pascale-Anne Brault and Peggy Kamuf (Paris: Seuil, 2019), 19–23; tr. Pascale-Anne Brault and Michael Naas as *Life Death* (Chicago: University of Chicago Press, 2020), 1–4, the deliberate lack of any conjugation in the phrase *life death* – to the degree that its possible hyphenation is replaced with a marked silence, a wordless trace or unmarked space – enables us to think it without an inevitable ontological *and* or *is*. It is Derrida's assertion that in Hegel's thought there is a latent translation from a thought in which life is considered in terms of the phrase *life and death* to a consideration of it as *life is death*, which allows for the speculative sublation of its apparent opposition, a move that Derrida wishes to put in question while suggesting his own unmarked non-relation. For Derrida, Hegel's sublation of the opposition between life and death exposes the reciprocity between the thought of ontology and that of the unconsidered opposition inherent to the thought of life *and* death.

5   As Hegel writes at the beginning of *Philosophie des Geistes*: 'finitude here has its meaning in the inadequacy of concept and reality, with the determination that it is a semblance held within the mind – a semblance that the mind sets up as a limit *in itself*, in order, through its sublation, to have and to be aware of freedom *for itself* as its essence, i.e. to be fully *manifested*' [ENZ: §386, 383–4/22].

6   It is important to recall that Hegel's understanding of this struggle would have drawn upon the social and political struggles relating to the emancipation of the peasantry, and the 'mediatisation' of imperial and ecclesiastical authority (*Herrschaft*), which created enormous turmoil in Germany in the period between 1790 and 1820. Indeed, it is difficult to overestimate the changes ongoing during this period in which 'Germany' came into being out of the destruction and

reorganization imposed by the French. To this degree, it is not too much to see that the roles of master and slave are reflected in the relations between France and Germany in this time, between the all-powerful French armies who had overcome the fear of death and the disparate German forces that chose subservience instead. (Hegel says as much in a letter to a student in 1807, shortly before the *Phänomenologie* was published, when he states that, thanks to the Revolution, the individual in France 'has shed the fear of death', see *Briefe von und an Hegel, Band I: 1785–1812*, ed. Johannes Hoffmeister (Hamburg: Felix Meiner, 1952), 138; *Hegel: The Letters*, tr. Clark Butler and Christiane Seiler (Bloomington: Indiana University Press, 1984), 123.) However, the notion of *Herrschaft* also designates the various forms of local authority (military, noble, commercial, or religious) that constituted the traditional bases of power across the German territories before the French invasions and domination. Thus, it is due to the abstraction of Hegel's description of the life and death struggle that it can be mapped across these different social, historical, and personal models. For more on the political background of this period see, especially, James J. Sheehan, *German History 1770–1866* (Oxford: Clarendon Press, 1989); Terry Pinkard, *Hegel: A Biography* (Cambridge: Cambridge University Press, 2000); and, Frank Ruda, *Hegel's Rabble* (New York: Continuum, 2011).

7 Michel Foucault, 'Dire et voir chez Raymond Roussel', in *Dits et écrits 1954–1988: I, 1954–1969*, ed. Daniel Defert, François Ewald, and Jacques Lagrange (Paris: Gallimard, 1994), 212; tr. Robert Hurley as 'Speaking and Seeing in Raymond Roussel', in *Aesthetics, Method, and Epistemology*, ed. James D. Faubion (London: Penguin, 1998), 27. This article appeared in 1962, nine months before Foucault published his book on Roussel, and some of its formulations are unique to it.

8 Foucault, 'Dire et voir chez Raymond Roussel', 213; 'Speaking and Seeing in Raymond Roussel', 28.

9 Foucault, *Raymond Roussel* (Paris: Gallimard, 1963), 23–5; tr. Charles Ruas as *Death and the Labyrinth: The World of Raymond Roussel* (London: Continuum, 2004), 17–18. The insights of these literary investigations come to a peak in the 1963 article 'Le langage à l'infini' in which Foucault proposes that his readings could introduce 'a formal ontology of literature', and for which he establishes a history stretching from Sade to Borges. See, 'Le langage à l'infini', in *Dits et écrits 1954–1988: I, 1954–1969*, 254; tr. Donald F. Bouchard and Sherry Simon as 'Language to Infinity', in *Aesthetics, Method, and Epistemology*, 93. For more on this period of Foucault's work see, especially, Jean-François Favreau, *Vertige de l'écriture, Michel Foucault et la littérature* (Lyon: ENS Éditions, 2012).

10 In his reading of this passage, Martin Heidegger terms the movement of consciousness a 'constant death', but then goes on to valorize this movement as that of a sacrifice in which consciousness offers up its own death *in order* to experience the resurrection of itself, see, *Holzwege*, ed. Friedrich-Wilhelm von Herrmann

(Frankfurt am Main: Vittorio Klostermann, 1977), 160–1; tr. Julian Young and Kenneth Haynes as *Off the Beaten Track* (Cambridge: Cambridge University Press, 2002), 120–1. Although this appears to follow Hegel's thought of experience, it significantly distorts what he is saying by imposing a reading in which there is the security of a voluntarist resolution, as if consciousness were able to perceive the resurrection before it experiences its death, which then becomes a guaranteed sacrifice, which is far from the ongoing anxiety that is experience. Such a reading is noteworthy, however, for the way that it affects later interpretations of Hegel.

11 Blanchot's key essay on Hegel, 'La littérature et le droit à la mort', will be examined in chapter four, which extends my earlier readings in *Aesthetics of Negativity: Blanchot, Adorno, and Autonomy* (New York: Fordham University Press, 2016), 199–209, and *Without End: Sade's Critique of Reason* (New York: Bloomsbury, 2018), chapter three.

12 Blanchot, 'Le "discours philosophique"', in *La Condition critique, articles, 1945–1998*, ed. Christophe Bident (Paris: Gallimard, 2010), 334–5. Blanchot refers in particular to a line from Maurice Merleau-Ponty, *Le Visible et l'invisible*, ed. Claude Lefort (Paris: Gallimard, 1964), 139; tr. Alphonso Lingis as *The Visible and the Invisible* (Evanston: Northwestern University Press, 1968), 102–3, which is also mentioned in Lefort's postface/foreword, 358/xxxi.

13 Hegel, *Grundlinien der Philosophie des Rechts*, ed. Klaus Grotsch and Elisabeth Weisser-Lohmann (Hamburg: Felix Meiner, 2009), 16; *Elements of the Philosophy of Right*, 23.

14 Blanchot, 'Le "discours philosophique"', 337.

15 See, for example, Foucault, *L'Ordre du discours* (Paris: Gallimard, 1971), 61; tr. Ian McLeod as 'The Order of Discourse', in *Untying the Text: A Post-Structuralist Reader*, ed. Robert Young (London: Routledge, 1981), 69. As Blanchot remarked later in reference to this lecture: 'The subject does not disappear: it is its unity, overdetermined, that is called into question, since what arouses interest and research is its disappearance (that is to say this new way of being that is disappearance) or even its dispersion that does not annihilate it, but offers us only a plurality of positions and a discontinuity of functions', see, *Une voix venue d'ailleurs* (Paris: Gallimard, 2002), 124–5; tr. Charlotte Mandell as *A Voice from Elsewhere* (Albany: SUNY Press, 2007), 112–13.

Chapter One: Roussel and Lautréamont

1 Foucault, *Raymond Roussel*, 37–8; *Death and the Labyrinth*, 27–8.
2 For background details on the genesis and publication of *Impressions d'Afrique* see Mark Ford, *Raymond Roussel and the Republic of Dreams* (London: Faber & Faber,

2000), 95–105; and, François Caradec, *Raymond Roussel*, tr. Ian Monk (London: Atlas Press, 2001), 95–101.
3   Hans-Georg Gadamer, *Hegel's Dialectic: Five Hermeneutical Studies*, tr. P. Christopher Smith (New Haven: Yale University Press, 1976), 95–6. Hegel's notion of the speculative sentence is open to much interpretation but the best commentaries are, Jere Paul Surber, 'Hegel's Speculative Sentence', *Hegel-Studien* 10 (1975): 211–30; Stephen Houlgate, *Hegel, Nietzsche, and the Criticism of Metaphysics* (Cambridge: Cambridge University Press, 1986), 145–66; and, Chong-Fuk Lau, 'Language and Metaphysics: The Dialectics of Hegel's Speculative Proposition', in *Hegel and Language*, ed. Jere O'Neill Surber (Albany: SUNY Press, 2006), 55–74. According to Adorno, the 'mode of presentation' of Hegel's thoughts 'has a sovereignly indifferent attitude to language', which seems at odds with the work presented here on speculative sentences [DS: 342/109]. But Adorno's point is that even with these linguistic developments Hegel's thinking does not go far enough, as it bears an excessive confidence in speculative thought realizing the universality of language and not enough recognition of the negativity of language that will always disrupt this realization, see also, Steven Helmling, 'How to Read Adorno on How to Read Hegel', *Postmodern Culture* 17.2 (2007).
4   I have discussed Adorno's thought on this point in *Aesthetics of Negativity*, 178–90.
5   Annie Le Brun, *Vingt milles lieues sous les mots, Raymond Roussel* (Paris: Pauvert, 1994), 102–3. Ford sees the *procédé* as 'underpinning' the excesses of Roussel's proliferating language, supporting and structuring its development as its essential lining (or *doublure*), see, *Raymond Roussel*, 57.
6   As Jean-François Lyotard writes in relation to Winston's diary in *Nineteen Eighty-Four*, but in terms that could apply to Roussel, 'Writing must perform on itself – in its detail, in the restlessness of words that appear or fail to appear, in its receptivity to the contingency of the word – the very work of exploring its own weakness and energy [...] One writes against language, but necessarily with it. To say what it already knows how to say is not writing. One wants to say what it does not know how to say, but what one imagines it should be able to say. One violates it, one seduces it, one introduces into it an idiom unknown to it. When this desire disappears – this desire for it to be able to say something other than what it already knows how to say – when language is felt to be impenetrable and inert, rendering all writing vain, it is called Newspeak', see *Le Postmoderne expliqué aux enfants: correspondance, 1982–1985* (Paris: Galilée, 1986), 140; *The Postmodern Explained: Correspondence 1982–1985*, tr. ed. Julian Pefanis and Morgan Thomas (Minneapolis: University of Minnesota Press, 1993), 89. This contingency comes to be the point of language's greatest weakness, but also greatest resistance to totalitarianism, digital or otherwise.
7   The first song appeared anonymously in August 1868 and was then revised for inclusion in the book a year later. Although the book was printed in 1869 with the

author's name as 'Comte de Lautréamont', the publisher refused to distribute it (a few copies were still circulated and notices of its forthcoming appearance were made); as a result, it was not actually published in France until 1890. Ducasse produced another work, the *Poésies*, in 1870, which appeared under his own name (and as 'author of *Maldoror*'), before he died at the age of twenty-four. The status of the author of *Les Chants de Maldoror*, 'Lautréamont', is thus as elusive as the work itself. Details on the appearance of the work can be found in the editorial comments of Steinmetz and Lykiard in their respective versions of the text. An extensive and very useful study of the history and reception of the work has been conducted by Andrea S. Thomas in *Lautréamont, Subject to Interpretation* (Amsterdam: Rodopi, 2015).

8 This discovery was made by Maurice Viroux in 'Lautréamont et le docteur Chenu', *Mercure de France* (décembre 1952): 632–42. As Steinmetz points out, the only alteration made by Lautréamont to Chenu's text is the addition of the adjective 'magnetic' (*aimanté*) in line five [CM: 411–12]. Lautréamont's own writing begins again with the sentence 'Despite this strange way . . .'. A very helpful analysis of this passage has been developed by Ora Avni in *Tics, tics, et tics: Figures, syllogismes, récit dans "Les Chants de Maldoror"* (Lexington, KY: French Forum, 1984), which compares the movement of the starlings with that of the cranes in the first song.

9 Blanchot's awareness of Hegel's discussion on this point is likely to have been informed by the analysis developed by Hyppolite [GS: 24–30/19–26].

10 It is from this association that Derrida's reading in 'Hors livre, prefaces' begins, in which he links the sense of heterogeneous exteriority in Lautréamont's writing to that which obtains between Hegel's prefaces and the works they introduce, where the preface is a pretext that cannot be avoided or left behind, although Derrida does not develop this point in relation to the formal notion of experience that is apparent in Blanchot's reading.

11 Marcelin Pleynet, *Lautréamont par lui-même* (Paris: Seuil, 1967), 107–46; Philippe Sollers, 'Lautréamont's Science', tr. Philip Barnard in *Writing and the Experience of Limits*, ed. David Hayman (New York: Columbia University Press, 1983), 135–84.

12 Hegel, 'Zur christlichen Religion', in *Frühe Schriften II*, ed. Walter Jaeschke (Hamburg: Felix Meiner, 2014), 240; tr. T. M. Knox as 'The Spirit of Christianity and its Fate', in *Early Theological Writings* (Chicago: University of Chicago Press, 1948), 251. When Jesus offered his companions bread and wine and said, 'this is my body, this is my blood', the feeling of communion was made objective through the objects and the linguistic act – in the shared experience of their copula as an actual relation – and then made subjective again as these objects were consumed. But this is not a comparison (*Vergleichung*) in which one object is simply likened to another, and that is thereby external to both; indeed, Hegel is very clear that the relation between the bread and the body is not metaphorical if one is to be considered the vehicle and the other the tenor, if one is the compared and the other the comparison.

This relation is not one in which objective and subjective are simply combined but one in which their 'difference is lost [*wegfällt*], so too the possibility of comparison. The heterogeneous are most intimately tied' [237/249]. Thus, when Hegel makes just such a comparison between reading and transubstantiation, it is because both offer merely provisional and inadequate comparisons, for even though he says that reading remains inadequate, since words do not disappear in the same way that the bread and wine vanish as objects (although this is not a perfect consumption either), the fact that the latter are consumed, and thus are confused rather than unified emblems, means that they cannot be divine as they lack the permanence and perfection of the properly religious symbol; their presence in the communion is inevitably mournful as they only reveal the lack of a real divine presence. In this way the comparison between transubstantiation and reading is made stronger, for as with the bread and wine, reading fails to achieve a permanent consummation, since its parts are brought together but remain unassimilated to each other, and it is here that the sense of this movement comes closer to Lautréamont's own notion of reading. As we have seen in reading Lautréamont, the objective text is emphatically not extinguished; rather, its literal sense is understood but risks drawing the mind of the reader into its own errant and obtrusive existence. Derrida discusses this passage from Hegel in *Glas* [G: 77–82/65–70]. See also Werner Hamacher, *Pleroma – Reading in Hegel*, tr. Nicholas Walker and Simon Jarvis (Stanford: Stanford University Press, 1998), 100–12. Hegel's study of the Last Supper, which Hamacher calls one of the first great speculative analyses of Hegel's thought, is fascinating precisely because it cannot bring itself to any speculative closure due to its material and symbolic diremption, and as a result neither Derrida nor Hamacher is required to do much more than to draw attention to this rupture.

13 In the rapacious movement that marks Lautréamont's understanding of reading, by which sense is torn or snatched away and replaced with another, the form of its inverted communion resembles that suffered by the blind seer, Phineus, in the *Argonautica* (II: 188–93). It will be recalled that Phineus had been cursed to endure the predations of the Harpies, who would snatch the food from his mouth whenever he tried to eat and befoul the rest of it. In doing so, Phineus experiences both the removal of sense and the rupture of materiality.

14 One is reminded here of the unusual expression that appears on Thomas's face at the end of the first chapter of *Thomas l'Obscur* and that equally disrupts any easy movement of reflection or illumination.

15 Bident, *Maurice Blanchot: A Critical Biography*, tr. John McKeane (New York: Fordham University Press, 2019), 206–7. Bident claims that, in his readings of Lautréamont, Blanchot was not only working out the form of his emergence as a writer but also working through his withdrawal from the violent politics of the extreme Right.

16 In discussing Pierre Fontanier's 1827 volume on the figures of discourse, Derrida highlights a passage in which Fontanier distinguishes between literal and figurative language and then suggests that a third term lies between them, an '*extended tropological sense*' or catachresis, which can only be regarded as 'a new kind of *proper sense*'. As Derrida comments, what is interesting here is the production of a new kind of sense, and a new sense of proper, 'by means of the violence of a catachresis whose intermediary status tends to escape the opposition of the primitive and the figurative', which thus demonstrates that this opposition itself is not pertinent [MP: 305-6/255-6]. Rodolphe Gasché discusses the notion of general metaphoricity in *The Tain of the Mirror: Derrida and the Philosophy of Reflection* (Cambridge: Harvard University Press, 1986), 293-318. It is no accident that his study ends on this point, for in many ways metaphor is at the heart of Derrida's approach – as an analysis of the nature, possibility, and limits of philosophical language – and is thus the basis for Gasché's introduction of the term 'quasi-transcendental'.

17 Indeed, for Hegel, materiality is defined in terms of resistance, and vice versa [ENZ: §265 Z, 50]. So, it is perhaps in relation to the resistance of the text that we should understand the sense of 'materiality' that Paul de Man speaks of when he writes about both 'a *material* vision' (or 'stony gaze') and 'the prosaic materiality of the letter', in *Aesthetic Ideology*, ed. Andrzej Warminski (Minneapolis: University of Minnesota Press, 1996), 82-3, 90, 127-8. However, it is notable that de Man's ideas about materiality largely derive from Kant's descriptions of the ocean in *Kritik der Urteilskraft* and, specifically, his suggestion that to judge the ocean sublime is possible only if we are able simply to behold it, without knowing or thinking but 'merely as the poets do', see *Critique of the Power of Judgment*, tr. Paul Guyer and Eric Matthews (Cambridge: Cambridge University Press, 2000), 152-3. See my *Aesthetics of Negativity*, 120-5, for an analysis of how sublime judgement unavoidably involves a literary subreption of thought, which suggests what this material vision may imply.

Chapter Two: Derrida: infinite outline

1 Derrida, 'The Time of a Thesis: Punctuations', tr. Kathleen McLaughlin in *Philosophy in France Today*, ed. Alan Montefiore (Cambridge: Cambridge University Press, 1983), 36-43.

2 Particularly important here are Derrida's 1964-5 course on Heidegger, which will be discussed further below, the 1969-70 course, *Théorie du discours philosophique: La métaphore dans la texte philosophique* (which is yet to be published), and the 1975-6 course, *La Vie la mort*. The latter two courses begin with brief but instrumental

examinations of Hegel; however, broader discussions were to arise in a course on Hegel's aesthetics from 1979–80, and a seminar in 1987 on Hegel and Blanchot. After *Glas*, Hegel more or less recedes from Derrida's publications: there is some discussion of his aesthetics in the first part of 'Le parergon', in *La Vérité en peinture*, and a reading of the right to philosophy in 'L'age de Hegel' from 1977, before the review of Catherine Malabou's *L'Avenir de Hegel* in 1998. It is only in his 1998-9 seminars on perjury and forgiveness that Hegel re-emerges as a major interlocutor through a discussion of the nature of reconciliation (*Versöhnung*), see *Le Parjure et le pardon II*, ed. Ginette Michaud, Nicholas Cotton, and Rodrigo Therezo (Paris: Seuil, 2020), 32–48 and 88–99, from which Derrida delivered an extract in his last lecture in 2004, see '*Versöhnung, ubuntu*, pardon: quel genre?', *Le Genre humain* 43 (2004): 111–56.

3   Leslie Hill discusses the ways in which Blanchot's later readings of Hegel respond to Derrida's works in 'From Deconstruction to Disaster (Derrida, Blanchot, Hegel)', *Paragraph* 39.2 (2016): 187–201.

4   In this course Derrida seems to subscribe to Heidegger's critique of Hegel as an idealist thinker of presence and teleology who understands being as concept, metaphysics as logic, and history and thought as eschatology, see *Heidegger: The Question of Being and History*, ed. Thomas Dutoit, tr. Geoffrey Bennington (Chicago: University of Chicago Press, 2016), 2–9, 36–9. That this is the case is supported by the way that Derrida's description of the relation of his thought to that of Hegel as one 'of almost absolute proximity' (in the 'Positions' interview) is foreshadowed in this earlier work by his description of the difference between Heidegger's and Hegel's thought as being 'as close as possible to *nothing*', an 'almost immaterial but decisive displacement' [9, cf. 149–50; P: 60/44]. There would appear to be a sleight of hand here for insofar as Derrida is discussing Heidegger, and the way that Heidegger distinguishes his thought from that of Hegel, he largely refrains from any critique of the image of Hegel that Heidegger develops, despite its evident partiality. But when Derrida does come to discuss Hegel, the terms in which this image is developed are mostly retained; the only point upon which he comes to critique Heidegger's interpretation is over Hegel's apparently vulgar concept of time [210], which if it were followed through would also undermine any description of Hegel's thought as that of presence and teleology, as Malabou has shown in her thesis. There are, however, two significant asides in this course [108, 175] where Derrida speaks very allusively to a possibility of rethinking Hegel by way of a renewed understanding of the finitude of meaning, which suggests much about the structure of *différance* that was beginning to emerge at this time.

5   Derrida, 'La parole soufflée', *Tel Quel* 20 (1965): 41–67 (60, 64); and, 'De la grammatologie II', *Critique* 22 (1966): 23–53 (46, 53) [cf. ED: 284–5/189–90, 290/193; DG: 125/84, 142/93]. In all other cases in these two essays, the use of

différance in the later books either revises earlier uses of 'difference' or appears in passages added to the earlier essays. It is interesting to note the Hegelian manner in which difference 'becomes' *différance* in this transition, as closer examination of the notion reveals how it changes itself by itself. (*N.B.* In citing Derrida, I will only italicize *différance* in those cases where he does.) Considering the way that the variable senses of *souffler* will be exploited by Derrida, it is surprising not to find a reference to Klossowski's 1960 novel *Le Souffleur*, especially as Foucault's 1964 article on Klossowski ends on an examination of the verb, see, 'La prose d'Actéon', in *Dits et écrits 1954–1988: I, 1954–1969*, 337; tr. Robert Hurley as 'The Prose of Actaeon', in *Aesthetics, Method, and Epistemology*, 134.

6   Critical readings of Derrida's essay can be found in Tony Corn, 'La négativité sans emploi (Derrida, Bataille, Hegel)', *Romanic Review* 76.1 (1985): 65–75; Joseph C. Flay, 'Hegel, Derrida, and Bataille's Laughter', in *Hegel and His Critics: Philosophy in the Aftermath of Hegel*, ed. William Desmond (Albany: SUNY Press, 1989), 163–79; Raphael Foshay, '"Tarrying with the Negative": Bataille and Derrida's Reading of Negation in Hegel's *Phenomenology*', *Heythrop Journal* 43 (2002): 295–310; Ryan Krahn, 'Aufhebung and Negativity: A Hegelianism Without Transcendence', *Cosmos and History* 7.1 (2011): 142–54. See also, more generally, David C. Durst, 'Hegel and Derrida on the Problem of Reason and Repression', *Continental Philosophy Review* 32 (1999): 1–17; Karin de Boer, 'Différance as Negativity: The Hegelian Remains of Derrida's Philosophy', in *A Companion to Hegel*, ed. Stephen Houlgate and Michael Baur (Oxford: Blackwell, 2011), 594–610; Joseph Cohen, 'The Event of a Reading: Hegel "with" Derrida', in *Hegel's Thought in Europe: Currents, Crosscurrents, and Undercurrents*, ed. Lisa Herzog (London: Palgrave, 2013), 250–61.

The literature on Derrida's relation to Hegel is of course extensive, but some of the most substantive discussions can be found in *Hegel After Derrida*, ed. Stuart Barnett (London: Routledge, 1998), especially the essay by Kevin Thompson, as well as: Jan Mieszkowski, 'Derrida, Hegel, and the Language of Finitude', *Postmodern Culture* 15.3 (2005); Catherine Kellogg, *Law's Trace: From Hegel to Derrida* (London: Routledge, 2010); Rocío Zambrana, 'Hegel's Logic of Finitude', *Continental Philosophy Review* 45 (2012): 213–33; Malabou, 'Philosophy in Erection', *Paragraph* 39.2 (2016): 238–48.

7   Derrida refers to Foucault here, in particular his discussion of the non-positive affirmation in Bataille's thought that takes place as transgression or contestation, although Derrida does not mention this last point, see 'Préface à la transgression', in *Dits et écrits 1954–1988: I, 1954–1969*, 238; tr. Donald F. Bouchard and Sherry Simon as 'A Preface to Transgression', in *Aesthetics, Method, and Epistemology*, 74–5.

8   Georges Bataille, *Œuvres complètes V* (Paris: Gallimard, 1973), 220; *Inner Experience*, tr. Stuart Kendall (Albany: SUNY Press, 2014), 195–6.

9   See Derrida's comments at the end of the discussion after his lecture, 'La "différance"', *Bulletin de la Société Française de Philosophie* 62.3 (1968): 101–20 (120); 'The

Original Discussion of "Différance" (1968)', tr. David Wood et al. in *Derrida and Différance*, ed. David Wood and Robert Bernasconi (Coventry: Parousia Press, 1985), 95. At the beginning of *Marges de la philosophie* he also notes, in reference to the fact that philosophy is always concerned with its limits, that 'in this book I will be examining almost constantly the *relevance* of this limit. And therefore re-launching in every sense the reading of the Hegelian *Aufhebung*, eventually beyond what Hegel, in inscribing it, understood himself to say or had intended to mean' [MP: ii/xi]. This is, as I have pointed out, part of what arises out of the experience of the speculative sentence for Hegel, and thus comprises the broader dimensions of his method of thinking and writing, see, in particular, Michael A. Becker, 'Method and the Speculative Sentence in Hegel's *Phenomenology of Spirit*', *Inquiry* (2019).

10 For instance, the study of the onto-theo-logical constitution of metaphysics in Heidegger's *Identity and Difference*, tr. Joan Stambaugh (New York: Harper & Row, 1969), 53–4, 120, provides an impetus for Derrida to read the apparent *telos* and *archē* of Hegel's thought as an underlying union in the all-consuming *Aufhebung* of the absolute. But in this text Heidegger's reading of Hegel is just as partial and tendentious as Kojève's, since he does not actually discuss *Wissenschaft der Logik* but simply draws out the supposedly essential relation between ontology and theology on the basis of a single parenthetical comment, which he then adduces to the constitution of metaphysics [WL2: 65/78]. And, as the latter is then worked out in terms of the ontico-ontological difference, it is clear that it is Heidegger's own understanding of being that is at issue, rather than Hegel's. The notion of an ontological difference does not play any part in Hegel's thought, indeed, ontology generally and the concept of being in particular are seen as largely empty pursuits, since what is at issue is rather the concrete unfolding of being over time rather than any abstract discourse around being as such. Hence the ontological criticisms of Hegel that Derrida draws from Heidegger are largely out of place; instead, the reading of being as presence or *parousia* needs to be replaced with a dialectical and speculative account of the metaphysics of becoming or development.

The same is true of Heidegger's ontological reading of the Introduction to the *Phänomenologie*, where he asserts – on the basis of Hegel's remark that the absolute is 'in and for itself already with us [*bei uns*]' – that Hegel's thought is oriented around a *parousia*, understood as being-with-us (*Bei-uns-sein*), or presencing-with-us (*Bei-uns-an-wesen*), *par-ousia*, see *Holzwege*, 130–1; *Off the Beaten Track*, 98 [PG: 53/47]. (See also the text of Heidegger's 1942 seminar on the *Phänomenologie* in *Hegel*, tr. Joseph Arel and Niels Feuerhahn (Bloomington: Indiana University Press, 2015), 63.) That the absolute is not simply equivalent to being or presencing should not need to be stressed, at least in part because the notion of that which is beside (*bei*) will come to inflect and divert any sense of presence, which is what is drawn out in the thought of the *Beispiel*. As will be shown, the appearance of the example

(*Beispiel*) is far from casual, especially as it concerns the act of reading in which the very role of the 'we' is actualized, and by which the experience of consciousness becomes known to it. That is, as phenomenologists, as readers of the *Phänomenologie*, we are not only led through descriptions of the various changes in consciousness but also (speculatively) bring them about, insofar as reading provides an exemplary perspective on this experience, on its temporal movement or becoming.

11 Heidegger, *Being and Time*, tr. Dennis Schmidt and Joan Stambaugh (Albany: SUNY Press, 2010), 406–13. This critique derives very closely from the sketch developed in the 1925-6 lecture course entitled *Logic: The Question of Truth*, tr. Thomas Sheehan (Bloomington: Indiana University Press, 2010), 209–21, where Heidegger dismisses Hegel's thinking of space and time as merely an empty and confused paraphrase of Aristotle's *Physics IV*. The point is then repeated in his lectures on the *Phänomenologie* five years later, see Heidegger, *Hegel's "Phenomenology of Spirit"*, tr. Parvis Emad and Kenneth Maly (Bloomington: Indiana University Press, 1988), 143–6.

12 The passages Derrida refers to can be found here: WL1: 251-2/841-2; PG: 429/487. In following directly from the *Enzyklopädie Logik*, the *Naturphilosophie* picks up the point from the end of *Wissenschaft der Logik* as well, so that the discussion of circularity in the latter leads into the analysis of space and time. Indeed, this is addressed in the last few paragraphs of the *Enzyklopädie Logik* where the apparent return to itself of the concept is also its ongoing realization as nature.

13 Derrida presented this paper at a seminar on Hegel's thought organized by Hyppolite (eleven days before the seminar where he would deliver the paper on *différance*). As he makes clear in his opening remarks, the paper is in effect an extrapolation of the chapter on sense in Hyppolite's *Logique et existence* and especially the following formulation and extension of Hegel's thought: 'Language precedes the thought of which it is nevertheless the expression, or, if you like, thought precedes itself in this immediacy. Language refers only to itself, sublates itself only in language' [LE: 38/31–2].

14 See also, Hegel, *Lectures on the Philosophy of Spirit 1827–8*, tr. Robert R. Williams (Oxford: Oxford University Press, 2007), 224.

15 The Zusatz to this point notes: 'Sound, for itself, is the self of individuality, not an abstract ideal like light, but as it were a mechanical light, produced only as the time of movement in coherence. Matter and form belong to individuality; sound is this total form that announces itself in time' [ENZ: §300 Z, 138].

16 Hegel, *Aesthetics*, 889–91. The account here is somewhat elliptical and relies on the understanding of sound developed in the *Naturphilosophie*. See also, John McCumber, 'Sound – Tone – Word: Toward an Hegelian Philosophy of Language', in *Hegel and Language*, 111–25; and, Peter Hanly, 'Hegel's Voice: Vibration and Violence',

Research in Phenomenology 39 (2009): 359–73. Derrida's insistence that Hegel denigrates writing in favour of speech is challenged by Andrew Cutrofello, 'A Critique of Derrida's Hegel Deconstruction', *Clio* 20 (1991): 123–37; and, Tanja Stähler, 'Does Hegel Privilege Speech Over Writing?', *International Journal of Philosophical Studies* 11.2 (2003): 191–204. See also the reading of Gérard Lebrun in *La Patience du concept, essai sur le discours hégélien* (Paris: Gallimard, 1972), which, although it does not refer to Derrida, contains a strong refutation of this charge of logocentrism.

17 Marian Hobson has explored the relation of Blanchot's syntax to Derrida's thinking in *Jacques Derrida: Opening Lines* (London: Routledge, 1998), especially chapter four.
18 de Man, *Blindness and Insight: Essays in the Rhetoric of Contemporary Criticism* (Minneapolis: University of Minnesota Press, 1983), 136–7.
19 As Giacomo Rinaldi emphasizes, this point derives from Hegel's desire to overcome the limited senses in which Kant and Fichte conceived the infinite as only abstract or ideal, whereas for Hegel it is both actual and ideal, the 'totality' of being as an endless process of becoming in which negation and position, finite and infinite are moments, see *A History and Interpretation of the Logic of Hegel* (Lewiston, NY: Edwin Mellen Press, 1992), 153–6; and, Houlgate, *The Opening of Hegel's "Logic"* (West Lafayette, IN: Purdue University Press, 2006), 421–5.

The notion that the true infinite is a totality lies behind Alain Badiou's rejection of the distinction between the bad and true infinite. For him, the basis of the argument lies in the fact that the bad infinite is purely quantitative while the true infinite represents the transition or sublation into quality in which the indeterminacy of the bad infinite is fully determined. However, Badiou claims that mathematical developments since Hegel's time have made it possible to consider the merely quantitative infinite as also determinable, thereby removing the difference between Hegel's two forms and negating the necessity of the apparent totalization that occurs in the form of the true infinite. See, *Being and Event*, tr. Oliver Feltham (London: Continuum, 2005), 161–70. This point is a key aspect of Badiou's argument that ontology must give way to mathematics, for in the latter he sees the possibility of a secular, non-transcendent, non-totalizing, and purely materialist determinability. It should be apparent that the true infinite is neither transcendent nor totalizing, but in finding the possibility of determination within the quantitative infinite Badiou has to some degree simply collapsed the differences between the two forms, which is precisely what Hegel finds in the true infinite. The distinction that remains is thus over the manner of this collapse and the use of mathematics, since Badiou assumes a mathematical reading of the infinite from the outset, whereas for Hegel this reading is only part of his understanding of the difference between the two forms, which also rests in the issue of finitude, which Badiou avoids. Fundamentally, Badiou is making a very different argument (about the form of ontology) and thus his reading of Hegel on this point is not essential to its success or failure. For a critical reading from Badiou's perspective, see Tzuchien Tho, 'The Good, the Bad, and the Indeterminate: Hegel and Badiou on the Dialectics of the Infinite', in *Badiou and Hegel: Infinity, Dialectics, Subjectivity*, ed. Jim Vernon and Antonio Calcagno (Lanham, MD: Lexington, 2015), 35–57; for a view more sympathetic to Hegel, see Simon Skempton, 'Badiou, Priest, and the Hegelian Infinite', *International Journal of Philosophical Studies* 22.3 (2014): 385–401.

20 Gasché helpfully explicates this structural or syntactic evasion of sense, which (re)marks the imbrication of the infinite and the finite in the fold, in his *Inventions of Difference* (Cambridge: Harvard University Press, 1994), 137–44. As Francesco Vitale shows in a commentary on this piece, this imbrication is also that of life and death, 'Finite Infinity: Reading Gasché reading Derrida reading Hegel', *New Centennial Review* 17.3 (2017): 43–61.

21 This distinction also casts light on the variable legacies of *différance* and *Aufhebung*, in that the focus on inscription in relation to the former has occasionally led to an over-focusing on the word to the extent of reducing it to a textual fetish, while the latter is often simplified as a thought of conceptual totalization in the all-encompassing syllogism of thesis-antithesis-synthesis. The task given to thinking by each (to think finite inscription and infinite reflection) is thus foreclosed.

22 Adorno, *Einführung in die Dialektik (1958)*, ed. Christoph Ziermann (Frankfurt am Main: Suhrkamp, 2010), 77; tr. Nicholas Walker as *An Introduction to Dialectics (1958)* (Cambridge: Polity, 2017), 51. Further along Adorno makes the important clarification that 'the reconciliation of the world cannot genuinely come about through any settlement located over and above its objectively contradictory character, but only in and through this contradictory character itself. This character, this development, this driving force, and ultimately also that which aims for reconciliation, is something itself harboured within the diremption, the negative, the suffering of the world, which is equally, as an experience of actuality, a sustaining element of the Hegelian dialectic' [108/73–4]. In an earlier essay, Adorno makes this point even more clear: 'Only in and through the becoming absolute of contradiction, not through its mitigation in the absolute, could it dissolve and perhaps one day still find that reconciliation that must have misled Hegel because its real possibility was concealed from him' [DS: 277/31].

23 See also Derrida's description of the *Aufhebung* in *De la grammatologie* as 'the dominant concept of nearly all histories of writing, even today. It is *the* concept of history and of teleology', which is unhelpful to the degree that it underestimates the ambivalence between concepts, history, and writing that he notes elsewhere [DG: 40/25]. By contrast, in *Glas*, he writes that the *Aufhebung*, 'the economic law of absolute reappropriation of absolute loss, is a family concept' [G: 152/133]. Thus,

although these quasi-definitions are sometimes crude, their proliferation can perhaps be seen as a deliberate strategic displacement.

24 Adorno makes an extended case for why the role of contradiction is more profound than that of difference in *Einführung in die Dialektik*, 44–55, 84–109; *An Introduction to Dialectics*, 27–34, 56–74. In doing so, he draws attention to the importance of the Kantian antinomies for the development of Hegel's thought, and the critical ontological point that what is, also is not, since it is precisely here that thought finds its imperative, which means that there is no complete union between concept and object and no thought that is not both true and false. It is in these terms that contradiction, for Adorno, becomes the nature of concrete reality, as it presents the negativity of the current state of things for which difference presents only a utopian image of heterogeneity. It is because contradiction plays such a decisive role in the development of logic (it is, as Adorno writes, its very organon) that it remains an aporia for thinking, since this also means that it is not capable of being taken as a principle for thinking. John Protevi makes a strong attempt to defend Derrida's reading of Hegel on this point in 'Derrida and Hegel: *Différance* and *Untershied*', *International Studies in Philosophy* 25.3 (1993): 59–71, but does so from a position that takes Derrida's reading of Hegel for granted, and so merely confirms the caricature of Hegel's thought as an onto-teleology of absolute assimilation. Considering that Derrida has overlooked Hyppolite's work on contradiction, there is some degree of irony in the fact that he later complains that Malabou does not refer to Hyppolite at all in her thesis, which Derrida had himself supervised, see 'A Time for Farewells', tr. Joseph D. Cohen in *The Future of Hegel: Plasticity, Temporality, Dialectic*, tr. Lisabeth During (London: Routledge, 2005), xxv.

25 This example comes from Alexandre Koyré's very influential 1934 article, 'Hegel à Jena', tr. Doha Tazi *Continental Philosophy Review* 51 (2018): 377–99 (387). In a discussion of the nature of the present in the Jena *Logik*, Hegel states that its moment is not multiple, as it is not an extended whole that contains a diversity, but nor is it simple, instead it has 'an absolutely different relation [*differente Beziehung*] to the simple', see *Jenaer Systementwürfe II*, ed. Rolf-Peter Horstmann and Johann Heinrich Trede (Hamburg: Felix Meiner, 1971), 194. In reference to the phrase '*differente Beziehung*', Koyré remarks that the French translation should perhaps be '*rapport différenciant*' (differentiating relation), in an active sense, rather than just 'different relation'. Derrida notes that if Koyré had written *différance* here, it would have made the translation of Hegel possible, at 'an absolutely decisive point of his discourse', without further notes or specifications [MP: 15/14].

26 Leonard Lawlor has shown how *Logique et existence* lies behind much of Derrida's early thought in *Derrida and Husserl: The Basic Problem of Phenomenology* (Bloomington: Indiana University Press, 2002), 89–104. Derrida confirms the

association of Hegel with Husserl in the preface to his 1954 dissertation, *The Problem of Genesis in Husserl's Philosophy*, tr. Marian Hobson (Chicago: University of Chicago Press, 2003), xxiv, which is repeated in his *Introduction to Husserl's "The Origin of Geometry"*, tr. John P. Leavey (Lincoln: University of Nebraska Press, 1989), 67 (where he explicitly recognizes Hyppolite's work as the basis for this reading), and then later in 'Le puits et la pyramide' [MP: 94/82]. It is not just the focus on the sign that marks this approach but also the idea that Hegel's thought holds an emphasis on the self-presence of the voice that colours Derrida's interpretation, as his rehearsal of the theme demonstrates:

> the thesis is familiar. Here we do not want to recall it but, in reformulating it, to reconstitute its configuration, to mark in what way the authority of the voice is essentially coordinated with the entire Hegelian system, with its archaeology, its teleology, its eschatology, with the will to parousia and all the fundamental concepts of speculative dialectics, notably those of negativity and of *Aufhebung*.
>
> MP: 102/88

27 On this point, and in relation to Bataille's thoughts in *Méthode de méditation*, Derrida remarks that sovereignty is not neutral, even if it neutralizes contradictions and oppositions in its discourse, since neutrality, as neither this nor that, bears a negativity that means it is still part of discursive knowledge, whereas although sovereignty is related to this work of neutralization in discourse it surpasses neutralization insofar as the latter remains work (*travail*) [ED: 402–3/274]. In this reading, Bataille's thought of neutrality would seem to differ from Blanchot's thought of the *neutre*, even though they arose together through their shared discussions. However, we need to distinguish between the sovereignty of neutral knowledge, which remains close to Hegel, and the thought of the *neutre* as sovereign, which is closer to what Blanchot finds in Sade and is irreducible to negativity. This latter thought is unremarked by Derrida, but in retrospect it indicates how closely Bataille's thought works to extricate itself from Hegel without just opposing him (there is a very brief comment by Derrida to this effect in *The Beast and the Sovereign: Volume 1*, ed. Michel Lisse et al., tr. Geoffrey Bennington (Chicago: University of Chicago Press, 2009), 230–1, to which he says he will return, but unfortunately never did). For the step that Bataille makes in his understanding of neutral knowledge is such that it is not reducible to the negative even if it bears some of its qualities, since to be neither this nor that is neither to be negative nor not to be so, which is how Blanchot begins to think the *neutre*. Thus, sovereignty cannot be separated from negativity even as it is not simply negative either, and this is the basis for Bataille's understanding of transgression and contestation as an experience of authority that expiates itself.

Chapter Three: Hegel: uneasy infinite

1. I will use 'supersession' as a translation of *Aufhebung* in this context as it is more relevant to the discussion of the now. Alongside Derrida's use of *relève*, de Man noted in passing that 'upheaval' could translate *Aufhebung*, perhaps following the Danish *ophævelse*, which would suggest that 'overhauled' could work as a translation of *aufgehoben*, see, *Aesthetic Ideology*, 111. The verb *heben* does refer to the action of heaving, so this elaboration would seem to be helpful. Although *ophæve* was used by Danish Hegelians as a translation of *aufheben*, its usage did not impress Kierkegaard who felt that it did not carry the same sense of contradictory meanings, see *Concluding Unscientific Postscript*, tr. Alastair Hannay (Cambridge: Cambridge University Press, 2009), 186–7. This passage is cited by Derrida in *Glas* [G: 224–5/200].
2. Miller translates Hegel's phrase (*an der er nur das Beiherspielende war*) as 'for which it was only the source of instances'; Baillie as 'was merely something alongside and by the way'; Pinkard as 'was only ancillary'; and Inwood as 'was only what was in play beside it'. For more on the relation between *Beispiel* and *Beiherspielende* see, Andrzej Warminski, 'Reading for Example', *Diacritics* 11.2 (1981): 83–94.
3. Jean-Luc Nancy, *La Remarque spéculative (Un bon mot de Hegel)* (Paris: Galilée, 1973), 44–5; tr. Céline Surprenant as *The Speculative Remark (One of Hegel's Bon Mots)* (Stanford: Stanford University Press, 2001), 29–30. Although this text is quite obviously Derridean in spirit, and was delivered at one of Derrida's seminars in March 1973 in explicit recognition of his papers on Bataille and Hegel, it is nevertheless distant from Derrida's reading of Hegel. It is likely that Nancy saw his work as simply continuing in the wake of Derrida's writings, and it certainly does not position itself in any way as a critique but this is still the result, since, by taking up the deconstruction of Hegel's thought that Derrida did not develop, Nancy implicitly shows the limits of Derrida's own readings. *Glas* appeared eighteen months after Nancy's presentation and, although it was based on a seminar given by Derrida in 1971–2, work on the book continued until early 1974 and yet there is no mention of Nancy in the final work, even though both works were produced by the same publisher (but then there is no mention of Lebrun's major work, *La Patience du concept*, either, although Derrida does take time to discuss Bernard Bourgeois's *Hegel à Francfort*, which is not nearly as significant).
4. As Adorno shows, this phrase is an anacolouthon, that is, it lacks completion and remains without consequence, a non sequitur; syntactically, nothing precedes or succeeds its fragmentarity [DS: 352/120]. This allows for a statement about being that is not contradicted by its form, which in turn reveals the limits of ontology as a discourse. As Houlgate remarks, in this opening fragment, 'Hegel indicates through his language that what we are to focus on is not a determinate subject of discourse or

"thing" nor a predicate of some assumed thing (such as the "Absolute") but rather utterly indeterminate being', *The Opening of Hegel's "Logic"*, 263.

5   This section in the remark on *aufheben* was added in the second edition of *Wissenschaft der Logik*, and Hegel refers the reader to the *Naturphilosophie* discussion of place and motion, which directly follows the passages on space and time, where he explains the transition from ideality to reality (as is found in the move from space and time to concrete reality) through a reference to mechanical phenomena, in which ideality can take the place of reality and vice versa, as is found in the use of a lever where distance can take the place of mass and vice versa, as 'a quantum of ideal moment produces the same effect as the corresponding real amount' [ENZ: §261, 253/42].

6   Hamacher, *Pleroma*, 208–20. See also John Russon, *Reading Hegel's "Phenomenology"* (Bloomington: Indiana University Press, 2004), 21. The importance of reading to Hegel's thinking becomes a central issue in response to Derrida's *Glas*, which is to some degree illegible since it is not possible to read the interplay between its columns and peepholes fully. To compose something that is resistant to reading in this way is, as Derrida suggests, to find a way to disrupt the dialectical movement of *aufheben*, as the different parts of the text cannot be made into an ordered whole, *il ne marche pas*. This raises a critical point, for the explicitly spatial and architectural features of *Glas* risk leaving it aporetic, as the insistent counterpoint that the binocular reading imposes is such that every point of Hegel's thought is both supported and distorted. This effect is, as Derrida would emphasize, perhaps inevitable in our relation to Hegel, but the strictures that it imposes on thought are also capable of bringing it to a halt, as is noted in relation to the static figure of Antigone [G: 187/166]. See, on this problem, the remarks by Geoffrey Bennington in 'Derridabase', in *Jacques Derrida* (Chicago: University of Chicago Press, 1993), 275–302, and the very interesting account in Johannes-Georg Schülein, *Metaphysik und ihre Kritik bei Hegel und Derrida* (Hamburg: Felix Meiner, 2016), chapter four. It is thus in relation to this aporia that Derrida will be concerned to examine the movement of Blanchot's spaces in 'Pas'.

7   Nancy, *La Remarque spéculative*, 110; *The Speculative Remark*, 86–7.

8   On the relation between restlessness and quality Hegel refers to the association made by Jakob Böhme between *qual* and quality, a relation of pain and materiality central to materialist thinking [WL2: 102/114; ENZ: §472, 470/209]. For example, in chapter six of *Die heilige Familie*, in his discussion of French and English materialism, Marx glosses this relation in terms of the differential position of pain: 'Among the qualities inherent in *matter, motion* is the first and foremost, not only in the form of *mechanical* and *mathematical* motion, but rather as a *drive, vital spirit, tension* [Trieb, Lebensgeist, Spannkraft], as a *qual* – to use Jakob Böhme's expression – of matter'. Friedrich Engels cites this passage in his *Socialism: Utopian*

and Scientific, tr. Edward Aveling (London: Allen & Unwin, 1892), x–xi, and goes on to explain the meaning of the last term: '*Qual* is a philosophical play upon words. *Qual* literally means torture, a pain that drives to action of some kind; at the same time the mystic Böhme puts into the German word something of the meaning of the Latin *qualitas*; his *qual* was the activating principle arising from and promoting in its turn the spontaneous development of the thing, relation, or person subject to it, in contradistinction to a pain inflicted from without'. Engels appears to have found this explanation in Hegel's remarks on Böhme in his *Vorlesungen über die Geschichte der Philosophie. Teil 4: Philosophie des Mittelalters und der neueren Zeit*, ed. Pierre Garniron and Walter Jaeschke (Hamburg: Felix Meiner, 1986), 82; tr. R. F. Brown and J. M. Stewart as *Lectures on the History of Philosophy 1825–26, Volume III: Medieval and Modern Philosophy*, ed. Robert F. Brown (Berkeley: University of California Press, 1990), 123; see also Derrida's 1971 lecture on Paul Valéry, 'Qual Quelle' [MP: 338–9/284–5].

9   Houlgate, 'Hegel, Derrida, and Restricted Economy: The Case of Mechanical Memory', *Journal of the History of Philosophy* 34 (1996): 79–94 (93). In *Philosophie des Geistes* Hegel discusses the relation of thought and language in terms of a form of memory (*Gedächtnis*) that he calls mechanical, in which words are internalized as 'senseless exteriorities' through their repetition into a 'space of names'. That is, such words have lost their meaning and representational sense and have become mere signs as 'true concrete negativity' – a notion that Blanchot would pick up. But, in being repeated (and recalling the movement of consumption from the analysis of the Last Supper), words themselves become the object (*Sache*) of thought, the thing itself, and thereby convey the union of thought and object, interiority and exteriority. For Hegel, such words generate an experience in the self of an 'empty bond'; that which finds and brings thoughts together as they endlessly appear and pass away, for in their abstraction from material reference they cannot be sustained otherwise [ENZ: §§462–3, 459–62/199–201]. This is an experience of being in its emptiness and indeterminacy, as it is an experience of subject and object in their bare unity, and it is thus that it becomes an experience crucial to the emergence of genuine thinking. The provocative aspect of this abstraction (despite its estranged passage through negativity) is the manner in which thought discovers these words as its *own*, that is, they bear a sense of property and belonging, which will enable the transition from subjective to objective spirit in which the will actualizes itself in private property and thereby demonstrates the rights of the private individual. See also, Hegel, *Jenaer Systementwürfe III*, ed. Rolf-Peter Horstmann (Hamburg: Felix Meiner, 1976), 185ff.; *Jena Lectures on the Philosophy of Spirit (1805–6)*, ed. and tr. Leo Rauch (Detroit: Wayne State University Press, 1983), 86ff.. Useful commentaries can be found in, McCumber, *The Company of Words: Hegel, Language, and Systematic Philosophy* (Evanston: Northwestern University Press, 1993), 229–38; and, Wendell

Kisner, 'Erinnerung, Retrait, Absolute Reflection: Hegel and Derrida', *The Owl of Minerva* 26 (1995): 171–86.

10 Duchamp, *Salt Seller: The Writings of Marcel Duchamp*, ed. Michel Sanouillet and Elmer Peterson (Oxford: Oxford University Press, 1973), 194.

11 Hegel, *Differenz des Fichte'schen und Schelling'schen Systems der Philosophie*, in *Jenaer Kritische Schriften*, ed. Hartmut Buchner and Otto Pöggeler (Hamburg: Felix Meiner, 1968), 16; *The Difference between Fichte's and Schelling's System of Philosophy*, tr. H. S. Harris and Walter Cerf (Albany: SUNY Press, 1977), 93–4.

12 Hyppolite's *Logique et existence* came out as Blanchot was starting work on *L'Espace littéraire*, having just completed *Celui qui ne m'accompagnait pas*, and he wrote a brief note in 1957 recommending it, precisely in reference to this discussion of alienation, see 'La grande tromperie', in *La Condition critique*, 244; tr. Ann Smock as 'The Great Hoax', in *The Blanchot Reader*, ed. Michael Holland (Oxford: Blackwell, 1995), 166. Aside from an earlier reference to Hyppolite's *Genèse et structure* as an 'important book', Blanchot seems to have made no other reference to his works [PF: 295/302]. However, Blanchot would have known of Hyppolite since at least the time of his translation of the *Phänomenologie* but also because of his involvement in Bataille's 'Discussion sur le péché' in March 1944, at which Blanchot was present and during which some of the most significant contributions came from Hyppolite, see, Bataille, *Œuvres complètes* VI (Paris: Gallimard, 1973), 337–43, 348–52; *The Unfinished System of Nonknowledge*, ed. and tr. Stuart Kendall (Minneapolis: University of Minnesota Press, 2001), 50–6, 62–6.

13 Adorno, *Einführung in die Dialektik*, 36; *An Introduction to Dialectics*, 20–1.

14 Hegel, *Jenaer Systementwürfe II*, 33–4; *Jena System, 1804–5: Logic and Metaphysics*, tr. ed. John W. Burbidge and George di Giovanni (Kingston: McGill University Press, 1986), 35. It is worth recalling that this discussion of a few pages is expanded into the whole first section of *Wissenschaft der Logik*, as the first part of the doctrine of being (which includes the transition from being and nothing to becoming and thence to determinate being and the relation of finitude and infinitude) is also the determination of quality.

15 The sense of this movement is what is captured in Hyppolite's rendering: 'Language precedes the thought of which it is nevertheless the expression, or, if you like, thought precedes itself in this immediacy. Language refers only to itself, sublates itself only in language' [LE: 38/31–2]. But this reformulation of teleology also indicates how closely Hegel is working in relation to the problem of teleology found in Kant's thought, where an equivalent understanding of the end is at stake, see Bennington, *Kant on the Frontier* (New York: Fordham University Press, 2017), chapter five.

There is not the space here to discuss Malabou's work in *L'Avenir de Hegel*, which seeks to go between and beyond the readings of Koyré and Kojève, but in her analysis of the plasticity of the future in Hegel's thinking she seeks to apply the speculative ambivalence of *aufheben* to futurity, its capacity to both form and be formed by its own movements, which leaves it open to contingency without falling into a bad infinite. While there is much here that is suggestive, particularly in its reformulation of the transcendental, the naturalizing tendency in Malabou's subsequent work in neurobiology leads to a very different sense of the experience of this futurity. For example, see the frank self-assessment in 'Deconstructive and/or "plastic" readings of Hegel', *Bulletin of the Hegel Society of Great Britain* 41–2 (2000): 132–41, in which dialectical reconciliation is understood in terms of the deformation of scar tissue.

16 This is one of the conclusions of Surber's analysis in 'Hegel's Speculative Sentence': '*The same sentence becomes speculative by virtue of the very manner in which we comprehend and reflect upon it*' (228). And, as Judith Butler explains in her reading of Hyppolite, its model also undermines any sense of Hegel's thought 'as a movement toward a determinate *telos*', see *Subjects of Desire* (New York: Columbia University Press, 1987), 87–8: 'the relation between substance and predicate is a double relation, one that, in this case, presents the infinite as an aspect of being and also presents being as an aspect of the infinite. The usual hierarchy between substance and predicate is subverted through a constant exchange of roles'. For Butler, this is the major significance of Hyppolite's reading of Hegel: that the infinite in its unrest inflects not just the character of life and desire but the very form of logic through its absolute negativity, which generates a structure of unceasing dissatisfaction and becoming.

Chapter Four: Blanchot: nothing doubled

1 Heidegger, *Wegmarken*, ed. Friedrich-Wilhelm von Herrmann (Frankfurt am Main: Vittorio Klostermann, 1976), 120; *Pathmarks*, ed. William McNeill (Cambridge: Cambridge University Press, 1998), 94–5.
2 Hegel, *Jenaer Systementwürfe II*, 33; *Jena System, 1804–5: Logic and Metaphysics*, 35.
3 Hyppolite, *Études sur Marx et Hegel* (Paris: Marcel Rivière, 1955), 180; tr. John O'Neill as *Studies on Marx and Hegel* (New York: Basic Books, 1969), 161. This essay first appeared in *Les Temps modernes* in 1947, in the same issue as an article by Blanchot, 'Le roman, œuvre de mauvaise foi', and the second part of Sartre's 'Qu'est-ce que la littérature?' Alongside Sartre's enquiry, Hyppolite's essay seems in many ways to be the basis for Blanchot's critical and speculative reflections in the two parts of 'La littérature et le droit à la mort', which would appear at the end of that year.
4 Hyppolite, *Études sur Marx et Hegel*, 176; *Studies on Marx and Hegel*, 157–8. The internal quotation about nothingness raising itself to the level of being comes from the last lines of Valéry's 1921 poem, 'Ébauche d'un serpent'.

5   Immanuel Kant, *Critique of Pure Reason*, ed. and tr. Paul Guyer and Allen W. Wood (Cambridge: Cambridge University Press, 1998), 212. The categories, or pure concepts of the understanding, are: Quantity (unity, plurality, totality); Quality (reality, negation, limitation); Relation (subsistence, causality, community); and Modality (possibility, existence, necessity). The manner in which Blanchot tacitly but persistently undermines the possibility of these categorical distinctions is compelling, for example, the fragmentary work is neither one nor many, neither parts nor a whole; it contests its own status, position, and extent; it lacks or undermines relation internally, externally, and reciprocally; and it renders complex and uncertain its own possibility, reality, and rationale. Such failures perhaps do not lie entirely with the work of literature but rather with Kant's schematic definitions.

6   Kant, *Critique of Pure Reason*, 382–3. As he writes, the development of the categories necessitates a further and more general distinction about the status of the object: 'Since the categories are the only concepts that relate to objects in general, the distinction of whether an object is something or nothing must proceed in accordance with the order and guidance of the categories'. Thus, the categories lead to their own inversion in terms of the equivalent determination of nothing as: an empty concept without an object (the nothingness of a concept of nothing, like zero); an empty object of a concept (the nothingness of a lack or absence, like darkness); an empty intuition without an object (the nothingness of sheer form, like space); an empty object without a concept (the nothingness of an object whose concept is impossible as it contradicts itself, like a square circle). The limitations of this model are evident from the way it has been developed from the prior categorization, but it still offers a useful starting point from which to explore the forms of nothingness in Blanchot's writings. Heidegger relates Hegel's thinking of negativity to this Kantian arrangement in his 1938 seminar, see *Hegel*, 20, 39.

7   See my initial examination of this topological transformation in Blanchot's thought and writings in *Blanchot and the Outside of Literature* (New York: Bloomsbury, 2019), chapter seven.

8   Friedrich Hölderlin had written that the immediate, strictly speaking, is impossible for mortals as for immortals, hence mediation is the law, see *Poems and Fragments*, tr. Michael Hamburger (London: Anvil, 1994), 638–9. Blanchot extends this account much further by claiming that, insofar as the immediate excludes both the immediate and the mediate through its strict impossibility, then it is only by way of this impossibility, that is, outside either mediacy or immediacy, that the immediate can be approached, although even 'approach' is not an accurate enough term for this irruption. As he writes, the expression 'presence (of) the immediate' lacks any meaning, for how could presence actualize the immediate, and how could the latter be present? The immediate is thus that which ruins the possibility of presence as present, such that it becomes an empty or infinite non-presence [EI: 66/440].

9 Marlène Zarader, *L'Être et le neutre, à partir de Maurice Blanchot* (Lagrasse: Verdier, 2001), 41–86; Mathieu Dubost, 'La littérature comme épreuve: Blanchot, lecteur de Hegel', in *Maurice Blanchot et la philosophie*, ed. Éric Hoppenot and Alain Milon (Paris: Presses universitaires de Nanterre, 2010), 87–101. In Zarader's understanding, the other night is a thought that originates in Blanchot's early writings as that which refuses the light of day, which in the 1960s changes into an understanding of the night as other, in line with the ethical discussions Blanchot pursued at this time. Although her reading is carefully developed in relation to Hegel's thought, it fails to grasp the greater uncertainty inherent in Blanchot's thinking, which places the night, as I have shown, at a distance from both the diurnal night and the night of pure indeterminacy. This failure is partly due to her lack of engagement with Blanchot's fictional writings but also because of the quasi-phenomenological approach to experience that she adopts, which is one of the readings that Blanchot is concerned to contest. He makes it quite clear that the experience of the other night is an experience of non-experience, in that it is an ineradicable encounter with the fact that everything has disappeared, an encounter with this disappearance as that which cannot be avoided. It is thus inaccessible and impure, as it is the combined appearance of disappearance, which can never complete itself in either aspect [EL: 169–70/163–4].

10 Alexandre Kojève, *Introduction à la lecture de Hegel*, ed. Raymond Queneau (Paris: Gallimard, 1947), 372–4; *Introduction to the Reading of Hegel*, ed. Allan Bloom, tr. James H. Nichols (New York: Basic Books, 1969), 140–2. Hegel's account of naming is found in *Jenaer Systementwürfe I*, 288; *"System of Ethical Life" (1802/3) and "First Philosophy of Spirit" (1803/4)*, 221, and the lines from the latter to which Blanchot refers are also mentioned by Hyppolite [GS: 228/237].

11 Hegel, *Jenaer Systementwürfe III*, 187; *Jena Lectures on the Philosophy of Spirit (1805–6)*, 87. Kojève cites this passage at the end of his book, *Introduction à la lecture de Hegel*, 574–5; 'The Idea of Death in the Philosophy of Hegel', tr. Joseph Carpino *Interpretation* 3 (1973): 114–56 (155–6). Blanchot refers to this passage in relation to the extract from *L'Entretien infini* cited earlier, where he likens it to the phrase, 'the night of language' [EI: 524/357]. In this case, it arises as a possible gloss on the problems of Novalis's *Monolog* in terms of its unplaceable voice.

12 Stéphane Mallarmé, 'Crise de vers', in *Œuvres complètes II*, ed. Bertrand Marchal (Paris: Gallimard, 2003), 213; 'Crisis of Verse', in *Divagations*, tr. Barbara Johnson (Cambridge: Harvard University Press, 2007), 210: 'Je dis une fleur! et, hors de l'oubli où ma voix ne relègue aucun contour, en tant que quelque chose d'autre que les calices sus, musicalement se lève, idée même et suave, l'absente de tous bouquets'. (I say, a flower! and, outside the oblivion to which my voice relegates any outline, as something other than known calyxes, arises musically and smooth, the idea itself, the one absent from every bouquet.)

13 Blanchot, 'L'étrange et l'étranger', in *La Condition critique*, 287. Emmanuel Levinas, 'Philosophy and the Idea of the Infinite', in *Collected Philosophical Papers*, tr. Alphonso Lingis (Dordrecht: Martinus Nijhoff, 1987), 50–3, and, *Totality and Infinity: An Essay on Exteriority*, tr. Alphonso Lingis (Dordrecht: Martinus Nijhoff, 1979), 42–6 and 298–9.

14 Heidegger, *Holzwege*, 205; *Off the Beaten Track*, 154.

15 See, for example, my discussion of the opening of *Thomas l'Obscur* in *Aesthetics of Negativity*; the openings of *Le Très-Haut* and *Le Dernier Homme* in *Blanchot and the Outside of Literature*; and the opening of *L'Arrêt de mort* in *Noir and Blanchot: Deteriorations of the Event* (New York: Bloomsbury, 2020).

16 Of particular significance, given Derrida's reading, is the remark by de Man in 1980 that 'in order to have memory one has to be able to forget remembrance and reach the machinelike exteriority, the outward turn, which is retained in the German word for learning by heart, *aus-wendig lernen*', see *Aesthetic Ideology*, 102. Interestingly, while Derrida passes over this discussion in *Mémoires: For Paul de Man* (New York: Columbia University Press, 1986), 51–5, 74–8, he does not make anything of this point, although his conclusion in regards to the allegorical, disjunctive structure of Hegel's thought (as formulated by de Man) is notable. However, this outward turn in which we learn by heart is central to Derrida's understanding of the experience of the poem, where it becomes the loss of sense that is the impossibly single trait, or spacing, of the poetic, see, 'Che cos'è la poesia?', tr. Peggy Kamuf in *Points . . . : Interviews, 1974–94*, ed. Elisabeth Weber (Stanford: Stanford University Press, 1995), 294–5.

17 Evidence for the significance of this syntactical reformulation of ontology can be found in Levinas's consideration of the notion of 'perhaps' (*peut-être*), as a relation 'irreducible to the modalities of being and certainty', see 'Enigma and Phenomenon', tr. Alphonso Lingis in *Basic Philosophical Writings*, ed. Adriaan T. Peperzak et al. (Bloomington: Indiana University Press, 1996), 71, 75. Although he discusses this as a new modality, its vagueness is left undeveloped and so it does not reach the level of disruption brought about by the use of *pas* and *sans* in Blanchot's writings. Shane Weller has attempted to provide a survey of Blanchot's use of syntactical negations in 'Voidance: Linguistic Negativism in Blanchot's Fiction', *French Studies* 69.1 (2015): 30–45 (expanded and revised in his *Language and Negativity in European Modernism* (Cambridge: Cambridge University Press, 2019), chapter five), but this account is problematized by his use of the figure of epanorthosis, 'the taking back of the said', or retraction, which he sees as 'the dominant stylistic strategy adopted by Blanchot in his [later] fiction' [41/146, in the book version he terms it 'the dominant form of linguistic negativism']. Two aspects of this figure suggest caution: its emphasis on speech rather than writing, and its figuration as an act of self-correction (this, no *this*), neither of which is sensitive enough to the complexity of negativity in

Blanchot's writings. For example, when it comes to the use of *sans*, Weller's preference for this figure of epanorthosis leads him to claim that the taking back of the said 'nonetheless leaves in place what has been said', since the phrases of *sans* only have a retrospective (that is, belated and thereby incomplete) rather than prospective negation, which was seemingly more in use in Blanchot's earlier fictional works where there was a heavier use of negative prefixes [43/152]. Setting aside the historical claims of this account, it is clear that it is the reading of phrases of *sans* as epanorthotic that leads to them being understood as retrospective but, as I have shown, the role of *sans* is much more disturbing since it operates forwards and backwards across the sentence, unsettling both subject and object. Reading a phrase like 'death without death' as epanorthotic leads to a foreclosure of its ambivalent multidimensionality, since it privileges the last word without giving any grounds for doing so, and thereby neglects the manner in which *sans* dislocates relation as such. As I have emphasized, it is more helpful to consider Blanchot's way of writing in the wake of and as an ongoing rethinking of Hegel's speculative sentences. Despite these concerns, Weller's essay is a bold and stimulating exercise and is one of the very few readings to have focused on the crucial significance of Blanchot's syntax.

18 Blanchot, *Aminadab* (Paris: Gallimard, 1942), 16, 40; tr. Jeff Fort as *Aminadab* (Lincoln: University of Nebraska Press, 2002), 9, 29. See my *Aesthetics of Negativity*, 147–8.

Chapter Five: Blanchot: wholly impossible

1 For example, Derrida writes the following in relation to Hegel's aesthetics: 'No doubt art figures one of those productions of spirit thanks to which the latter returns to itself, comes back to consciousness [*reprend connaissance*] and comes into its proper place by *returning* to it, circularly. That which *calls itself* spirit is that which says to itself "come" in order to hear *itself* already saying "come back". The spirit only is what it is, only says what it means, *in returning*. Retracing its steps [*Sur ses pas*], and in a circle', see *La Vérité en peinture* (Paris: Flammarion, 1978), 31–2; tr. Geoff Bennington and Ian McLeod as *The Truth in Painting* (Chicago: Chicago University Press, 1987), 26. Derrida is here recapping one of the major lines of enquiry in *Glas*, of which this section of *La Vérité en peinture* seems to be an appendix. It is notable that this concern with circularity is also the focus of de Man's early article on Blanchot, although he does not recognize how far the modulation of this Hegelian theme is already underway in Blanchot's writings, see *Blindness and Insight*, 75–7. As a preliminary understanding consider how the image of the circle becomes more complex when it is understood dialectically, as Adorno explains in regard to the moments of identity and non-identity in the interchange between being and nothing:

> only when identified with each other, by means of their synthesis, would the moments become non-identical. From this the assertion of their identity gains that restlessness that Hegel called becoming: it trembles in itself. As the consciousness of non-identity through identity, dialectics is not only a progressive but at the same time a retrograde process; to this extent the image of a circle describes it accurately. The development of the concept is also a reaching back, its synthesis the determination of the difference that sank, "disappeared", into the concept; almost, as with Hölderlin, as an anamnesis of the natural that had to go down. Only in the completed synthesis, the union of the contradictory moments, is their difference revealed. Without that step being would be the same as nothingness, both would be indifferent to each other, to use a favourite term of Hegel; only when they are supposed to be the same, do they become contradictory.
>
> ND: 160/157

It is from this more complex image that Blanchot's later writings on the fragmentary will depart even further in their modulation of the scope and process of dialectical thinking.

2 The faith in the spread of information technologies becomes totalitarian when it reaches a point of ideological closure, when it is not only seen as inevitable but also beneficial, when the only possible future has also become the best possible future, so that the only responsibility of humans is to submit to its immanent control. In this way the faith in question resembles that which once surfaced in relation to the Party, which knows everything and also knows best, as well as that which arises in the panglossian caricatures of Right Hegelianism. Any possibility of real change, of a future that could be differently imagined, is foreclosed. While there may be an illusion of freedom in the endless variety and novelty on offer through information technology, there is no freedom to pursue a different kind of future, and this lack of future is masked by endless activity. The role of thought is thus diminished when the basic functioning of the state is no longer in question and, as a result, it becomes possible to imagine that politics and economics can be handed over to technocrats.

The necessity is to break this cycle of activity, to force a rupture in which thought can re-emerge, to create an aporia that cannot be read or paraphrased. The 'system' cannot be made to change by large-scale actions, only by recognizing and propagating the fact that it is not a system. One thinks here, in anticipation of the demand to render oneself unreadable, of the occasion when Blanchot was interrogated in relation to the 'Manifeste des 121' in September 1960, and persistently refused to have his words paraphrased by the investigating judge Jean Pérez, see *Cahiers de l'Herne Maurice Blanchot*, ed. Éric Hoppenot and Dominique

Rabaté (Paris: L'Herne, 2014), 81–5. It is palpable that something of the same resistance is underway in the broken dialogues of *L'Attente l'oubli*, but today there is a greater necessity to break the very programme of discourse as it has become manifest in contemporary media, for which Blanchot finds a parallel in the operations of cancer:

> "Cancer" would symbolise (and "realise") the refusal to respond: here is a cell that does not hear the command, which develops outside the law, in a way that is called anarchic – it does more: it destroys the idea of the programme, rendering doubtful the exchange and the message, the possibility of reducing everything to the simulacra of signs. Cancer, from this perspective, is a political phenomenon, one of the rare ways of dislocating the system, of disarticulating through proliferation and disorder the universal programming and signifying power – a task once accomplished by leprosy, then by the plague. Something that we cannot understand maliciously neutralises the authority of a master-knowledge.
>
> EDB: 137/86–7

In the documentary *Autour du Groupe de la rue Saint-Benoît de 1942 à 1962* (Jean Mascolo and Jean-Marc Turine, 1993), the surrealist writer Gérard Legrand recalls Blanchot saying in 1958 that de Gaulle's military coup 'was in reality a nothingness to which must be opposed our own nothingness'. While this point recalls the general argument of 'La perversion essentielle' (see *Écrits politiques, 1958-1993*, ed. Michel Surya (Paris: Léo Scheer, 2003), 19–20; *Political Writings, 1953-1993*, tr. Zakir Paul (New York: Fordham University Press, 2010), 11–12), Legrand also refers to a note denouncing de Gaulle that Blanchot apparently attached to an article on Proust in the Gaullist *NRF* shortly after the coup. However, this seems to be referring to an article on Nietzsche entitled 'Passage de la ligne', which appeared in September 1958, to which Blanchot added a postscript – responding to some comments by the editors in the previous issue of the *NRF* who had criticized those who despaired of France – stating that 'it is hopeless that the people and the country have no other hope than an occasional man [*homme épisodique*]'. (This date was significant as it was just before the referendum that de Gaulle had called to seek approval for the new constitution that would found the Fifth Republic.) Nevertheless, the remark recalled by Legrand is highly interesting as it would seem to have been used by Blanchot twice, once in terms of politics and again in terms of writing, for later on, in reference to Nietzsche's fragmentary writing, he speaks of articulating the void by a void, which demonstrates the ambivalent force and inescapable necessity of negativity that links both fields [EI: 254/169]. A reference to Blanchot's remark about the coup is also made in Laure Adler, *Marguerite Duras* (Paris: Gallimard, 1998), 606; tr. Anne-Marie Glasheen as

Marguerite Duras: A Life (London: Victor Gollancz, 2000), 399, but without any note as to its source.

3. Adorno cites here two passages from the *Enzyklopädie* that state points that are neither contradictory nor identical, firstly from the *Logik*, that truth consists 'in the agreement of the object with itself, i.e., with its concept'; and secondly, from *Philosophie des Geistes*, that truth 'means agreement of the concept with its actuality' [ENZ: §172 Z, 250; §379 Z, 7]. In alluding to these points Adorno is also indicating how the circularity and teleology of the whole yields a different sense of the whole, which is in part derived from Hegel's revision of the autonomy and purposiveness evident in Kant's notion of organization in the third *Kritik*. That is, in the actualization of the concept the whole that takes place does so through and as its self-determination and concretization, thereby reformulating the sense of natural purpose that had so troubled Kant's analysis of organized bodies, whether natural or artistic. On this point see Karen Ng, 'Life and the Space of Reasons: On Hegel's Subjective Logic', *Hegel Bulletin* 40.1 (2018): 121–42, and, more suggestively, in terms of the role that it sketches out for the aesthetic, my *Aesthetics of Negativity*, 37–40.

4. Allen, *Noir and Blanchot*, 125. Adorno's fuller version of this dialectic comes from his 1932 lecture, 'Die Idee der Naturgeschichte', in *Philosophische Frühschriften*, ed. Rolf Tiedemann (Frankfurt am Main: Suhrkamp, 1973), 354–5; tr. Robert Hullot-Kentor as 'The Idea of Natural-History', in his *Things Beyond Resemblance: Collected Essays on Theodor W. Adorno* (New York: Columbia University Press, 2006), 260.

5. Adorno, *Zur Lehre von der Geschichte und von der Freiheit (1964/65)*, ed. Rolf Tiedemann (Frankfurt am Main: Suhrkamp, 2001), 182; tr. Rodney Livingstone as *History and Freedom: Lectures 1964–1965* (Cambridge: Polity, 2006), 126. These lectures were drawn from the first drafts of the third part of Adorno's *Negative Dialektik*, which was published in 1966 [e.g. ND: 353/360]. It is intriguing to note that this lecture course was delivered at the same time as Derrida's lectures on Heidegger, since their approaches are sometimes parallel in that Derrida uses Heidegger to criticize Hegel over the question of history, while Adorno does exactly the reverse.

6. Blanchot, *Le Livre à venir* (Paris: Gallimard, 1959), 85; tr. Charlotte Mandell as *The Book to Come* (Stanford: Stanford University Press, 2003), 60–1. These points draw out the ways that *Un Coup de dés* ends, which on the one hand, as is well known, culminates with the announcement that 'nothing will have taken place but the place except perhaps a constellation', and on the other hand, in its last line, reverses this discovery as 'every thought emits a throw of the dice'.

7. This thought of the relation between the one and the two is a crucial problem inherited by dialectics, particularly in Maoist thought, as Badiou points out: 'Dialectics states that there is the Two, and intends to infer the One from it as a moving division. Metaphysics posits the One, and forever gets tangled up in deriving

from it the Two', see *Theory of the Subject*, tr. Bruno Bosteels (London: Continuum, 2009), 22, and, *The Century*, tr. Alberto Toscano (Cambridge: Polity, 2007), 59–61. This formulation was derived from a debate in 1964 among members of the Chinese Communist Party over the meaning of a passage from Lenin's 1915/25 article 'On the Question of Dialectics', which summarized his notes on Hegel's *Wissenschaft der Logik*, concerning whether one should divide into two, or two should merge into one, and the concomitant question of whether the transition from quantity to quality occurred through the sharpening or alleviation of contradiction. Mao, like Lenin, believed that it was only by the former path that transition was possible. As such, there is no suggestion that Blanchot was familiar with this debate, but it is significant that in his own rethinking of dialectics it is not only the issue of the division or gathering of the whole that should become critical but also the very issue of number: of the one as well as the two.

8   Hill provides information on the history of this phrase in *Maurice Blanchot and Fragmentary Writing: A Change of Epoch* (London: Continuum, 2012), 282–3. Ninety years earlier Hegel made a similar remark, see 'Aphorisms from the Wastebook', *The Independent Journal of Philosophy* 3 (1979): 3.

9   Adorno, 'Die Aktualität der Philosophie', in *Philosophische Frühschriften*, 338; tr. Benjamin Snow as 'The Actuality of Philosophy', in *The Adorno Reader*, ed. Brian O'Connor (Oxford: Blackwell, 2000), 34.

10 Adorno, 'Der Essay als Form', in *Noten zur Literatur*, ed. Rolf Tiedemann (Frankfurt am Main: Suhrkamp, 1974), 32; tr. Shierry Weber Nicholsen as 'The Essay as Form', in *Notes to Literature: Volume I* (New York: Columbia University Press, 1991), 22; 'Die Aktualität der Philosophie', 343; 'The Actuality of Philosophy', 38. This necessary disjunction would again be remarked at the end of his career, when he wrote: 'Praxis is a source of power for theory but cannot be prescribed by it. It appears in theory only, although necessarily, as a blind spot, as an obsession with what is being criticized; no critical theory is carried out in particulars that does not overestimate the particular, but without particularity it would be nothing', see, 'Marginalien zu Theorie und Praxis', in *Kulturkritik und Gesellschaft II*, ed. Rolf Tiedemann (Frankfurt am Main: Suhrkamp, 1977), 782; tr. Henry W. Pickford as 'Marginalia to Theory and Praxis', in *Critical Models: Interventions and Catchwords* (New York: Columbia University Press, 1998), 278.

11 Max Horkheimer and Adorno, *Dialektik der Aufklärung. Philosophische Fragmente*, ed. Rolf Tiedemann (Frankfurt am Main: Suhrkamp, 1980), 26–7; tr. Edmund Jephcott as *Dialectic of Enlightenment: Philosophical Fragments* (Stanford: Stanford University Press, 2002), 7.

12 Blanchot, 'L'expérience magique d'Henri Michaux', in *Chroniques littéraires du "Journal des débats" avril 1941-août 1944*, ed. Christophe Bident (Paris: Gallimard, 2007), 666; 'The Magical Experience of Henri Michaux', in *Death Now: Chronicles of*

Intellectual Life, 1944, tr. Michael Holland (New York: Fordham University Press, 2019), 172; and, 'Il m'a toujours paru que le mot magie . . .', in *La Condition critique*, 227–8.

13 Adorno, 'Musik, Sprache und ihr Verhältnis im gegenwärtigen Komponieren', in *Musikalische Schriften 1-3*, ed. Rolf Tiedemann (Frankfurt am Main: Suhrkamp, 1978), 651; 'Music, Language, and Composition', tr. Susan H. Gillespie in *Essays on Music*, ed. Richard Leppert (Berkeley: University of California Press, 2002), 115.

14 Adorno, 'Voraussetzungen', in *Noten zur Literatur*, 433; tr. Shierry Weber Nicholsen as 'Presuppositions', in *Notes to Literature: Volume II* (New York: Columbia University Press, 1992), 97.

15 Horkheimer and Adorno, *Dialektik der Aufklärung*, 35; *Dialectic of Enlightenment*, 13–14.

16 Perhaps it was for this reason that when Blanchot sent a copy of *L'Attente l'oubli* to Bataille, he inscribed it with the line 'Dans la pensée du but qui nous est commun' (Thinking of the goal that we share), cited in Bident, *Maurice Blanchot*, 348. But a few months earlier he had written to Bataille and said the following: 'in these days of distress, these entirely ordinary days therefore, something has been given to us in common, to which we must also respond in common, as though, at the extreme limit of our strength, we had each silently to continue to keep watch over this relation with I know not what that is very lowly (perhaps physical, perhaps metaphysical, and necessarily both)', cited in Hill, *Nancy, Blanchot: A Serious Controversy* (London: Rowman & Littlefield, 2018), 60.

17 It is important to recall the period in which Blanchot was working as he wrote this book, which was the busiest social and political time for him since his journalistic work in the late 1930s. His previous narrative work, *Le Dernier Homme*, came out in early 1957 and the first appearance of a piece that would later emerge in *L'Attente l'oubli* was published in August 1958. After de Gaulle's return to power earlier that summer, Blanchot started an association with the journal *Le 14 Juillet* edited by Dionys Mascolo and Jean Schuster, for which he wrote the articles, 'Le refus' and 'La perversion essentielle'. This journal closed after one year and Blanchot then became involved with writing and defending the *Déclaration sur le droit à l'insoumission dans la guerre d'Algérie* in 1960. This project led into the more ambitious idea of an international review, upon which he worked until negotiations about its aims and structure collapsed in 1963. Each of these ventures was not only a political challenge but also sought to develop a new mode of political authorship that would be collective, anonymous, and fragmentary, and each was, to differing degrees, unable to fully actualize these demands. Thus, *L'Attente l'oubli* can be seen as an account of these years with all their frustrations and expectations, which gives an insight into a different kind of illegibility that the book makes apparent: the personal and historical events that formed the milieu of Blanchot's thought but that have become invisible over time.

1961 in particular was an exceptionally busy year with Blanchot struggling to organize the launch of the *Revue internationale*, while the OAS, the FPA, and the FLN staged more and more bloody encounters on the streets of Paris, following a failed coup attempt by a group of retired generals in Algiers in April. It was also the year of the Bay of Pigs fiasco, the Eichmann trial, the appearance of the Berlin Wall, and Gagarin's trip into space. And then, in the winter of 1961–2, the OAS set off hundreds of bombs in Paris and elsewhere, attacking the offices of various newspapers, the French Foreign Ministry, as well as the homes of pro-independence figures like Malraux and Sartre. As a result, the publication of *L'Attente l'oubli* in March 1962, after the massacres at pont Saint-Michel (17 October 1961) and the Charonne metro station (8 February 1962) – where protests against the oppression of Algerians were brutally crushed by the Parisian police – would have cast its scenario in a very different, and much more politically sombre, light. Blanchot's awareness of these events is hardly in doubt as the flat on rue Saint-Benoît, where Mascolo and Duras lived and where he was often a visitor, was also a storehouse for funds and papers for the FLN, and one of the scenes of the massacres on the night of 17 October took place on the place Saint-Sulpice, just around the corner from Blanchot's flat and next to a café that he often visited. Useful contemporary reports on these days can be found in the diaries of Simone de Beauvoir, *Force of Circumstance*, tr. Richard Howard (London: André Deutsch, 1965), 598–617; and, Janet Flanner, *Paris Journal: 1944–1965*, ed. William Shawn (London: Victor Gollancz, 1966), 490–514. For a more historical analysis see, especially, Jim House and Neil MacMaster, *Paris 1961: Algerians, State Terror, and Memory* (Oxford: Oxford University Press, 2006).

18 Blanchot, 'Prière d'insérer pour *L'Attente l'oubli*', in *La Condition critique*, 301–2.
19 Iain Macdonald, *What Would be Different: Figures of Possibility in Adorno* (Stanford: Stanford University Press, 2019), chapter two, is particularly strong on explaining how the question of the modality of existence is critical to Adorno's response to Hegel, insofar as Hegel assumes that all possibilities must be actualized, so that what is actual is inevitably true to the essence of what is as it leaves no unactualized possibilities. It is this sense of closure that Adorno criticizes as insufficiently dialectical, as it fails to take account of the persistence of the negative, and the non-identical, as that which is not actualized and always offers possibilities for things to be otherwise [ND: 161–2/159–60].

Macdonald only mentions it in passing [89], but there is also an important thinking of impossibility in Adorno's writings that goes beyond the impossibility of that which has been ideologically prohibited. In particular, in his discussions of the virtuoso or tour de force artwork he indicates the modal transformation at issue, where it is precisely a question of the 'constitutive impossibility' of the work. In his words, virtuosity 'bears into appearance the paradoxical essence of art, the impossible as possible' [AT: 415/279]. What is intriguing about this description is how it arises out of an association between the artist and the circus performer, who champions the idea of art as audacity by contesting the law of logical consequence. As he says: 'Works that are made as a tour de force, a balancing act, bring to light something about all art: the actualization of the impossible' [AT: 162/106]. In this association, the absolute risk involved in the artwork – in which everything is at stake, both the work and the artist – makes it clear that its modal transformation occurs by a complete reconfiguration of the subject position, that is, the impossible is not made possible, rather, the work exists in the mode of impossibility. This means that it is not a question of saying that the work is or is not possible, but that there is (in the work) impossibility. As Blanchot indicated in his explication of Bataille's thought of the impossible, 'possibility is not the sole dimension of our existence' [EI: 307/207].

20 Foucault, 'Entretien avec Michel Foucault', in *Dits et écrits 1954–1988: IV, 1980–1988*, ed. Daniel Defert, François Ewald, and Jacques Lagrange (Paris: Gallimard, 1994), 41–7; tr. Robert Hurley as 'Interview with Michel Foucault', in *Power*, ed. James D. Faubion (London: Penguin, 1998), 239–46.

21 Blanchot, letter to Bataille, 6 January 1962, see, Bataille, *Choix de lettres, 1917–1962*, ed. Michel Surya (Paris: Gallimard, 1997), 595. This was one of Blanchot's last letters to Bataille, who died six months later. The whole passage is worth citing: 'René Char wrote me a very sombre letter evoking the universal disaster. It is true, but what is terrible is not the weakness, it is the inexorable hope that nevertheless keeps us standing. I should add that friendship is also the truth of disaster. You know mine'. These lines should be considered alongside the following thought, which was developed by Robert Antelme in a letter written to Mascolo around 1949–50, cited in Dionys Mascolo, *Autour d'un effort de mémoire, sur une lettre de Robert Antelme* (Paris: Maurice Nadeau, 1987), 23–4:

> I would like to say that I do not think of friendship as a positive thing, I mean as a value, but rather more as a state, an identification, thus a multiplication of death, a multiplication of interrogation, the most miraculously neutral site from which there is the perception and feeling of the constantly unknown, the site where the difference in which it is most acute – as one understands it at the "end of history" – only lives, flourishes in the heart of its opposite – the proximity of death.

22 Blanchot, *L'Amitié* (Paris: Gallimard, 1971), 130; tr. Elizabeth Rottenberg as *Friendship* (Stanford: Stanford University Press, 1997), 111. This piece was first published in October 1958.

23 Blanchot, *Thomas l'Obscur, nouvelle version* (Paris: Gallimard, 1992), 130; tr. Robert Lamberton as *Thomas the Obscure*, in *The Station Hill Blanchot Reader: Fiction and*

Literary Essays, ed. George Quasha (Barrytown, NY: Station Hill Press, 1999), 125; *Thomas l'Obscur, première version, 1941* (Paris: Gallimard, 2005), 316.

24 Blanchot, *Thomas l'Obscur, nouvelle version*, 137; *Thomas the Obscure*, 128; *Thomas l'Obscur, première version*, 323. Derrida has made much of the watery aspects of Blanchot's novel in 'Pas'.

25 This allows for a clarification in relation to the work of Giorgio Agamben, for whom shame takes on a central role in his *Remnants of Auschwitz*, tr. Daniel Heller-Roazen (New York: Zone Books, 1999), 103–30. Agamben draws upon many writers and thinkers for this rather hasty and confused analysis to claim that 'shame is truly something like the hidden structure of all subjectivity and consciousness' [128]. This is the case for Agamben, as shame takes the form of the relation and non-relation between the living being and the speaking being, insofar as it takes place as the disparity between subjectification and desubjectification that occurs in the event of speech, and that constitutes subjectivity. That is, in being called to give an account of oneself the subject experiences its own desubjectification, which manifests itself as shame; the experience of the inability to be and to bear witness at the same time. By making subjectivity dependent on the event of speaking, which is then revealed by shame as an ontology of presence (however fractured), the distance from Blanchot's thought is made obvious, where the very possibility of such an ontological account of subjectivity is put in question. To some degree Blanchot's version resembles the early understanding of shame developed by Levinas in 'De l'évasion' (which Agamben briefly mentions), in which shame is the appearance of 'the fact of being riveted to oneself, the radical impossibility of fleeing oneself to hide from oneself', see, *De l'évasion*, ed. Jacques Rolland (Montpellier: Fata Morgana, 1982), 87; tr. Bettina Bergo as *On Escape* (Stanford: Stanford University Press, 2003), 64. But Blanchot has radicalized this suggestion by showing how even this thought of relation is disrupted by literature – which is seemingly what is at stake in the last chapter of *Thomas l'Obscur*, as an exposure of the literary half-life of unfulfilled death and survival – thereby indicating that it is not just a literary phenomenon but, as he emphasizes, that which is insinuated into the world by way of literature.

26 Karl Marx, letter to Arnold Ruge, March 1843, in *Early Writings*, tr. Rodney Livingstone (London: Penguin, 1975), 200. Marx is recalling Hegel's thought that shame 'is an incipient, subdued anger of man against themselves; for it involves a reaction to the contradiction between my appearance and what I ought and want to be' [ENZ: §401 Z, 80].

Index

abstraction 12, 14–15, 112, 131–2, 175, 202
Adorno, Theodor W. 32, 84, 104, 108, 113, 170–3, 182–6, 193, 220n.22, 221n.24, 223–4n.4, 234nn.3–5, 235n.10
Aesthetics of Negativity (Allen) 15
affinity 15, 25–6, 29, 33, 35, 89
Agamben, Giorgio 205, 239n.25
alienation 42, 52, 110–12, 120, 123, 125, 130, 133, 139
Also 96–7
Althusser, Louis 16
Aminadab (Blanchot) 128, 154, 165
Aristotle 96
Artaud, Antonin 58, 60–1, 69–70, 72
'Aspekte' (Adorno) 170
atheism 69
aufheben
  and Blanchot 127–8, 134, 147, 159
  and Derrida 55, 58, 66, 70–1, 72–85, 87, 89–90
  and Hegel 91–7, 97–108, 111, 113–14, 116, 121, 223n.1
  introduction 15
Aufhebung 72–90, 96, 98, 101–3, 107–8, 159, 217–18nn.10, 12–13, 16, 220–1n.23, 221–2nn.26–7
Au moment voulu (Blanchot) 150, 155

Bataille, Georges 58, 60, 67–77, 89–90, 104, 123, 147–9, 162, 164, 198, 201
Baudelaire, Charles 39
Beiherspielende 95–6
being and beings 61–2, 127
being and nothing 96, 98–107, 130
Being and Time (Heidegger) 73, 76, 218n.11
Benjamin, Walter 172
Bident, Christophe 51, 213n.15
Bildungsroman 41, 43
Blanchot, Maurice
  coda 202–6, 239n.25

and Derrida 55–9, 61, 69, 72, 80, 89–90
and Hegel 102–3, 105, 110–11, 113, 117, 121–4
marks of experience 2–10, 12, 15–19, 21, 210nn.12, 15
negativity in language 127–49
a neutral relation 149–54
opening lines 154–65, 230–1nn.16,17
out of circulation 167–74, 232–4n.2
parataxis of relation 188–202, 236n.16, 238n.21
Roussel and Lautréamont 21, 35–9, 42–4, 46–7, 50–1, 211–12n.7
rupture of actualization 182–8, 236–7n.17
transitions and transcriptions 174–82, 234–5nn.6–7
blank 79, 81–3, 117, 119
bondsman 10–11, 132–3

'Canada is large' 29–30
catachresis 52, 214n.16
Celui qui ne m'accompagnait pas (Blanchot) 150, 155
Chenu, Jean-Charles 39–40
Chiquenaude (Roussel) 21–4
Christianity 49
circularity 39, 71–7, 81–3, 88, 103–4, 133–4, 167, 167–8
Comment j'ai écrit certains de mes Livres (Roussel) 23–4
consciousness 9–10, 14–15, 129–30, 139, 144
Cratylism 10–15, 25, 184
Cratylus (Plato) 12
Critique of Pure Reason (Kant) 131, 228n.5–6

Dasein 10–11, 78, 99
Das Schloß (Kafka) 152
death 2–14, 66, 111–12, 130, 137, 143–6, 163

De la grammatologie (Derrida) 61, 65
De l'economie restreinte à l'economie générale' (Derrida) 56
Deleuze, Gilles 32
de Man, Paul 80
Der Process (Kafka) 205–6
Derrida, Jacques
    and *aufheben see aufheben*
    and *Aufhebung* 72–90, 217–18nn.10, 12–13, 16, 220–1n.23, 221–2nn.26–7
    and Blanchot 160–2, 164, 202
    and *différance* 15, 56, 58–76, 80, 84–9, 117, 159, 215–16nn.4–5, 216–17n.9, 220n.21
    and Hegel 103, 108–9, 112–13, 117, 146, 153–4, 167, 231–2n.1
    infinite outline 55–9, 214–15n.2
    introduction 7, 15, 19, 208n.4
    Roussel and Lautréamont 49, 51–2, 212n.10, 214n.16
dialectics 5, 14–16, 179, 234–5n.7
différance 15, 56, 58–76, 80, 84–9, 117, 159, 215–16nn.4–5, 216–17n.9, 220n.21
differente Beziehung 88, 221n.25
digital totalitarianism 171, 232–4n.2
Discours, figure (Lyotard) 87
Ducasse, Isidore 44, 50
Duchamp, Marcel 23, 26, 109

Encyclopédie d'histoire naturelle (Chenu) 39
entendre 158–9
Enzyklopädie Logik (Hegel) 100, 136
epanorthosis 6–7, 230–1n.17
eroticism 46, 90

fan 82–3
fausse note tibia/Phonotypia 26, 28–9, 31–2
Faux pas (Blanchot) 3
Fichte, Johann Gottlieb 62
Foucault, Michel 10–14, 16, 19, 176, 198–9, 208nn.7–9
fragmentation 149, 158, 168, 174–5, 187, 190
freedom 2, 3, 5, 9–10, 108, 111
Freud, Sigmund 59, 87, 89, 113

Gadamer, Hans-Georg 31, 211n.3
Gasché, Rodolphe 82, 220n.20
Glas (Derrida) 55–6, 58
'God is being' 29–30
Goethe, Johann Wolfgang von 172

Hamacher, Werner 105, 224n.6
Hegel, Georg Wilhelm Friedrich
    Aufheben at the limits of language 108–18, 226n.14
    Aufheben in the form of language 118–25, 227n.16
    Aufheben in logic 97–108, 224–5n.8
    Aufheben in sense-certainty 91–7, 223n.2
    and Blanchot 127, 131–8, 140–4, 146, 148, 152–3, 159–61, 167–5, 180–2, 189, 191, 193, 199, 202, 231–4nn.1–2
    and Derrida 55–9, 59–72, 61, 73–8, 80–90, 112–13, 217–18nn.10, 15, 219–20n.19, 221n.15
    marks of experience 2–10, 15, 17, 19, 207n.1, 208–9nn.3, 5–6
    Roussel and Lautréamont 21, 29–31, 33, 35, 40, 42–4, 48–51, 212–13n.12, 214n.17
Heidegger, Martin
    and Blanchot 140, 192
    and Derrida 57, 59, 61–2, 73, 75–6, 89, 217–18nn.10–11
    and Hegel 113, 118, 127, 131, 156
    introduction 10–11, 15, 209–10n.10
here 92–3
Hill, Leslie 181, 235n.8
Histoire de la folie (Foucault) 198
Hölderlin, Friedrich 56, 72, 134–5, 202, 228n.8
Holzwege (Heidegger) 73
Horkheimer, Max 185
'Hors livre' (Derrida) 55–6, 62–3, 153
Houdebine, Jean-Louis 85, 88
Houlgate, Stephen 108, 225n.9
Husserl, Edmund 7, 55, 57, 59, 63–5, 86, 89
hymen 74, 82, 85
Hyppolite, Jean 55, 87–9, 96, 108–13, 118, 120–1, 130–1, 135, 226n.12, 226–7n.15, 3–4

Identity and Difference (Heidegger) 73, 217–18n.10
Impressions d'Afrique (Roussel) 5, 13–14, 22–9, 35
In der Strafkolonie (Kafka) 34
inframince 23, 109
intuition 77–8, 92, 119, 132, 135
irony 38, 46, 48, 94

Jena *Logik* (Hegel) 114, 120, 129

Kafka, Franz 21, 34, 59, 139, 152, 179, 205–6
Kant, Immanuel 51, 55, 62, 131, 228n.5
Kierkegaard, Søren 113
Klossowski, Pierre 77
knowledge 40–3, 66, 69, 71, 96, 173, 198
Kojève, Alexandre 116, 118, 136–7, 141, 147, 229nn.10–11
Koyré, Alexandre 116–18, 203

labour 10, 14, 45, 65, 74, 111, 170
'La "différance"' (Derrida) 77
La Disparition (Perec) 28
'La double séance' (Derrida) 85
La Folie du jour (Blanchot) 154–5
'L'age de Hegel' (Derrida) 56
'La littérature et le droit à la mort' (Blanchot) 19, 51, 56, 112, 117, 134, 136, 144
'La parole soufflée' (Derrida) 59, 215–16n.5
La Part du feu (Blanchot) 56
'La pharmacie de Platon' (Derrida) 77
L'Arrêt de mort (Blanchot) 42, 154, 161
Last Supper 75, 94, 212–13n.12
L'Attente l'oubli (Blanchot) 113, 128, 150, 155, 157, 161, 175–6, 179, 181–2, 186, 188–91, 195, 199, 201, 236n.16
Lautréamont, Comte de 15, 21, 35–52, 139, 202, 203, 211–12nn.7–8, 213n.13
Lautreamont et Sade (Blanchot) 51
L'Avenir de Hegel (Malabou) 117, 226–7n.15
La Voix et le phénomène (Derrida) 63
Lawlor, Leonard 221–2n.26
Le Brun, Annie 33–4, 211n.5
L'Écriture du désastre (Blanchot) 3, 57, 162, 194

Le Dernier Homme (Blanchot) 150, 155
Leiris, Michel 26
Le Livre à venir (Blanchot) 175, 234n.6
L'Entretien infini (Blanchot) 42, 57, 127–9, 154–6, 162, 168, 178
'Le parergon' (Derrida) 56
Le Pas au-delà (Blanchot) 15, 57, 113, 149, 151, 156, 159, 161
'Le puits et la pyramide' (Derrida) 56, 62–3, 89, 108, 164
Le Ressassement éternel (Blanchot) 156
Les Chants de Maldoror (Lautréamont) 35–8, 41–50
Les Mots et les choses (Foucault) 19
L'Espace littéraire (Blanchot) 3, 162
Le Très-Haut (Blanchot) 46, 154
Levinas, Emmanuel 59, 128, 150, 180–1, 201
limit-experience 147–8, 198
L'Instant de ma mort (Blanchot) 156
Locus Solus (Roussel) 14
Logique et existence (Hyppolite) 88, 221–2n.26, 226n.12
logocentrism 78–9, 219n.16
logos 62, 109–10, 203
Lukács, György 182
Lyotard, Jean-François 35, 87, 211n.6

Macdonald, Ian 237–8n.19
Malabou, Catherine 107, 116, 118
Mallarmé, Stéphane 56, 58, 79–83, 102, 112, 122, 145–6, 175, 182, 202, 205, 229n.12
Maoism 89
Marges de la philosophie (Derrida) 75, 77
Marx, Karl 16, 86, 88, 111–12, 170, 183, 206, 239n.26
Mascolo, Dionys 201
materiality 52–3, 214n.17
Maurice Blanchot and Fragmentary Writing (Hill) 181, 235n.8
melancholia 93
memory 28, 62–4, 75, 77–8, 89, 108–9, 136
Menge 115
Merleau-Ponty, Maurice 16–17, 69
metamorphosis 45–6
metaphoricity 41, 45, 52

metaphysics 56–61, 70, 173
Méthode de méditation (Bataille) 90, 222n.27
Mitvollzug 185–6
moment 104–6

Nancy, Jean-Luc 103–4, 106–7, 223n.3
Naturphilosophie (Hegel) 75, 78
Negative Dialektik (Adorno) 183
negativity 13139, 144, 159, 202
neutre 90, 150, 159, 16162, 164, 181
Nietzsche, Friedrich 57, 77, 113, 134–5, 192
nothingness 127, 130–1, 135, 144

Oulipo, the 26–8
'Ousia et grammē' (Derrida) 73, 75, 77

paranoia 57–8
'Parmi les Noirs' (Roussel) 23
parousia 62, 77, 81
pas 80, 162–3
Paulhan, Jean 201
Perec, Georges 26, 28
Phänomenologie (Hegel) 91–2, 95, 97, 100–1, 103, 114, 117–20, 123
  Blanchot 134, 136, 144, 152, 156, 167, 172, 191
  Derrida 66–7, 74, 76–7
  Roussel and Lautréamont 40–1, 44
pharmakon 74
phenomenality 67
Philosophie des Geistes (Hegel) 77, 108–9, 136, 225–6n.9
Pindar 134
Plato 204
Pleynet, Marcelin 47
Poésies (Ducasse) 44, 47, 50–1
point 75–6
Poulet, Georges 168
procédé 22–9, 31–4

rapport sans rapport 162
relève 64, 75, 78, 85, 87

Revolution 202
Roussel, Raymond 5, 10–16, 208n.9
  and Blanchot 184
  and Derrida 82–3
  and Foucault 176
  and Lautréamont 15
  speculative sentences 27–35
  torn lining 21–7

Sade, Marquis de 44, 51, 202
Sartre, Jean-Paul 130
Saussure, Ferdinand de 89
Scarpetta, Guy 85
scepticism 121, 134, 182
Socrates 12
Sollers, Philippe 47
sound 78–9, 218–19n.16
sovereignty 46, 51, 59, 67–71, 77
space 75–9, 81–2, 84, 128
speculative sentences 27–35
Surveiller et punir (Foucault) 198

teleology 78–9, 84, 90, 113, 128
temporality 7, 57, 63, 75–8, 103, 206
'the other night' 135
Thomas l'Obscur (Blanchot) 3, 50, 149, 154, 156, 202–6, 213n.14
time 75–7, 116
torn lining 21–7
transcendence 8, 59, 63, 81, 102, 120, 127
transubstantiation 49

Un Coup de dés (Mallarmé) 175
Une scène primitive (Blanchot) 155–6

viens 160, 160–2
'Violence et métaphysique' (Derrida) 56
viscous reading 35–53

Wissenschaft der Logik (Hegel) 74–7, 86, 95–6, 98, 132–3, 167, 172, 188, 191
Without End (Allen) 15

www.ingramcontent.com/pod-product-compliance
Lightning Source LLC
Chambersburg PA
CBHW062134300426
44115CB00012BA/1916